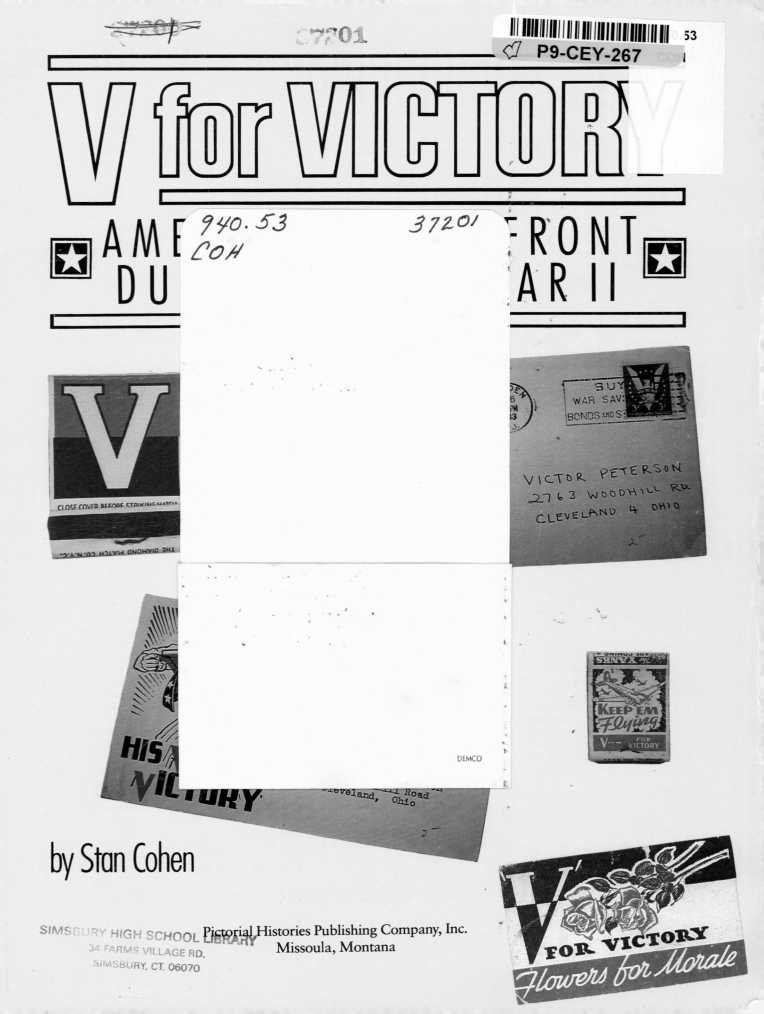

V for VICTORY

AMERICA'S HOME FRONT DURING WORLD WAR II

by Stan Cohen

Pictorial Histories Publishing Company, Inc.
Missoula, Montana

LIBRARY OF CONGRESS
CATALOG CARD NUMBER 91-60428

ISBN 0-929521-51-X

First Printing September 1991
Second Printing February 1992
Third Printing July 1993
Fourth Printing October 1994
Fifth Printing July 1995

Cover Art Work:
Stan Hughes, Missoula, Montana
Typography:
Leslie Over, Missoula, Montana

Printed in U.S.A.

Book Trade Distribution by:

PICTORIAL HISTORIES PUBLISHING CO., INC.
713 So. Third West
Missoula, Montana 59801

Introduction

Restating Charles Dickens' oft-quoted cliché, "It was the best of times; it was the worst of times," accurately describes America in the years of World War II, which was the last "good war" and the last "Great Patriotic War" to borrow Russia's name for it. It was a time of great personal sacrifice by American mothers and fathers, wives, children and friends who saw their loved ones go off to war.

But, at that, America was lucky. She was the only major Allied power whose home soil was not devastated to a greater or a lesser degree. The worst that happened within American boundaries were a few minor attacks by Japanese submarines on the Pacific Coast and the ineffectual Japanese balloon bomb attacks late in the war. Off the shores of both coasts, however, a fierce battle raged between Allied ships and Axis submarines.

Nevertheless, the war affected virtually every man, woman and child in the United States. While the young men were overseas or stationed at military camps throughout the country, the children were doing their part by collecting scrap, buying war stamps and helping their elders in many other ways. The older generation assisted the war effort in a variety of ways from serving on selective service boards and manning civilian defense jobs to rolling bandages, working in servicemen's canteens and buying and selling war bonds. The men who stayed on the "Home Front" for any number of reasons and the millions of women who joined the work force for the first time produced war materials, kept the transportation systems running and provided the countless other functions needed to run the country. Each man, woman and child on the "Home Front" contributed in his or her own way.

Sacrifices reduced Americans' standard of living which was higher than that in other countries. Most goods were rationed, and travel and entertainment were curtailed. War news was brought into most homes by newspapers and radios, and it was a traumatic time for all, especially for those families whose loved ones were off to war. It was probably the last time that America was totally committed to a common cause - the defeat of the Axis dictators - and the cause succeeded because of the strong will of the people and their leaders and because the country proved to be overwhelmingly capable in producing war material.

There was, of course, a dark side. America had its share of war profiteers, black markets, hate mongers, bigots and gangsters. But these were all overshadowed by the patriotic fervor that swept the country.

It is hard today to comprehend the degree of hatred whipped up by the government against the Axis powers, especially the Japanese, when one considers the extent of cooperation and intertwining of economics that exist now. The Japanese were singled out because they had made an unprovoked attack against the United States, and because they weren't Caucasian, whereas the Germans and Italians had been in this country for most of its history and were assimilated into its culture. The Russians became our allies only after Germany attacked the U.S.S.R. in June 1941.

Now Germany is one country again; Japan is a world economic leader; most of the world has discarded its yoke of communism, and Russia is looking to the West for economic survival.

How the world has turned and history come full circle!

I did not write this book to be the definitive chronicle of the war years. There are many books listed in the bibliography for this purpose. However, I feel that this is an accurate visual record of the subject and hope it will bring back that time for those who lived through it and teach the younger generations what those days were like for their parents and grandparents. Any one of the book's chapters could be expanded into a book on its own, and I hope the pictures and narrative will stimulate further research by those interested. The "Home Front" was a vital part of the war effort, and this book is a collection of images of those who took part in that effort.

Stan Cohen
1991

Acknowledgments

So many individuals and organizations throughout the country assisted with this project that it is impossible in this limited space to mention them all. There are some, however, that I must give credit to.

Gil and Joanne Mangels who operate the Miracle of America Museum in Polson, Mont., provided most of the artifacts pictured in this book. Their museum is well worth a stop for any reader traveling in western Montana.

The assistance of staff members at the FDR Library in Hyde Park, N.Y., and the Library of Congress and National Archives was essential to the book's production. I am indebted also to the staffs of many national, state, county, university and private libraries and historical societies nationwide.

Further thanks go to William Martin, of Ashland, Ky., who provided photos from the Frank B. Elam collection, to *The Californians* magazine, and to Richard Andre, Lloyd Clark, Edward Polic, Jack Jaunal, Eleanor Bishop, Ed Bearss and Dr. Robert Conte who wrote segments of the text.

Others who helped with photos or information include: Bonnie Brow, Powell, Wyo.; Mitch Reis, Windsor, Ct.; Betty Zuck, Twin Falls, Idaho; Elizabeth Hooks, American Red Cross; Don Young, Rancho Palos Verdes, Calif.; Pat Gibson, Ocracoke, N.C.; Arue Szura, Castro Valley, Calif.; John Deere Co.; Kraft Food Co.; USO national headquarters; C&O Historical Society; Ft. Stevens State Park, Astoria, Ore.; La Valencia Hotel, La Jolla, Calif.; The Grove Park Inn, Asheville, N.C.; The Greenbrier Resort, White Sulphur Springs, W.Va.; The Homestead, Hot Springs, Va.; Bob Chenoweth, U.S. Army Museum, Hawaii; Union Pacific Railroad; Don Thomas, Dunedin, Fla.; Bob Stephens, Kalispell, Mont.; George Bragg, Glen Jean, W.Va.; Wolf's Head Books, Morgantown, W.Va.; Welfred Stahl, Largo, Fla.; Kermit Edmonds, Missoula, Mont.; YMCA; Boy Scouts of America; Girl Scouts of America; Jim Reesdorff, David City, Neb.; Al Lloyd, Seattle, Wash.; White Sands Missile Range, N.M.; Michael Wiener, Albuquerque, N.M.; Robert Stinnett, Oakland, Calif.; Mr. and Mrs. William Tunstall; Martin Cole and Friedl Pfeifer.

Technical assistance was provided by Leslie Over, office manager of Pictorial Histories Publishing Co., who typeset the manuscript, Jacquelyn McGiffert, of Missoula, Mont., who edited the manuscript and Chris Harris, also of Missoula, who proofread the manuscript.

And finally, a much-deserved thank-you goes to my wife, Anne, who has suffered through the many years that went into collecting, writing and producing this book on her "Home Front."

About the Photographs

The photographs in this book were collected from various federal, state and private archives throughout the country. Many of them have never been published before and were picked to portray the nationwide effect of the war on every aspect of American life. Photo credit abbreviations are as follows:

NA - National Archives, Washington, D.C.

LC - Library of Congress, Washington, D.C.

DSA - Delaware State Archives, Dover, Del.

FDR - Franklin D. Roosevelt Library, Hyde Park, N.Y.

OHS - Oregon Historical Society, Portland, Ore.

USN - United States Navy, Washington, D.C.

Photos not credited are from the author's collection.

Americans had a daily dose of war news in their newspapers for more than six years.

EXTRA Seattle Post-Intelligencer

SEATTLE, MONDAY, DECEMBER 13, 1937

AMERICAN GUNBOAT SUNK BY JAPANESE AIR BOMB

SOLDIERS HURL GAS BOMBS TO QUELL RIOTERS

Sloan Donates 10 Million for Research
Foundation Will Make Study of Economics

U.S. WARSHIPS ARRIVE TO AID WRECK VICTIMS

Man Saved by Aged Couple In Fire
Trio Trapped in Blaze; Door Kicked Down

FLOOD WATERS IMPERIL 5,000 IN CALIFORNIA

Mercer Bridge Plan Opposed at Meet

WAR EXTRA! WAR EXTRA!

Seattle Post-Intelligencer

SEATTLE, MONDAY, DECEMBER 8, 1941

JAPAN, U.S. AT WAR
104 DIE IN HAWAII RAID; S. TRANSPORTS SUNK

BRITAIN GETS

Two American

TOKYO SAYS AT

President Drafting

The Montana Record-Herald
HELENA, MONTANA, THURSDAY, DECEMBER 11, 1941 — CITY EDITION
PRICE FIVE CENTS

BATTLE RAGES AT WAKE ISLAND
U.S. NOW AT WAR WITH GERMANY

President Asserts Delay Would Have Held Danger
Swift Congressional Action Brings Passage of War Resolutions; Formal Signing Is This Afternoon

SENATOR FLAYS NAVAL CHIEF AS INEFFICIENT
Tobey Declares Listening Devices Not Working When Hawaii Was Attacked

Hitler Raps F.D.R. in War Speech
Announces New Military Alliance With Japan, Italy for Finish Fight

Late War Bulletins

Japanese And Destroy Are Sunk b
Navy Announces Four Sep On Outpost in Pacific Landing Atten

FINAL EDITION The Missoula Sentinel
The Only Afternoon Paper in Western Montana With FULL ASSOCIATED PRESS News Service. Always Reliable
MISSOULA, MONTANA, TUESDAY EVENING, MARCH 17, 1942

MACARTHUR IN AUSTRALIA
German Moves Indicate Imminent Attack in North
Strong Nazi Point on Leningrad Front Falls

NORWAY PORTS CLOSED; NAVAL UNITS ACTIVE

Reds Draw Noose Tighter Around Trapped Germans

BIG FORCE OF YANKS ARRIVES "DOWN UNDER"

SUPREME COMMANDER

Philippines Hero High Commander Of Pacific Forces

EXTRA THE DAILY MISSOULIAN
Missoula, Montana, Tuesday Morning, June 6, 1944

ALLIED INVADERS SMASHING IN

Greatest Fleet In History Launches Blow

Beachhead Secured fo Liberation of Europe
Supreme Headquarters, Allied Expeditionary Force, June 6.—(AP)—Al

---

Nasi Radio Reports . . .

ADOLF HITLER DEAD, DOENITZ TAKES OVER

London Dubious of Tale Fuehrer Died in Battle; Reds Say He Fled Berlin

The Oregonian
PORTLAND, OREGON, WEDNESDAY, MAY 2, 1945

Weather Report

Churchill Hints Allies To Set V-E

War Dead

Two Down and One to Go—Box Score on Dictators

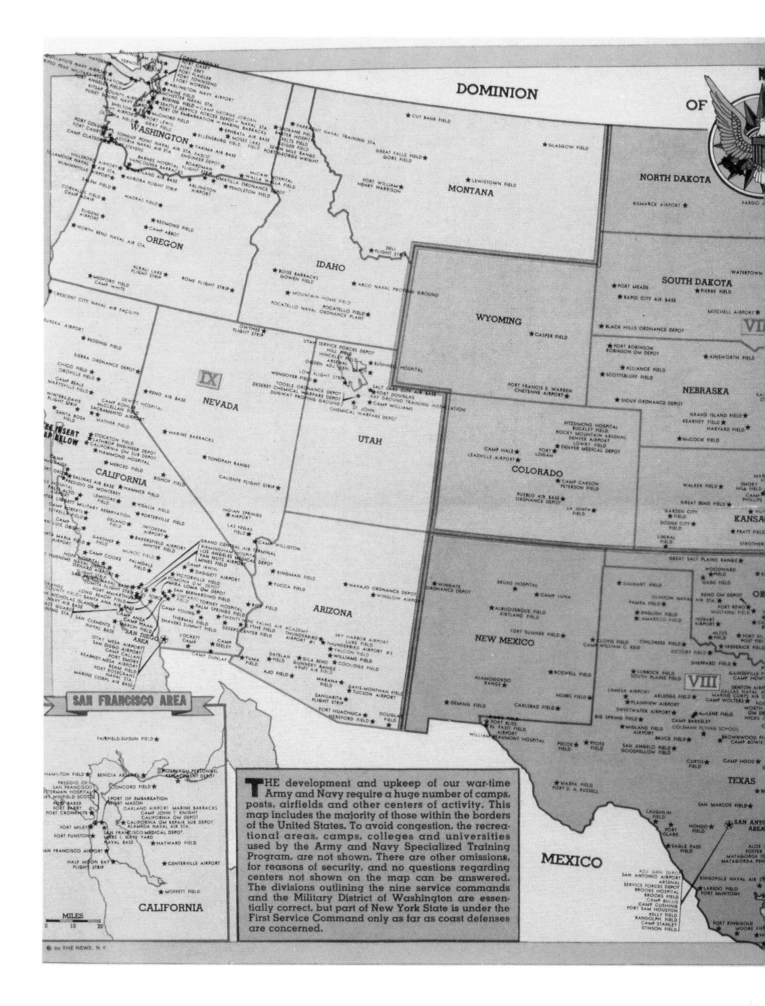

THE development and upkeep of our war-time Army and Navy require a huge number of camps, posts, airfields and other centers of activity. This map includes the majority of those within the borders of the United States. To avoid congestion, the recreational areas, camps, colleges and universities used by the Army and Navy Specialized Training Program, are not shown. There are other omissions, for reasons of security, and no questions regarding centers not shown on the map can be answered. The divisions outlining the nine service commands and the Military District of Washington are essentially correct, but part of New York State is under the First Service Command only as far as coast defenses are concerned.

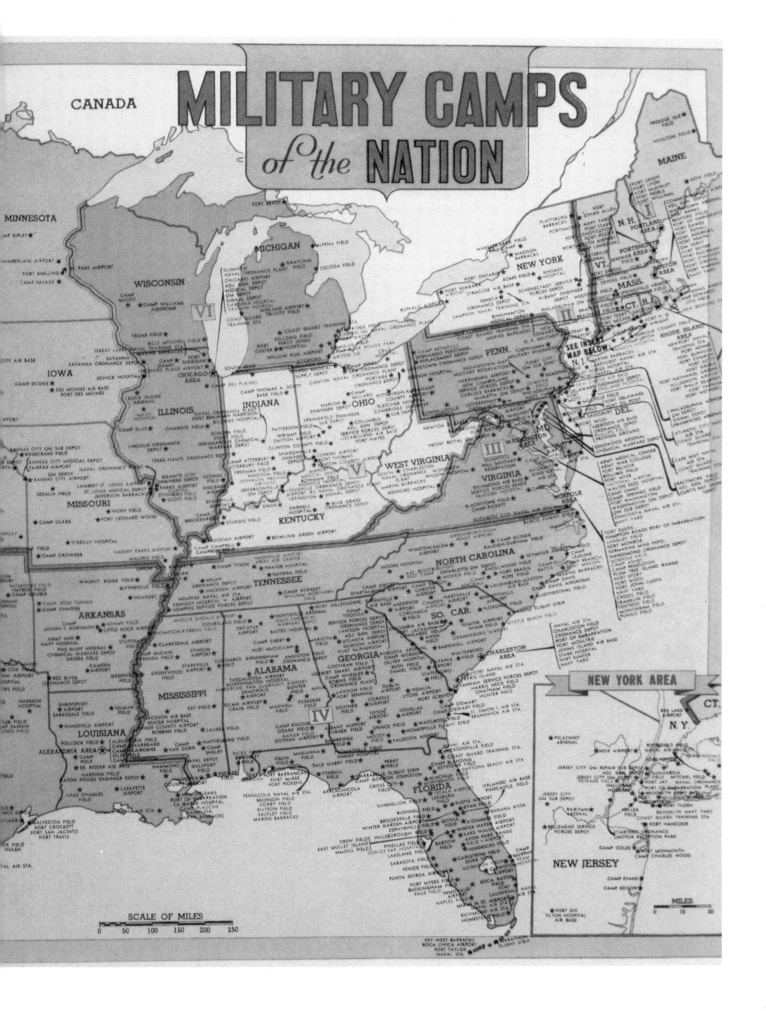

MILITARY CAMPS of the NATION

Table of Contents

America First

PREWAR
1939-1941

KEEP the
LIGHT of PEACE
BURNING

GIVE
YOUR DONATION
IS NEEDED
LARGE
OR SMALL
EVERYTHING
HELPS
BRITISH
WAR RELIEF ASS'N

KEEP U.S.
OUT OF WAR
BE
NEUTRAL

Peace pickets in front of the White House in 1941. A
soldier is apparently grabbing one of the pickets' signs.
FDR

PREWAR

Germany's invasion of Poland in September 1939 prompted Britain and France to declare war officially starting World War II. Japan had been fighting in China since the 1930s and was in the process of fortifying its mandated islands in the Pacific. It was a time of stress around the world, stress that the United States was trying to stay out of. America was in an isolationist mood, and President Roosevelt reiterated that the nation's sons would not be sent overseas again to settle Europe's troubles.

But by the spring of 1940, Hitler's armies had overrun most of western Europe and threatened to invade Britain. If Britain fell, America would stand alone against the Nazi menace (Russia was still allied with Germany at this time). Help was urgently needed to counteract German aggression, and in the spring of 1941 the Lend-Lease bill was signed providing aid to Britain although America technically remained a neutral power. This aid was also subsequently given to China and Russia.

The United States went to drastic measures to retain an outward show of neutrality, even while supplying Britain with as much necessary war material as possible. Fifty aged destroyers were traded to Britain in exchange for the use of bases in Britain's Caribbean colonies. Airplanes were trucked up to the Canadian border and physically towed across by Canadians, so as not to present an appearance of blatant help to the British. Eventually, however, the United States Navy had to institute patrols in the North Atlantic and establish bases in Iceland to protect its shipping. This produced some clashes with the Germans even before war was declared on Dec. 10, 1941.

The military buildup in the United States increased rapidly in 1940 and 1941, despite the country's professed neutrality. The National Guard was called up in 1940 for federal duty, and the first peacetime draft took place in October 1940. The Pacific fleet was moved from its home port in California to Hawaii in order to "show the flag" closer to the western Pacific and hopefully thwart Japanese aggression. Defense industries geared up not only to supply increased American military demands but also to supply the besieged nations of Europe.

Isolationist views were still strong in the United States even while shiploads of war material were sailing to Europe. Organizations such as America First continued to preach the theme

The *Great Pacific War*, by Hector Bywater, was published in 1925, one year after new immigration laws in the United States limiting Asian immigration sparked anti-American sentiment in Japan. The book told the story of a hypothetical war between the United States and Japan in 1931-33. In the novel the Japanese captured Guam and the Philippines, sank ships off the California coast and bombed San Francisco, Oakland and Los Angeles with seaplanes. Japanese living on Oahu rose up and took over the island, and Americans captured under arms were sent to Panama to work as laborers. Ultimately, however, the Americans won the war. Even at this early date, some authors could foresee trouble with the Japanese.

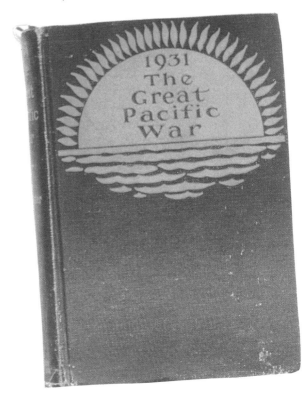
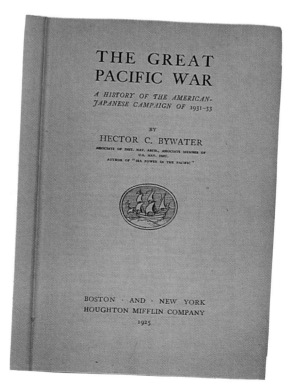

of non-involvement in foreign wars right up to December 1941. In August 1941, however, President Roosevelt met British Prime Minister Winston Churchill aboard a warship in a Newfoundland harbor and drew up the Atlantic Charter, proclaiming their vision of a world built on democratic principles. This placed America squarely on the side of Britain in the impending conflict.

In the Far East, Japan increased its militancy in the late 1930s and early '40s. In September 1940 she joined with Germany and Italy in signing the Tripartite Pact, thus aligning herself with Europe's two aggressors. In April 1941 Japan signed a nonaggression pact with Russia, freeing her from "that possible military threat." Secretary of State Cordell Hull told President Roosevelt that "Japan's military leaders are bent on conquest - just as are Germany's." When Japan moved further in China and then-occupied French Indochina, Roosevelt retaliated by freezing all Japanese assets in the United States, halting trade between the two countries and cutting off oil exports to Japan.

By fall, Japan and the United States had reached an impasse - and both knew it. As the Japanese would not step back from its aggressive plans, neither would the United States stand aside to let them proceed. Japan was already planning a surprise attack on several American military establishments and aggressive attacks against British and Dutch interests in Asia.

Thus as 1941 drew to a close, the world was on the brink of a true world war, involving most of the countries in the world.

A 1939 Army poster in front of the Tyler, Texas, post office. The military buildup was beginning to change the lifestyle of Americans two years before Pearl Harbor. These idyllic travel scenes would soon be replaced with battle scenes for millions of soldiers who would fight and die in every corner of the world. LC-USF33-12480-M2

Father Coughlin, a Catholic priest, was one of America's most vocal isolationists. Every week his radio broadcast preached to Americans to stay out of the European War. He was passionate anti-British, anti-Semitic and anti-Roosevelt. He edited the magazine *Social Justice* with a circulation of half a million.

Front page of West Virginia University's paper, *Daily Athenaeum*. Student editors were so upset with Hitler's Nazi government that, according to Al Volker, the paper's editor at the time, they sent a copy of this front page to the Führer and a German newspaper. "As we put the paper to bed," Volker said, "six of us chipped in for a cablegram to Germany that read: 'West Virginia students hereby sever diplomatic relations with Germany.' That took all ten words, so we couldn't add the customary 'love.'" Jan. 5, 1939. WEST VIRGINIA UNIVERSITY

News of the Sino-Japanese conflict was followed closely by San Francisco's Chinatown residents. Chinese men are seen here reading news of the surrender of Canton in November 1938. Most of the city's Chinese were Cantonese. LC-USZ62-70696

German-American Bund

Fritz Kuhn (1896-1951)

In 1936 a group of American Nazi supporters met in Buffalo, N.Y., to form the German-American Bund. Fritz Kuhn, a convicted racketeer, was elected Bundesführer and called for a "socially just, white, gentile-ruled United States." The Bund established paramilitary training camps and anti-Semitic newspapers but by 1938 authorities in Germany disavowed the organization as it was considered too damaging to German-American relations. Kuhn was indicted for embezzling Bund funds, imprisoned and deported to Germany after the war. The Bund never posed any real threat to United States security.

German American Youth

Here's Where You Belong!

Over 20,000 people packed Madison Square Garden on Feb. 20, 1939, for a pro-Nazi, anti-Semitic rally with a 30-foot tall George Washington banner in the background. FDR

A Bund camp somewhere in the eastern United States. Nazi symbolism and mass rallies used so effectively in Germany were also employed in the United States on a smaller scale. FDR

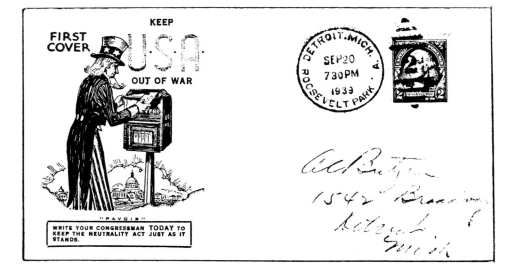

A TIME-TABLE OF DICTATORSHIP

*THE STEPS	FRANCE	GERMANY	ITALY	MEXICO	UNITED STATES
Wasteful Public Works	Yes	Yes	Yes	Yes	Yes
Concentrate Power in One Man	Yes	Yes	Yes	Yes	Yes
Undermine and Control Courts	Yes	Yes	Yes	Yes	Yes
Excessive Subsidies	Yes	Yes	Yes	Yes	Yes
Government by Executive Orders	Yes	Yes	Yes	Yes	Partly
Encourage Subversive Forces	Yes	Yes	Yes	Yes	Yes
Impose Confiscatory Taxes	Yes	Yes	Yes	Yes	Yes
Restrict Private Investments	Yes	Yes	Yes	Yes	Yes
Pile Up Debts and Deficits	Yes	Yes	Yes	Yes	Yes
Impose Planned Economy	Yes	Yes	Yes	Yes	Yes
Foster Class Conflicts	Yes	Yes	Yes	Yes	Yes
Government Controls Banks	Yes	Yes	Yes	Yes	Yes
Paralyses Industry	Yes	Yes	Yes	Yes	Yes
Excessive Borrowing	Yes	Yes	Yes	Yes	Yes
Increases Government Jobholders	Yes	Yes	Yes	Yes	Yes
Huge National Debt	Yes	Yes	Yes	Yes	Yes
Conscripts Army	Yes	Yes	Yes	Yes	Yes
Weakens Private Business	Yes	Yes	Yes	Yes	?
Destroys Labor Unions	Yes	Yes	Yes	No	
Regiments Farming	Yes	Yes	Yes	Yes	
Regiments Labor	Yes	Yes	Yes	Yes	
DICTATORSHIP	Yes	Yes	Yes	Yes	

IT IS LATER THAN YOU THINK! Every dictatorship that has been established maintains the appearance of legality in the country in which it exists!

Prepared from material in Congressional Record. © M. R F. MAGAZINE

There was considerable opposition to Roosevelt's domestic policies and his reputed slide towards dictatorship as described by his most ardent critics.

Members of the Mothers' Crusade Against Lend-Lease kneel in prayer near the nation's capitol to plead with Congress to kill the newly enacted Lend-Lease bill. BETTMANN ARCHIVE

America and the War

Address by Robert M. Hutchins, president, University of Chicago

This address was broadcast over the NBC (Red) Network, January 23, 1941

I speak tonight because I believe that the American people are about to commit suicide. We are not planning to. We have no plan. We are drifting into suicide. Deafened by martial music, fine language and large appropriations, we are drifting into war.

I address you simply as an American citizen. I do not represent any organization or committee. I do not represent the University of Chicago. I am not a military expert. It is true that from the age of eighteen to the age of twenty I was a private in the American army. I must have somewhere the very fine medal given me by the Italian government of that day in token of my co-operation on the Italian front. But this experience would not justify me in discussing tactics, strategy, or the strength to which our armed forces should now attain.

I wish to dissociate myself from all Nazis, Fascists, Communists, and appeasers. I regard the doctrine of all totalitarian regimes as wrong in theory, evil in execution, and incompatible with the rights of man.

I wish to dissociate myself from those who want us to stay out of war to save our own skins or our own property. I believe that the people of this country are and should be prepared to make sacrifices for humanity. National selfishness should not determine national policy.

It is impossible to listen to Mr. Roosevelt's recent speeches, to study the lease-lend bill, and to read the testimony of cabinet officers upon it without coming to the conclusion that the President now requires us to underwrite a British victory, and apparently a Chinese and a Greek victory, too. We are going to try to produce the victory by supplying our friends with the materials of war. But what if this is not enough? We have abandoned all pretense of neutrality. We are to turn our ports into British naval bases. But what if this is not enough? Then we must send the navy, the air force, and, if Mr. Churchill wants it, the army. We must guarantee the victory.

We used to hear of "all aid short of war." the words "short of war" are ominously missing from the President's recent speeches. The lease-lend bill contains provisions that we should have regarded as acts of war up to last week. The conclusion is inescapable that the President is reconciled to active military intervention if such intervention is needed to defeat the Axis in this war.

I have supported Mr. Roosevelt since he first went to the White House. I have never questioned his integrity or his good will. But under the pressure of great responsibilities, in the heat of controversy, in the international game of bluff, the President's speeches and recommendations are committing us to obligations abroad which we cannot perform. The effort to perform them will prevent the achievement of the aims for which the President stands at home.

If we go to war, what are we going to war for? This is to be a crusade, a holy war. Its object is moral. We are seeking, the President tells us, "a world founded on freedom of speech, freedom of worship, freedom from want, and freedom from fear." We are to intervene to support the moral order. We are to fight for "the supremacy of human rights everywhere."

With the President's desire to see freedom of speech, freedom of worship, freedom from want, and freedom from fear flourish everywhere we must all agree. Millions of Americans have supported the President because they felt that he wanted to achieve these four freedoms for America. Others, who now long to carry these blessings to the rest of the world, were not conspicuous on the firing line when Mr. Roosevelt called them, eight years ago, to do battle for the four freedoms at home. But let us agree now that we want the four freedoms; we want justice, the moral order, democracy, and the supremacy of human rights, not here alone, but everywhere. The question is whether entrance into this war is likely to bring us closer to this goal.

How can the United Stats better serve suffering humanity everywhere: by going into this war, or by staying out? I hold that the United States can better serve suffering humanity everywhere by staying out.

But can we stay out? We are told it is too late. The house is on fire. When the house is on fire, you do not straighten the furniture, and clean out the cellar, or ask yourself whether the house is as good a house as you would like. You put out the fire if you can.

The answer is that the house is not on fire. The house next door is on fire. When the house next door is on fire you do not set fire to your own house, throw the baby on the floor, and rush off to join the fun. And when you do go to quench the fire next door, you make sure that your bucket is full of water and not oil.

But, we are told, we are going to have to fight the Axis some time. Why not fight it now, when we have Britain to help us ? Why wait until we have to face the whole world alone?

Think of the mass of assumptions upon which this program rests. First, we must assume that in spite of its heroic resistance and in spite of the enormous supplies of munitions which it is yet to receive from America the British Empire must fall.

Second, we must assume that the present rulers of totalitarian states will survive the conflict.

Third, we must assume that if these regimes survive they will want to attack us.

Fourth, we must assume that they will be in a position to attack us. This involves the assumptions that they will have the resources to do so, that their people will consent to new and hazardous ventures, that their task of holding down conquered nations will be easily completed, and that the ambiguous attitude of Russia will cause them little concern.

Next, if Britain falls, if the totalitarian regimes survive, if they want to attack us, if they are in a position to do so, we must further assume that they will find it possible to do so. The flying time between Africa and Brazil, or Europe and America, does not decide this question. The issue is what will be at the western end of the line?

This will depend on our moral and military preparedness. A lone squadron of bombers might conquer a continent peopled with inhabitants careless of safety or bent on slavery. We cannot assume that any combination of powers can successfully invade this hemisphere if we are prepared to defend ourselves and determined to be free.

On a pyramid of assumptions, hypotheses, and guesses therefore, rests a decision to go to war now because it is too late to stay out. There is no such inevitability about war with the Axis as to prevent us from asking ourselves whether we shall ' serve suffering humanity better everywhere by going into this war or by staying out.

The chances of accomplishing the high moral purposes which the President has stated for America, even if we stay out of war, are not bright. The world is in chaos. We must give our thought and energy to building our defenses. What we have of high moral purpose is likely to suffer dilution at home and a cold reception abroad. But we have a chance to help humanity if we do not go into this war. If we do go into it, we have no chance at all.

The reason why we have no chance to help humanity if we go into this war is that we are not prepared. I do not mean, primarily, that we are unprepared in a military sense. I mean that we are morally and intellectually unprepared to execute the moral mission to which the President calls us.

A missionary, even a missionary to the cannibals, must have clear and defensible convictions. And if his plan is to eat some of the cannibals in order to persuade the others to espouse the true faith, his convictions must be very clear and very defensible indeed. It is surely not too much to ask of such a missionary that his own life and works reflect the virtues which he seeks to compel others to adopt. If we stay out of war, we may perhaps some day understand and practice freedom of speech, freedom of worship, freedom from want, and freedom from fear. We may even be able to comprehend and support justice, democracy, the moral order, and the supremacy of human rights. Today we have barely begun to grasp the meaning of the words.

Those beginnings are important. They place us ahead of where we were at the end of the last century. They raise us, in accomplishment as well as in ideals, far above the accomplishment and ideals of totalitarian powers. They leave us, however, a good deal short of that level of excellence which entitles us to convert the world by force of arms.

Have we freedom of speech and freedom of worship in this country? We do have freedom to say what everybody else is saying and freedom of worship if we do not take our religion too seriously. But teachers who do not conform to the established canons of social thought lose their jobs. People who are called "radicals" have mysterious difficulties in renting halls. Labor organizers sometimes get beaten up and ridden out of town on a rail. Norman Thomas had some troubles in Jersey City. And the Daughters of the American Revolution refused to let Marian Anderson sing in the national capital in a building called Constitution Hall.

If we regard these exceptions as minor, reflecting the attitude of the more backward and illiterate parts of the country, what are we to say of freedom from want and freedom from fear? What of the moral order and justice and the supremacy of human rights? What of democracy in the United States?

Words like these have no meaning unless we believe in human dignity. Human dignity means that every man is an end in himself. No man can be exploited by another. Think of these things and then think of the sharecroppers, the Okies, the Negroes, the slum-dwellers, downtrodden and oppressed for gain. They have neither freedom from want nor freedom from fear. They hardly know they are living in a moral order or in a democracy where justice and human rights are supreme.

We have it on the highest authority that one-third of the nation is ill-fed, ill-clothed, and ill-housed. The latest figures of the National Resources Board show that almost precisely 55 per cent of our people are living on family incomes of less than $1250 a year. This sum, says Fortune Magazine, will not support a family of four. On this basis more than half our people are living below the minimum level of subsistence. More than half the army which will defend democracy will be drawn from those who have had this experience of the economic benefits of "the American way of life."

We know that we have had till lately nine million unemployed and that we should have them still if it were not for our military preparations. When our military preparations cease, we shall, for all we know, have nine million unemployed again. In his speech on December 29, Mr. Roosevelt said, "After the present needs of our defense are past, a proper handling of the country's peacetime needs will require all of the new productive capacity-if not still more." For ten years we have not known how to use the productive capacity we had. Now suddenly we are to believe that by some miracle, after the war is over, we shall know what to do with our old productive capacity and what to do in addition with the tremendous increases which are now being made. We have want and fear today. We shall have want and fear "when the present needs for our defense are past."

As for democracy, we know that millions of men and women are disfranchised in this country because of their race, color, or condition of economic servitude. We know that many municipal governments are models of corruption. Some state governments are merely the shadows of big-city machines. Our national government is a government by pressure groups. Almost the last question an American is expected to ask about a proposal is whether it is just. The question is how much pressure is there behind it or how strong are the interests against it. On this basis are settled such great issues as monopoly, the organization of agriculture, the relation of labor and capital, whether bonuses should be paid to veterans, and whether a tariff policy based on greed should be modified by reciprocal trade agreements.

To have a community, men must work together. They must have common principles and purposes. If some men are tearing down a house while others are building it, we do not say they are working together. If some men are robbing, cheating, and oppressing others, we should not

say they are a community. The aims of a democratic community are moral. United by devotion to law, equality, and justice, the democratic community works together for the happiness of all the citizens. I leave to you the decision whether we have yet achieved a democratic community in the United States.

In the speech in which Mr. Roosevelt told us, in effect, that we are headed for war, he said, "Certainly this is no time to stop thinking about the social and economic problems which are the root cause of the social revolution which is today a supreme factor in the world." But in the same speech he said, "The need of the moment is that our actions and our policy should be devoted primarily-almost exclusively to meeting this foreign peril. For all our domestic problems are now a part of the great emergency." This means-and it is perfectly obvious-that if any social objective interferes with the conduct of the war, it will be, it must be instantly abandoned. War can mean only the loss of "social gains" and the destruction of the livelihood of millions in modest circumstances, while pirates and profiteers, in spite of Mr. Roosevelt's efforts to stop them, emerge stronger than ever.

The four freedoms must be abandoned if they interfere with winning a war. In the ordinary course of war most of them do interfere. All of them may. In calmer days, in 1929, the New York Times said, "War brings many collateral disasters. Freedom of speech, freedom of the press suffer. We think we shall be wiser and cooler the next time, if there is one; but we shan't." The urge to victory annihilates tolerance. In April, 1939, Alfred Duff-Cooper said that "hatred of any race was a sign of mental deficiency and of lack of a broad conception of the facts of the world." In April, 1940, Mr. Duff-Cooper said that the crimes of the German militarists were the crimes of the whole people and that this should be kept in mind when the peace treaty was written.

We cannot suppose, because civil liberties were restricted in the last war and expanded after it, that we can rely on their revival after the next one. We Americans have only the faintest glimmering of what war is like. This war, if we enter it, will make the last one look like a stroll in the park. If we go into this one, we go in against powers dominating Europe and most of Asia to aid an ally who, we are told, is already in mortal danger. When we remember what a short war did to the four freedoms, we must recognize that they face extermination in the total war to come.

We Americans have hardly begun to understand and practice the ideals that we are urged to force on others. What we have, in this country, is hope. We and we alone have the hope that we can actually achieve these ideals. The framework of our government was designed to help us achieve them. We have a tremendous continent, with vast resources, in a relatively impregnable position. We have energy, imagination, and brains. We have made some notable advances in the long march toward justice, freedom, and democracy.

If we go to war, we cast away our opportunity and cancel our gains. For a generation, perhaps for a hundred years, we shall not be able to struggle back to where we were. In fact, the changes that total war will bring may mean that we shall never be able to struggle back. Education will cease. Its place will be taken by voca-

tional and military training. The effort to establish a democratic community will stop. We shall think no more of justice, the moral order, and the supremacy of human rights. We shall have hope no longer.

What, then, should our policy be? Instead of doing everything we can to get into the war, we should do everything we can to stay at peace. Our policy should be peace. Aid to Britain, China, and Greece should be extended on the basis most likely to keep us at peace, and least likely to involve us in war.

At the same time we should prepare to defend ourselves. We should prepare to defend ourselves against military or political penetration. We should bend every energy to the construction of an adequate navy and air force and the training of an adequate army. By adequate I mean adequate for defense against any power or combination of powers.

In the meantime, we should begin to make this country a refuge for those who will not live without liberty. For less than the cost of two battleships we could accommodate half a million refugees from totalitarian countries for a year. The net cost would not approach the cost of two battleships, for these victims, unlike battleships, would contribute to our industry and our cultural life, and help us make democracy work.

But most important of all, we should take up with new vigor the long struggle for moral, intellectual, and spiritual preparedness. If we would change the face of the earth, we must first change our own hearts. The principal end that we have hitherto set before ourselves is the unlimited acquisition of material goods. The business of America, said Calvin Coolidge, is business. We must now learn that material goods are a means and not an end. We want them to sustain life, but they are not the aim of life. The aim of life is the fullest development of the highest powers of men. This means art, religion, education, moral and intellectual growth. These things we have regarded as mere decorations or relaxations in the serious business of life, which was making money. The American people, in their own interest, require a moral regeneration. If they are to be missionaries to the world, this regeneration must be profound and complete.

We must try to build a new moral order for America. We need moral conviction, intellectual clarity, and moral action: moral conviction about the dignity of man, intellectual clarity about ends and means, moral action to construct institutions to bring to pass the ends we have chosen.

A new moral order for America means a new conception of security. Today we do not permit men to die of starvation, but neither do we give them an incentive to live. Every citizen must have a respected place in the achievement of the national purpose.

A new moral order for America means a new conception of sacrifice, sacrifice for the moral purposes of the community. In the interest of human dignity we need a rising standard of health, character, and intelligence. These positive goals demand the devotion and sacrifice of every American. We should rebuild one-third of the nation's homes. We must provide adequate medical care in every corner of the land. We must develop an education aimed at moral and intellectual growth instead of at making money.

A new moral order for America means a new conception of mastery. We must learn how to reconcile the machine with human dignity. We have allowed it to run wild in prosperity and war and to rust idly in periodic collapse. We have hitherto evaded the issue by seeking new markets. In an unstable world this has meant bigger and bigger collapses, more and more catastrophic war. In Europe and Russia the efforts to master the machine are carried out by methods we despise. America can master the machine within the framework of a balanced democracy, outdistance the totalitarian despotisms, and bring light and hope to the world. It is our highest function and greatest opportunity to learn to make democracy work. We must bring justice and the moral order to life, here and now.

If we have strong defenses and understand and believe in what we are defending, we need fear nobody in the world. If we do not understand and believe in what we are defending, we may still win, but the victory will be as fruitless as the last. What did we do with the last one? What shall we do with this one? The government of Great Britain has repeatedly refused to state its war aims. The President in his foreign policy is pledged to back up Great Britain, and beyond that, to the pursuit of the unattainable. If we go to war, we shall not know what we are fighting for. If we stay out of war until we do, we may have the stamina to win and the knowledge to use the victory for the welfare of mankind.

The path to war is a false path to freedom. A new moral order for America is the true path to freedom. A new moral order for America means new strength for America, and new hope for the moral reconstruction of mankind. We are turning aside from the true path to freedom because it is easier to blame Hitler for our troubles than to fight for democracy at home. As Hitler made the Jews his scapegoat, so we are making Hitler ours. But Hitler did not spring full-armed from the brow of Satan. He sprang from the materialism and paganism of our times. In the long run we can beat what Hitler stands for only by beating the materialism and paganism that produced him. We must show the world a nation clear in purpose, united in action, and sacrificial in spirit. The influence of that example upon suffering humanity everywhere will be more powerful than the combined armies of the Axis.

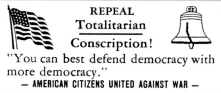

America First

The America First group was organized by isolationist people on Sept. 4, 1940, to counter the growing involvement of the United States in the European conflict. One strong catalyst for the committee to organize was the destroyer-for-bases trade two days before between Britain and the United States.

Famous aviator, Charles Lindbergh, along with other vocal isolationists in business, industry and politics pushed hard for total neutrality of the United States in regards to Germany's invasion of European states and, to a lesser degree, Japan's intrusion into China.

Their positions were made known through the various news media and public forums including many speeches by Lindbergh himself to large audiences around the country.

As the months of 1940 and 1941 passed by it became harder and harder for the committee to convince the nation to adhere to a strait neutrality policy as the Axis powers proceeded to overrun country after country. The Pearl Harbor attack, of course, put an end to the committee's activities and even Lindbergh volunteered his time and expertise to the war effort.

Senator Burton K. Wheeler of Montana was one of the leaders in Congress in favor of staying out of the European War. Here he is reading mail sent to the America First Committee. FDR

The America First Committee in Washington, D.C., December 1940. FDR

Famous aviator, Charles A. Lindbergh, speaking to an America First Committee meeting in Des Moines, Iowa, Sept. 11, 1941. FDR

Why Congress Should Investigate Lindbergh

Is the "Lone Eagle" a fascist? Lets find out—democratically

by Samuel Grafton

Charles Lindbergh was strongly denounced throughout the country for his isolationist views and his membership in the "America First Committee." These are advance proofs of an article that appeared in the Aug. 12, 1941, issue of *Look* magazine. FDR

-12-

STOP
HIM
Mr. Congressman

This is from the folks back home

We are not neutral. As freedom-loving citizens of the United States, we recognize that our liberty, that democracy everywhere will be ended unless the menace of Hitlerism is smashed.

We, therefore, petition the Congress of the United States TO REPEAL OUR SUICIDAL, HYPOCRITICAL AND DANGEROUS NEUTRALITY ACT, to remove the prohibition against arming our merchant ships, and dissolve the ban which prevents vessels flying the American flag from sailing the seven seas.

American policy has traditionally been that of freedom of the seas. Our Congress must reassert and uphold that right. Our Congress has pledged our resources to those nations fighting Axis aggression, and must reinforce that pledge by quaranteeing that our goods arrive at their destination in the hands of our allies.

We deplore the spectacle of resorting to the subterfuge of shipping our aid to the beleaguered nations resisting Nazi aggression under the flag of another country. The time for hypocrisy is ended. If we are to win the fight for freedom, the United States must reassert a brave and honest course.

The great majority of American people have shown, time after time, that they support the foreign policy of the President of the United States. The Congress of this nation must now be truly representative, must act and act quickly to carry out the will of the people of this nation.

SIGNATURE	STREET ADDRESS (I AM AN AMERICAN CITIZEN)	CITY & STATE

SIGNATURE	STREET ADDRESS (I AM AN AMERICAN CITIZEN)	CITY & STATE

(OVER)

FIGHT FOR FREEDOM
(NATIONAL OFFICES)

1270 Sixth Avenue　　:　　:　　:　　:　　:　　New York, N. Y.

(Please Place Your Local Chapter Address Here)

Surrounded by representatives of 20 Latin American republics in the East Room of the White House, President Roosevelt broadcasts to the nation and the world his proclamation that an "unlimited national emergency exists," May 27, 1941.

Prime Minister's meeting with President Roosevelt — Aug. Draft of Joint Declaration —

COPY NO: 1

M O S T   S E C R E T

NOTE: This document should not be left lying about and, if it is unnecessary to retain, should be returned to the Private Office.

P R O P O S E D   D E C L A R A T I O N

~~ALTERNATIVE VERSION~~ VERSION "A" ~~INCORPORATING NEW PARAGRAPH PROPOSED BY CODE IN A BY TELEGRAM NUMBER - 31~~

The President of the United States of America and the Prime Minister, Mr. Churchill, representing His Majesty's Government in the United Kingdom, being met together, deem it right to make known certain common principles in the national policies of their respective countries on which they base their hopes for a better future for the world.

First, their countries seek no aggrandisement, territorial or other;

Second, they desire to see no territorial changes that do not accord with the freely expressed wishes of the peoples concerned.

Third, they respect the right of all peoples to choose the form of government under which they will live; and they wish to see self-government restored to those from whom it has been forcibly removed.

Fourth, they will endeavour, with due respect to their existing obligations, to further the enjoyment by all peoples of access, on equal terms, to the trade and to the raw materials of the world which are needed for their economic prosperity.

Fifth, they fullest collaboration between all Nations in economic field with object of securing for all peoples improved labour standards, economic advancement and social security.

Sixth, they hope to see established a peace, after the final destruction of the Nazi tyranny, which will afford to all nations the means of dwelling in security within their own boundaries, and which will afford assurance to all peoples that they may live out their lives in freedom from fear.

Seventh, such a peace for all the high seas and oceans.

Eighth, they believe that all of the nations of the world must be guided in spirit to the abandonment of the use of force. No future peace can be maintained if land, sea or air armaments continue to be employed by nations which threaten, or may threaten, aggression outside of their frontiers, they believe that the disarmament of such nations is essential pending the establishment of a wider and more permanent system of general security. They will further the adoption of all other practicable measures which will lighten for peace-loving peoples the crushing burden of armaments.

Private Office.
August 12, 1941

Although America was not at war when this secret agreement was signed on board the cruiser, *Augusta*, in Newfoundland in August 1941, it was a strong statement as to where the sentiments of Roosevelt's administration lay, if not those of the population as a whole.

Franklin D. Roosevelt (1882-1945), served as President of the United States, 1933-1945.

Bundles For Britain

Bundles For Britain was founded by Mrs. Walls Latham on Jan 15, 1940. Its purpose was to provide non-military aid to the British people who were beseiged by the German military forces. Items such as medicine, clothing and blankets were collected from American citizens and shipped to Britain.

Students at Dupont High School in Wilmington, Del., collected gifts for the people of Britain in the fall of 1941. DSA

Bundles For Britain warehouse in Wilmington, Del. DSA

WE CAN HELP

"WHEN A FELLER NEEDS A FRIEND"

(Drawing Reprinted by permission of Shoemaker, Chicago Daily News)

Yes, We Can Do Something — Promptly and Practically By Giving Today To

THE BRITISH WAR RELIEF SOCIETY
INCORPORATED
730 FIFTH AVE., NEW YORK CITY

Registered with U. S. State Dept. No. 208

While there was a strong isolationist movement in the United States prior to the Pearl Harbor attack, there was a deep sympathy for the plight of the British undergoing heavy air bombardment and economic strangling by German submarines. Many Americans, anxious to enter the fight early, went North to join the Royal Canadian Air Force while some went directly to England to join the Royal Air Force.

The world situation was grave by late 1940. Most of Europe was occupied by German forces; Italy was entrenched in parts of North Africa; and Japan had closed most of China's entry points. In January 1941 President Roosevelt proclaimed that the United States would be the "Arsenal of Democracy" and asked Congress to authorize the lending of arms to nations threatened by the Axis powers. The Lend-Lease Act was passed in March 1941 with seven billion dollars appropriated, thus permitting direct military aid to be sent to Great Britain. On Oct. 30, 1941, the United States granted aid to the beleaguered Soviet Union. By November 1941 virtually all restrictions of military aid to friendly nations, including China, were lifted, thus putting the United States on a direct war footing before war was actually declared in December 1941.

After America's entry into the war, Lend-Lease material was greatly increased. These crates of knocked-down fighter planes and motors are slung from the deck of a lighter alongside an American cargo carrier ready to leave for Europe. FDR

Tanks and airplanes bound for the Soviet Union through Lend-Lease. The Soviet Union was attacked by Germany in June 1941. FDR

The Office of Production Management (OPM) was established in January 1941 to insure a steady flow of war material for the Lend-Lease program.

Machine tools from the
United States, shipped
under Lend-Lease, arrive
at a central ordnance
depot in England. FDR

Lend-Lease material
bound for Russia. FDR

Cases of T.N.T. gunpowder,
shipped from the United
States under Lend-Lease,
are stacked 100 feet
underground in a tunnel
dug out of solid rock in
western England. Lend-
Lease materials shipped to
England, Russia and
China helped to keep these
countries from falling to
the Axis powers.

Drawing the first number in the national call-up of 1940 at the state capitol in Frankfort, Ky. KENTUCKY STATE ARCHIVES

Manpower

In 1939 the U.S. Army numbered just 174,000 men. By the end of the war in 1945, over 11 million men and women were in uniform.

The first peacetime conscription in the nation's history, only a one-year draft, took place on Oct. 29, 1940. Over 16 million males aged 21-36 signed up and received numbers between 1 and 7,836. Secretary of War Henry L. Stimson drew the first number - 158 - from the same fishbowl used in the 1917 draft. President Roosevelt read it aloud.

Standards were not high for draftees: minimum height and weight (five feet and 105 pounds), correctable vision, at least half of one's natural teeth and no flat feet, hernias, or venereal diseases. Yet even with these simple criteria, about 50 percent of the applicants were rejected. In fact, the draft exposed one of the country's internal weaknesses traceable in part to the economic depression of the 1930s. Hundreds of thousands of physically acceptable recruits were turned down because they could not read or write.

Form. 15,112-11

NOTICE TO REGISTRANT
TO APPEAR FOR
PHYSICAL EXAMINATION
(Date of mailing)

You are directed to report for physical examination by the local board examiner at the time and place designated below:

_____Court House, Fort Thomas,_____ Ky._____
(Place of examination)

at __7:00__ P. m., on __Tues., Apr.___ 6th_____, 19__43

This examination will be of a preliminary nature, for the purpose of disclosing only obvious physical defects, and will not finally determine your acceptance or rejection by the armed forces.

If you are so far from your local board area that reporting for the above physical examination will constitute a hardship, you may submit a request to your local board for reference to another local board for preliminary physical examination. Your request must include the following information:
1. The reasons for your request for reference to another local board.
2. The designation (name and location) of the local board having jurisdiction over the area in which you are now located.

Failure to comply with this notice will result in your being declared delinquent and subjected to the penalties provided by law.

D. S. S. Form 201
(Rev. 4-1-42)

_____ Member-Clerk of Local Board.

Over 34 million men registered for the draft during the war. Of these, 72,354 applied for conscientious objector status. The army placed 25,000 in noncombatant service with 6,086 imprisoned for their refusal to participate in any form of service.

Olathe Company of the
Kansas State Guards, Sept.
6, 1941. KANSAS STATE
HISTORICAL SOCIETY

Kansas State Guards.
KANSAS STATE HISTORICAL
SOCIETY

The Delaware State Guard
being inspected in the
Wilmington Armory, Oct.
21, 1941. DSA

Members of the Delaware National Guard saying goodbye to their families. Scenes like this were repeated throughout the country when National Guard units were called to active duty in 1940. DSA

Members of the West Virginia National Guard leave for active duty from Clarksburg in 1940 wearing mostly World War I uniforms. CLARKSBURG ENGRAVING CO.

Naval construction increased considerably in 1940 and 1941 to counter aggressive Japanese intrusions in the Pacific, but naval forces would be no match for the future enemy until months after the Pearl Harbor attack. One of the newer battleships was the *USS South Dakota*. SOUTH DAKOTA STATE ARCHIVES

Scrap metal destined for Japan is piled up on a dock in Portland, Ore., in 1940 or early 1941. Scrap metal and oil, which fueled the Japanese war machine was finally embargoed by the United States government in 1941.

The United States embargoed silk from Japan in 1941 to try and pressure the country to come to terms with its demands for a less aggressive attitude.

The United States tried to avert war until the last moment but refused to back down from its demands that the Japanese withdraw their aggressive forces from China and Indo-China. This paper was printed the night before the dawn attack on Pearl Harbor.

THE FIRST DAYS: December 1941

LOCAL AIRCRAFT WARNING SERVICE IN OPERATION

The Searchlight

SECOND EXTRA

JAPS DECLARE WAR. ATTACK U.S.

Wake Reported Taken By Japanese

Hawaiian Island Bases Are Bombed

Jap Bombs Kill 350 At Airport

Newspaper extra on Dec. 7, 1941, in Redding, Calif. LC-USF34-71206-D

DAY OF INFAMY*

Originally published by the National Archives Trust Fund Board in 1988. Written by Raymond H. Geselbracht

At 9:30 p.m. on the night of December 6, 1941, a navy commander climbed the stairs to the second story of the White House, entered a large oval study, and gave President Franklin D. Roosevelt an intercepted and decoded cable from the Japanese Government to its ambassador in Washington. The President read over the rather lengthy cable for about 10 minutes, then handed it to Harry Hopkins, his chief foreign policy aide. Hopkins read over with dismay what amounted to a Japanese rejection of any attempt to resolve peacefully the differences between the United States and Japan. He handed the cable back to the President, a moment passed. Then Roosevelt turned to Hopkins and said, in substance, "This means war." Hopkins agreed, and added that the Japanese would strike when they were ready and wherever they chose. It was unfortunate, he suggested to the President, that the United States could not itself strike first, since the alternative was to suffer surprise attacks on its own Pacific interests or on those of the European nations fighting Germany. "No," Roosevelt replied, "we can't do that. We are a democracy and a peaceful people." The United States could not strike first, it would have to wait for the blow which would turn the wars in Europe and Asia into a World War. Neither Roosevelt nor Hopkins understood, as they discussed the issue late in the night of December 6, 1941, that the nation's wait would be over in only a few hours.

The United States had spent the two decades preceding its entry into World War II trying to avoid the mistakes that led to World War I. During the 1920s, the government participated in international conferences designed to avoid the arms buildup and formation of mutually hostile alliances that

had precipitated the outbreak of war in 1914. During the 1930s, this disenchantment with war spread throughout the country and became an outright disillusionment with everything having to do with World War I, and particularly with the kind of international idealism which President Woodrow Wilson had used to lead the country into the war. A so-called isolationism — a belief that America should keep free of European "entanglements" and concentrate on building and strengthening its democratic institutions at home — became dominant throughout the country.

This was the state of American public opinion when world order began to disintegrate in the 1930s under the pressures brought about by an international economic depression. In Europe, militaristic dictatorships in Germany and Italy, became increasingly able to send their armies across borders to seize territory, on one pretext or another, for the "fatherland." In Asia, Japanese military leaders argued that economic hard times required that new territories be conquered to serve both as sources of raw materials and markets for finished Japanese products. Japanese armies went first into Manchuria, then southward into other areas of China, and in 1940, into French Indochina. On September 27, 1941, Japan allied itself with Germany and Italy by signing at Berlin a pact pledging the three countries to a common military response against any country declaring war on any of the three countries. The politics of aggression and militaristic expansion in Europe and Asia were now clearly linked.

Despite the strongly isolationist views that most Americans held in the 1930s and despite a series of neutrality acts that isolationists in Congress had forced on him, President Roosevelt sought to encourage a spirit of resistance to the aggression of Germany, Italy, and Japan. In a speech delivered on October 5, 1937, he called for an international quarantine of the aggressors, and he hoped that the slogan "Quarantine the Aggressors" would be taken up by the American people

and be repeated so often that it would help shift public opinion away from isolationism. This did not happen, and instead the hostile reaction that his speech received proved to Roosevelt how strong isolationist sentiment was.

When Britain and France declared war on Germany in September 1939, Roosevelt warned the American people in a radio address that "when peace has been broken anywhere, the peace of all countries everywhere is in danger." His response to the outbreak of war was not to try to bring the United States into it; he knew public opinion would never support such an attempt. But he succeeded, after about a year's effort, in convincing the country that it must give all the help it could, short of actually going to war, to Britain and France. Most importantly, the United States, he said in a December 1940 radio address, must become "the great arsenal of democracy" providing the weapons and equipment which Britain, now standing alone against Germany, needed to win the war. By the fall of 1941, American actions to aid Britain were so substantial that the country was engaged in what was essentially an undeclared war with Germany.

Asia was considered to be of secondary importance in the period 1939-41. Roosevelt hoped Japan would keep more or less quiet while he pursued his main goal of preventing a German victory in Europe. He pursued a course of protracted negotiations with Japan without any real hope that they would bring lasting peace in the Pacific. It would be enough, he felt, if they gave the country a little additional time to build its munitions factories, to build up its armed forces, and to equip Britain and, beginning in the summer of 1941, Russia to resist Germany. The negotiations accomplished this goal, but they also allowed Japan to prepare its strike against the United States in the Pacific with great care.

In the days before the attack at Pearl Harbor, American and British military planners tried to determine where the inevitable Japanese strike would occur. Every logical target was in the western Pacific — in Southeast

Newspapers throughout the country put out extras for the "Day of Infamy," Dec. 7, 1941.

Asia or the Indonesian islands. When, in later November and early December, the possibility of a surprise attack on Hawaii was raised during American military planning discussions, the idea was dismissed as highly improbable. The things the Japanese needed to fuel their wartime economy and supply their armed forces — the oil, rubber, and other raw materials which they required — were all to be found in Southeast Asia and the Indonesian islands. An attack any closer to the United States would be, it was felt, illogical.

Japan's military planners, however, were not logical in the way American and British planners assumed them to be. In fact, during the same few days in later November and early December when American and British intelligence experts were studying maps of the western Pacific, trying to identify potential Japanese targets, a large Japanese fleet was bearing down on the Hawaiian Islands. At approximately 7:55 Sunday morning, Hawaiian time, December 7, 1941, a wave of 190 Japanese dive bombers, torpedo planes, and fighters struck the American naval base at Pearl Harbor. Not long after, a second wave of 170 planes joined in the surprise attack. The American forces were caught completely off their guard. The battle fleet, lined up in the harbor like targets at a shooting gallery, was largely destroyed

or put out of commission, as were most of the army and navy aircraft on Oahu; 2,403 Americans were killed. The Japanese attack planes flew back to their aircraft carriers almost without casualty. The attack had lasted about 2 hours.

It was early afternoon in Washington when the Pearl Harbor attack began. Roosevelt and Hopkins were sitting around the desk in the oval study, having lunch and giving barely a thought, for the moment, to the troubled world. The telephone rang, and Roosevelt learned from his Secretary of War that Honolulu was under attack. Hopkins could not believe the report: Japan would never attack Honolulu; it simply made no sense. The President disagreed: This was exactly the kind of unexpected thing the Japanese would do — attack out of the dawn at a place considered an illogical target, and at almost precisely the moment when their ambassadors were to meet with the Secretary of State to discuss peace.

For the rest of the afternoon and evening, news of the Japanese attack was relayed to the White House by telephone from the Navy Department. Grace Tully, the President's secretary, wrote down each message in shorthand as it came over the telephone, then transcribed it on the typewriter. By this time all of Roosevelt's major

military advisors had come together in the oval study. They stood around Tully's typewriter, watching in disbelief as the messages took form on the typed pages. Slowly, the dimensions of the terrible disaster became clear. The President, Tully later remembered, "maintained greater outward calm than anybody else but there was rage in his very calmness. With each new message he shook his head grimly and tightened the expression of his mouth."

Winston Churchill called from England to say that British colonies in Southeast Asia had also been attacked and that Britain would declare war on Japan the next morning. Roosevelt replied that he would go to Congress the next day to request a declaration of war. "This certainly simplifies things," Churchill told the President. "To have the United States at our side," he later wrote of his feelings during this telephone conversation, "was to me the greatest joy....Now at this very moment I knew the United States was in the war, up to the neck and in to the death. So we had won after all!...Hitler's fate was sealed. Mussolini's fate was sealed. As for the Japanese, they would be ground to powder."

Shortly before 5 p.m., the meetings for the moment over, the advisors, except Hopkins, gone, Roosevelt asked Grace Tully to take down a dictated

Residents of a New York City neighborhood discuss world events in Washington Square on Dec. 6, 1941. Little did they know that this was the last day of peace for America for almost four years. LC-USF34-12891-D

draft of his war message to Congress. His Secretary of State was adamant that the message be a long and detailed account of Japan's perfidious behavior toward the United States, but Roosevelt had decided on a brief message, describing the premeditated invasion of American territory on that day and requesting that Congress respond with a declaration of war on Japan. Tully recalled that Roosevelt dictated in the same calm tone that he used with his everyday correspondence. "Only his diction was a little different," she remembered, "as he spoke each word incisively and slowly, carefully...specifying each punctuation mark and paragraph." The most famous phrase of the finished address — one of the most famous phrases ever spoken by an American President — was not in the original dictation. "Yesterday, December 7, 1941," the original draft read, "a date which will live in world history, the United States of America was simultaneously and deliberately attacked by naval and air forces of the Empire of Japan." Roosevelt's orator's ear told him that "world history" would not do; he scratched out this wording and wrote in its place, "a date which will live in infamy."

This first sentence was in effect the entire substance of the war message. It made precisely the one, simple point that Roosevelt wanted to make to the American people. He was intensely conscious, as he prepared the address, that he had spent two years and more trying to lead his nation toward participation in a conflict that in their hearts they did not consider their own and did not want to enter. He had agonized, in the months prior to the Pearl Harbor attack, about what he should do if Japan struck — not at American territory — but at European colonies in the western Pacific. Surely our interest was involved in the well-being of the British empire in the Pacific, at least as long as Britain was fighting Germany. But would the American people understand this? Would they support their President if he wanted to fight to protect British interests? He was not sure. But the Pearl Harbor attack removed the agony from his decision making, and he wanted to convey, as briefly and directly as possible, the simplicity of the situation. The United States had been brutally and infamously attacked; we had no choice but to declare war on Japan. The rest of this brief message — it is under 500 words long and required about six minutes to read — was in-

Honolulu newspapers the day after the attack reported renewed Japanese attacks, which were, of course, erroneous.

THE SAGA OF NOMURA AND KURUSU

Kickisaburo Nomura was a Japanese admiral and ambassador to the United States in 1941. He was a naval attaché, a delegate to the 1919 Versailles Peace Treaty Conference and the 1922 Washington Naval Conference.

Saburo Kurusu was sent to the United States in November 1941 as a special envoy to help Nomura. He was the Japanese ambassador to Germany and signed the Tripartite Pact in 1940. He was married to an American, Alice Jay in 1914. She spent the next 27 years following him around the world while he was in the diplomatic corps. Their son was a Japanese military pilot who made a forced landing in Japan, and since he looked like an American, was beaten to death by the local peasants.

Both Nomura and Kurusu were interned after Pearl Harbor and repatriated in 1942. Nomura died in 1964, Kurusu in 1954.

Japanese Ambassador Nomura and Special Envoy Kurusu are shown leaving the White House about Nov. 26, 1941, after receiving rejections on proposals that they had hoped would avert war. The two diplomats were interned at The Homestead.

President Roosevelt, in the House
Chamber, asks Congress for a Decla-
ration of War against the Japanese,
Dec. 8, 1941. NA 208-CN-3992

VICTOR

For best results use
RCA Victor Needles

27734-A

PRESIDENT ROOSEVELT'S ADDRESS
TO THE CONGRESS OF THE
UNITED STATES
as broadcast to the Nation
on December 8, 1941
(Part 1)

RCA MANUFACTURING CO., INC., CAMDEN, N. J., U. S. A.

President Roosevelt signs the Declaration of War in his office on Dec. 8, 1941.
FDR

tended to portray in starkly contrasting colors the immorality of the enemy and the righteous position of the United States. "No matter how long it may take us to overcome this premeditated invasion," the address reads near its conclusion, "the American people in their righteous might will win through to absolute victory." According to Grace Tully, Roosevelt dictated the address to her "without hesitation, interruption or second thoughts."

By Monday morning, December 8, 1941, extra police had surrounded the White House, sentry boxes were under construction at the several entrances to the White House grounds, blackout curtains were being measured for the mansion's large windows, and a White House bomb shelter, to be built underneath the adjacent Treasury building, was being planned. The White House staff were being fitted for gas masks. At 12:30 in the afternoon, Roosevelt went before a joint session of Congress and read his war message. Congress promptly, almost unanimously, voted a Declaration of War. Roosevelt signed the declaration at 4 p.m. During the signing ceremony the President, despite being deeply worried about the seriousness of the defeat at Pearl Harbor, was vocally optimistic and portrayed a relaxed confidence as photographers took their pictures. The United States was at war with Japan.

Roosevelt's war message was almost entirely his own composition, the product of the immediate blaze of passionate anger and outrage that he felt when he learned of the attack on Pearl Harbor. "I do not think there was another occasion in his life," one of his speech writers, Robert Sherwood, later wrote of Roosevelt's delivery of the war message, "when he was so completely representative of the whole people." The American people, along with their President, felt a sense of relief that the war issue had been settled so definitely, and both, as Sherwood said, "recognized Pearl Harbor as a tragedy and a disgrace — and that recognition provided a boost to national pride which expressed itself in tremendous accomplishment." The United States, Roosevelt told the

American people in both the content of his address and in the confident manner of his delivery, would win this war.

Samuel Rosenman, a senior aide and friend of the President's, went to the White House to see Roosevelt late that same night. He was in his oval study sitting alone as his desk, working on his stamp collection. "There was a man at a big desk," Rosenman later remembered, "smoking a cigarette, poring over his stamps. There was concern, yes, deep concern; but it was a calm concern. He was worried, deeply worried; but there was no trace of panic. His face was resolute, even grim; but it was confident and composed. He knew by this time all the damage that had been done to us a Pearl Harbor. Yet I felt, as I looked at him, that he was confident that ultimate victory...was certain."

On December 11, Germany and Italy declared war on the United States. Until then, Roosevelt pointedly spoke only of the war with Japan in his public statements. He was still worried about isolationist feeling in the country. Japan had attacked the United States, Germany and Italy had not. As Roosevelt explained to the British ambassador just after the declaration of war on Japan, "I seem to be conscious of a still lingering distinction in some quarters of the public between war with Japan and war with Germany." Germany's and Italy's declarations of war on the United States settled the problem. The contestants in what had now become World War II were fully engaged.

Roosevelt did not live quite long enough to see the country through to the end of the war that his "Day of Infamy" speech had begun. He led his people through the difficult early days of 1942, through the liberation of North Africa, the invasion of Italy, the D-Day invasion of France, and the sea and island battles against Japan in the Pacific. Germany was all but beaten when Roosevelt died on April 12, 1945, and Japan, which would hold out until August, was already on the way to being, as Churchill put it, "ground to powder." In a radio address to the

nation given two days after the Pearl Harbor attack, Roosevelt made two promises. "We are going to win the war," he had said, "and we are going to win the peace that follows." He kept his first promise, despite his untimely death. The second, even had he lived longer, would probably have remained beyond his power to keep.

The typescript of the "Day of Infamy" address which the President used on December 8, 1941, called the "reading copy," suffered a peculiar fate for a rather long period. To begin with, it was "lost." When Roosevelt returned to the White House after having delivered his war message, Grace Tully, looking at him with alarm, asked, "Where is the speech, Mr. President?" But Roosevelt did not know where it was. According to the account in her memoirs, Tully asked practically everyone on the White House staff where the manuscript was, but no one knew. She was furious and asked a Secret Service agent to investigate the disappearance of the document. The agent reported that James Roosevelt, the President's son, had picked up the manuscript after Roosevelt had finished delivering his address and brought it back to the White House; he had entered by the front door, according to this account, turned to the right, and put both his coat and the manuscript on the coat rack. That was the end of the trail, as far as the Secret Service agent had been able to follow it. No one had seen the document since that moment when it lay on the coat rack. As late as 1981, when the Franklin D. Roosevelt Library tried to locate it for inclusion in an exhibit commemorating Roosevelt's centennial, the manuscript was still "missing."

The mystery was solved in 1984. In March of that year, an archivist who was aware that many people regarded the reading copy of the "Day of Infamy" speech as missing found it in the records of the United States Senate. It had never been truly lost or missing at all; it had merely been oddly placed. Roosevelt had not followed his normal practice of bringing his reading copy back to the White House for inclusion

Continued on page 32

The first radio news flash of the attack
was reported at 2:25 p.m. EST from the
Oval Office of the White House.

By Monday, Dec. 8, 1941, the country knew it was in a
global war, although Germany would not officially
declare war until Dec. 10. This is the scene on the
corner of Montgomery and Market streets in San
Francisco. NA 171-G-11L-1

in his own files. Instead, he had either handed the document to a Senate clerk when he was finished speaking, or the clerk had picked it up from the lectern from which the President spoke. The clerk then endorsed the reverse of the document, "Dec 8, 1941, Read in joint session," and filed it with the records of the United States Senate.

Crowds gather around a sound truck in New York City on Monday, Dec. 8, 1941, to hear President Roosevelt's war message to Congress. BETTMANN ARCHIVE

The Washington Monument, blacked out except for an airplane beacon on top of the obelisk, right after the Pearl Harbor attack. An anti-aircraft gun can be seen on the roof of an adjacent government office building. FDR

Key areas in Washington, D.C., were placed under heavy armed guard immediately following the Japanese attack on Pearl Harbor. These soldiers stand guard at the entrance to East Executive Avenue. BETTMANN ARCHIVE

Anti-aircraft guns, which were emplaced around Washington, D.C., shortly after Pearl Harbor to guard against another possible enemy air attack. BETTMANN ARCHIVE

Duke University students listen to President Roosevelt's Declaration of War speech, Dec. 8, 1941. Soon most of these students would be marching off to war.
DUKE UNIVERSITY ARCHIVES

Scene in the House of Representatives on Dec. 10, as Irving W. Swanson, House Reading Clerk, read a message from President Roosevelt asking Congress to declare war on Germany and Italy, after both of those nations had formally declared war on the U.S. earlier in the day.

The United States declared war on Germany and Italy on Dec. 10, thus opening up a second front for all the nations.

Jeannette Rankin, the first woman to serve in the U.S. Congress, was elected by the state of Montana in 1916, four years before women were allowed to vote. In Congress she voted against America's entry into World War I because, she stated, the war was being fought to preserve democracy, but women were denied the right to participate in the democratic process. She was defeated in 1919 because of her unpopular vote. She ran again and was elected in 1941, ironically just before America's entry into World War II and just in time to cast the only vote against a declaration of war, the day after the Pearl Harbor attack. Thus she held the distinction of being the only member of Congress to vote against entry into both World Wars. She was again defeated for re-election but went on to become a vocal advocate for peace throughout her lifetime. She died at the age of 93, two years before the end of the Vietnam War, in 1973. MONTANA HISTORICAL SOCIETY

TO THE CONGRESS OF THE UNITED STATES:

Yesterday, December 7, 1941 — a date which will live in infamy -- the United States of America was suddenly and deliberately attacked by naval and air forces of the Empire of Japan.

The United States was at peace with that nation and, at the solicitation of Japan, was still in conversation with its Government and its Emperor looking toward the maintenance of peace in the Pacific. Indeed, one hour after Japanese air squadrons had commenced bombing in Oahu, the Japanese Ambassador to the United States and his colleague delivered to the Secretary of State a formal reply to a recent American message. While this reply stated that it seemed useless to continue the existing diplomatic negotiations, it contained no threat or hint of war or armed attack.

It will be recorded that the distance of Hawaii from Japan makes it obvious that the attack was deliberately planned many days or even weeks ago. During the intervening time the Japanese Government has deliberately sought to deceive the United States by false statements and expressions of hope for continued peace.

The attack yesterday on the Hawaiian Islands has caused severe damage to American naval and military forces. Very many American lives have been lost. In addition American ships have been reported torpedoed on the high seas between San Francisco and Honolulu.

— 2 —

Yesterday the Japanese Government also launched an attack against Malaya.

Last night Japanese forces attacked Hong Kong.

Last night Japanese forces attacked Guam.

Last night Japanese forces attacked the Philippine Islands.

Last night the Japanese attacked Wake Island.

This morning the Japanese attacked Midway Island.

Japan has, therefore, undertaken a surprise offensive extending throughout the Pacific area. The facts of yesterday speak for themselves. The people of the United States have already formed their opinions and well understand the implications to the very life and safety of our nation.

As Commander-in-Chief of the Army and Navy I have directed that all measures be taken for our defense.

Always will be remembered the character of the onslaught against us.

No matter how long it may take us to overcome this premeditated invasion, the American people in their righteous might will win through to absolute victory.

I believe I interpret the will of the Congress and of the people when I assert that we will not only defend ourselves to the uttermost but will make very certain that this form of treachery shall never endanger us again.

Hostilities exist. There is no blinking at the fact that our people, our territory and our interests are in grave danger.

— 3 —

With confidence in our armed forces -- with the unbounding determination of our people -- we will gain the inevitable triumph -- so help us God.

I ask that the Congress declare that since the unprovoked and dastardly attack by Japan on Sunday, December seventh, a state of war has existed between the United States and the Japanese Empire.

Franklin D Roosevelt

THE WHITE HOUSE,
December 8, 1941.

This is Roosevelt's edited version of his famous "Day of Infamy" speech delivered to a joint session of Congress on Dec. 8, 1941. NA

DECEMBER 1941

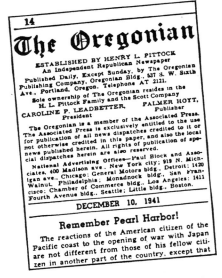

First to claim they had coined the battle cry "Remember Pearl Harbor" was the *Portland Oregonian* newspaper. Although dated Dec. 10 on the copy of the editorial page where it first appeared, the paper actually hit the streets at 4:45 p.m. on Dec. 9, 1941.

Two Americans viewed the start of the Japanese attack on Pearl Harbor from the air. At 7:58 a.m. on Dec. 7, a small Aeronca airplane, piloted by Honolulu lawyer Roy Vilusek with his 17-year-old son as a passenger, was in the sky over Honolulu when the Japanese attacked.

The Dow Jones average fell 2.5 percent the day after the Pearl Harbor attack and ultimately fell 20 percent in the next six months. It rallied 77 percent by the end of the war.

Army Insists Jap Planes Over S.F.

Air raid alarms have sounded east and west, 3000 miles apart, but as yet the continental United States has not been under attack by the enemy.

Last night the Mendicino County Sheriff's office was in-vestigating "mysterious flares" reported off the coast in the vicinity of Fort Bragg, one of the loneliest sections of Califor-nia's coast line.

High Army and Navy author-ities at San Francisco still in-sisted last night that the West Coast signals of Monday night and early yesterday were genu-ine, that it was not a test.

DEATH AT ANY MINUTE

"I tell you that Japanese planes were over this commu-nity," Lieutenant General John L. DeWitt emphatically told a session of the civilian defense organization at San Francisco. "Death and destruction are likely to come to this city at any minute."

President Roosevelt with his War Cabinet photographed at a meeting in the White House, Dec. 19. From left to right around the table: Harry Hopkins, Lend-Lease Administrator; Frances Perkins, Secretary of Labor; Col. Philip B. Fleming, Federal Works Administrator; Vice President Henry A. Wallace; Fiorello LaGuardia, Civil Defense Administrator; Paul V. McNutt, Federal Security Administrator; Jesse Jones, Secretary of Commerce and Federal Loan Administrator; Secretary of Interior Harold Ickes; Postmaster General Frank C. Walker; Secretary of War Henry L. Stimson; Secretary of State Cordell Hull; President Roosevelt; Secretary of Treas-ury Henry Morgenthau; Attorney General Francis Biddle; Secretary of Navy Frank Knox and Secretary of Agriculture Claude R. Wickard.

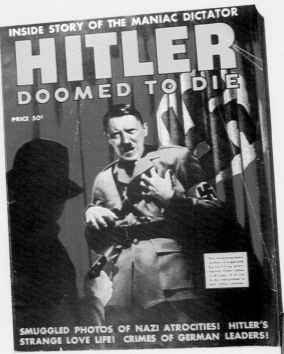

INSIDE STORY OF THE MANIAC DICTATOR
HITLER
DOOMED TO DIE
PRICE 50¢

SMUGGLED PHOTOS OF NAZI ATROCITIES! HITLER'S STRANGE LOVE LIFE! CRIMES OF GERMAN LEADERS!

ONE NATION INDIVISIBLE 1943-44

COUNCIL AGAINST INTOLERANCE IN AMERICA

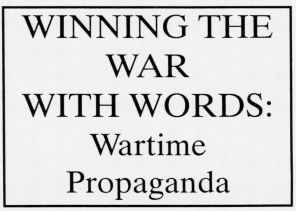

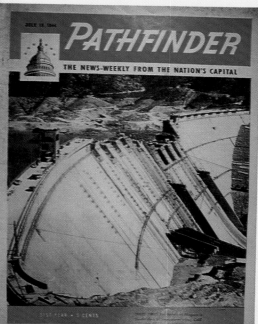

PATHFINDER
THE NEWS-WEEKLY FROM THE NATION'S CAPITAL

LET'S PULL TOGETHER

See WHAT HAPPENS TO ADOLF !
INSTRUCTIONS:
LIFT HEEL FROM BOTTOM..... AND PREPARE FOR A SURPRISE!
HEEL HITLER

WE WONT FORGET THE STAB IN THE BACK
* REMEMBER * PEARL HARBOR
Buy DEFENSE BONDS and STAMPS Now
DOUGLAS

We CAN'T win this war without sacrifice on the home front, too.

Managing the News

Soon after America's entry into the war, President Roosevelt realized that news would be very important for the American people and the conduct of the war. News came from a variety of sources, both public and private, and tended to be confusing. One agency was needed at the highest level of government to manage information.

Agencies already in existence included The Office of Facts and Figures, headed by Archibald MacLeish; the Office of Government Reports, headed by Lowell Mellett; the Office of the Coordinator of Information, headed by "Wild Bill" Donovan (who would soon be tapped to head the new Office of Strategic Services, the OSS); and the Office of Emergency Management, headed by Robert Horton.

All of these agencies were consolidated into one and called the Office of War Information, headed by a slow-talking, unpretentious CBS radio commentator named Elmer Davis. Davis' mandate was to tell the American people as much as possible, as fast and as be-lievably as possible, without compromising the safety of the armed forces.

Propaganda, of course, had to be built into some dispatches, but by and large Americans got factual and detailed information that brought the fighting forces closer to the people on the home front.

The Office of War Information, or OWI, was established early in the war to coordinate all war information released to the American public and the world at large. Elmer C. Davis, at the extreme right in the photo, was the agency's director for its duration. LC-USW3-28635-D

The news bureau of the Office of War Information (OWI) disseminated war news to both the domestic and overseas news media. While America adhered to its principles of freedom of speech and of the press, a central distribution center for war news was deemed necessary. FDR

Rehearsal for a radio program, "You Can't Do Business with Hitler," written and produced by the radio section of the Office of War Information. At the microphone, left to right, are: Col. Charles Ferris, Doris McWhirt and Virginia Moore. In the control room with script and talk-back microphone in hand is director Frank Telford. FDR

An American customer finds a choice of foreign language newspapers as well as American publications. Censorship may have been widespread abroad, but here the only censorship was for defense purposes. FDR

HITLER THE AXIS WAR MONSTER

A float in an anti-Nazi demonstration on Fifth Avenue
at 42nd Street, New York City, 1942. BETTMANN ARCHIVE

Hanging Hitler in effigy in
Ashland, Ky. FRANK B. ELAM
PHOTO

REMEMBER PEARL HARBOR

A street corner in Bridge-port, Conn., in 1944. FDR

Advertising poster in front of the TransLux Theater in Washington, D.C., July 1943. LC-USF34-11597-D

Clerks at a film counter promote stamps and bonds as well as film. OHS

Some propaganda, sponsored both by the government and private institutions, may have exceeded the bounds of good taste. FDR

A billboard in Aberdeen, S.D., February 1942. LC-USF34-64636-D

The back of a tractor-trailer in Charlotte, N.C., March 1943. LC-USW3-21981-D

LOOSE TALK

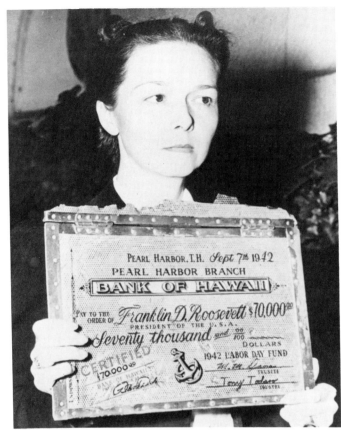

Miss Myrtle Bergheim, White House secretary, holds a check for $70,000 written on a wood and metal wing flap of a Japanese airplane shot down during the Pearl Harbor attack. The workers at the Pearl Harbor Navy Yard, instead of accepting their wages for working on Labor Day, sent them to the President in the form of this unique check, which was turned over to the U.S. Treasury. FDR

A mother proudly holds the pillow sent by a son in the service. American women participated in the war by giving up sons, husbands, brothers and fiancés, by working in defense plants, canteens, and war-related organizations, and by keeping the home fires burning. FDR

PROPAGANDA POSTCARDS

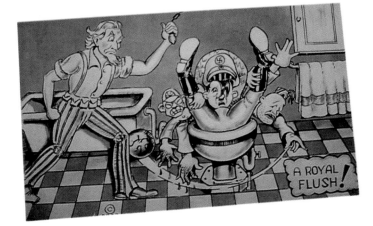

Mrs. Colin P. Kelly, mother of America's first outstanding hero of WWII, the late Colin P. Kelly, Jr., receives the first "V-HOME" certificate in her hometown of Madison, Fla., and one of the first in the nation. To qualify for a certificate, a family had to comply with instructions of the air raid warden regarding protection and blackout, conserve and salvage essential materials, refuse to spread rumors and buy War Savings Bonds and Stamps regularly. NA 171-G-12C-1

America's first war hero, Colin Kelly died a hero's death, but not exactly as the media portrayed it. He was cited as the country's first Medal of Honor winner who had single-handedly sunk the battleship, *Haruna*. Actually, he was shot down in his B-17 in the vicinity of the Philippines on Dec. 12, 1941, by a Zero fighter after sinking an enemy transport. America needed a hero, and Kelly fit the bill. He was awarded the Distinguished Service Cross, posthumously, and was lionized by the press. A liberty ship was even named for him.

HELP BRING THEM BACK TO YOU!

- Find time for war work
- Raise and share food
- Walk and carry packages
- Conserve everything you have
- Save 10% in War Bonds

DAVE AND SALLY MAKE THEIR

The Joseph C. Gardner family of Bethesda, Md., a suburb of Washington, have a Victory Home that David, 13, and Sally, 11, did much to make. David is in the ninth grade. Sally is in the sixth grade. Mr. Gardner is a landscape architect at the big, new War Department building. Mrs. Gardner is President of the Parent-Teacher Association at Sally's school. Joseph, Jr., a high school senior, is studying aeronautics and will register for the draft on his next birthday. With Dave and Sally setting the pace, the Gardners are saving and salvaging to, bring victory sooner.

V HOME

The (name of organization) is assisting in the V-Home Program sponsored by the U. S. Office of Civilian Defense and adopted by the Defense Councils of many communities to help every household give its best to winning the war. Dave and Sally show on these pages the part they took in the five-point program which won a sticker like the one above for their home.

This publication was distributed by Candid Features, Inc., in 1938 to warn Americans of the persecution of Jews in Germany and the possibility of similar events occurring in the United States.

This banner signifies that this home had a son in the Army engineers.

On June 9, 1942, the Germans destroyed the Czechoslovakian village of Lidice in reprisal for the assassination of S.S. Gen. Reinhard Heydrich, protector of Czechoslovakia. All males in the village over 15 years of age were shot, all females were sent to concentration camps and all children were sent to Germany for adoption. This action, outraged the Allies and in memorial, a town in Mexico and this one in Illinois, changed their names to Lidice.

POSTERS

WHAT CAN YOU SPARE THAT THEY CAN WEAR?

GIVE clothing for War Relief

APRIL 1 to 30

UNITED NATIONAL CLOTHING COLLECTION
for Overseas War Relief
HENRY J. KAISER, National Chairman

WE'VE MADE A MONKEY OUT OF YOU!

AMERICANOS TODOS ★ LUCHAMOS POR LA VICTORIA

★ AMERICANS ALL ★
LET'S FIGHT FOR VICTORY

For THINE is the KINGDOM and the POWER and the GLORY FOREVER

Give as the FAITH and COURAGE of our FOREFATHERS

PROTECT YOUR AMERICA

★ ★

FIGHT
COMMUNISM
FASCISM-NAZISM

CHRISTMAS GREETINGS
FROM Stewart Morse
SEAMAN SECOND CLASS
ONE OF OUR 400 BOYS IN SERVICE
STARR
COMMONWEALTH FOR BOYS
ALBION, MICH.

-GIT MAD-
WE GOTTA' LICK 'EM
LET'S GO ALL OUT FOR VICTORY!

Guns Blast Corregidor Invasion

© Gum, Inc.

Bubblegum card

A victory pot holder

AXIS BLASTER BANK

- BLAST THE AXIS FROM YOUR OWN HOME

JOKER

JOKER

WE GAVE

FOR OUR OWN — FOR OUR ALLIES

Match books

Flower vase

OUR CARELESSNESS
Their Secret Weapon

PREVENT FOREST FIRES

U. S. DEPT. OF AGRICULTURE
Forest Service

STATE
Forest Service

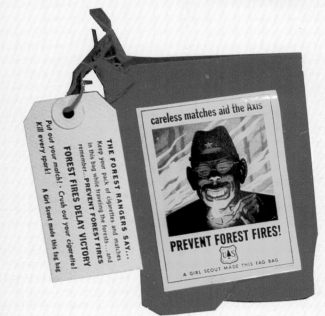

A sign in San Francisco, Calif., in April 1942. LC-USZ62-47276

TO YOU in the AIR FORCE!

GEE! The crowds were sure terrific! Their antics were a sin,

They stuck their elbows in my ribs
And kicked me in the shin!
In fact they were so WHACKY
And PUSHED and SHOVED
SO HARD —
I'm "IN THE AIR" myself, ol' Boy
BUT HERE'S YOUR CHRISTMAS CARD!

Valentine Greetings
TO ONE IN THE AIR CORPS

An EASTER Message to You In The Service

A HOLIDAY GREETING for You
in your COUNTRY'S SERVICE

Valentine Greetings to YOU in the SERVICE

UNCLE SAM IS PROUD OF YOU BECAUSE YOU'RE SURELY ONE SWELL GUY... AND KNOW HE NEEDS YOU, TOO!

A "Hello" to YOU In the SERVICE!

THIS FRIENDLY CARD IS BRINGING YOU A BIG HELLO TODAY AND I AM SENDING IT BECAUSE I THINK YOU'RE JUST...

Hi, SOLDIER!

HERE'S A VALENTINE "HELLO!"

CHEERIO!

It's "TAILOR-MADE" and a PERFECT FIT —

For a VERY FINE GIRL who is "DOING HER BIT"!

FINANCING THE WAR

FOR DEFENSE

BUY UNITED STATES SAVINGS BONDS AND STAMPS

OUR POST OFFICE OR BANK

COURTESY WOLF'S HEAD BOOKS, MORGANTOWN, W.VA.

Keep us flying!

BUY WAR BONDS

ST. VALENTINES DANCE
Student Body Cards Free
General Admission 11c
3:00 P.M. To 6:00 P.M.
Red Cross Benefit

I'M BUYING BONDS
OREGON SHIPBUILDING CORPORATION

St. Valentine's Day dance at the high school in
Emeryville, Calif., Feb. 14, 1942, promoting war bonds.
Notice the price for general admission - 11 cents.
OAKLAND TRIBUNE

Financing the War*

The problem of financing a global conflict of the magnitude of World War II staggers the imagination, even in retrospect, not merely because of the tremendously high cost of modern war equipment, such as aircraft carriers, ships, tanks, and planes, but because this high cost was largely borne by one country, the United States, called the "Arsenal of Democracy," but just as appropriately, the "Arsenal of Finance." The direct cost of World War II to the United States was estimated by the Treasury Department in 1947 to be $350,500,000,000, compared to $24,807,000,000 for World War I, and a total of $33,332,234,713, for all other wars of the United States, including World War I. Much of this disbursement was to Allies in the form of various types of equipment and supplies, including food.

Herculean efforts were made by the Treasury Department to meet some portion of these costs. Although the Federal public debt rose from $56.3 billion in 1941 to $252.7 billion in 1945, a large proportion of the war costs was met by tax levies. Federal taxes were collected at the source, with current payments; income tax personal exemptions were lowered; a special Victory Tax of five percent, later three percent and still later repealed, was levied; and income tax rates were raised markedly. During the period from 1940 to 1946, the Government relied on three general types of taxes to provide cash and reduce purchasing power. They were the personal income tax, which accounted for 37.1 percent of the receipts; the corporate income and excess profits taxes, which accounted for 32.9 percent of receipts; and levies on production, sale, or use of a number of goods and services, accounting for 14.1 percent of receipt. The remaining 16 percent included employment taxes, estate and gift taxes, capital stock taxes, customs, stamp taxes, and the like. The Treasury policy was to keep inflationary pressures under control.

Inflation was a pressing danger all through the war period. War wages were high and employment at top level. The various devices of Price and Rent Control, of Rationing and the like, were put into operation, but on the other hand there was a huge excess of ready cash in pay envelopes. Payment of income and other taxes, while satisfying to the deep instincts of loyalty and patriotism, was seldom or never glamorous; the call to buy War Bonds with surplus cash at intervals during the war offered the opportunity to those at home to do their bit, to let off steam, and to show how warmly and devotedly they were behind the men in the field.

Treasury estimates for 1943 show the enormity of the task of financing World War II. In preparation for the Third War Loan Drive, it was revealed that at the current wage levels more than $135 billion would pour into the pockets of American workers and salaried people in 1943. The war costs for that year were estimated to be $100 billion, and Secretary Henry Morgenthau Jr., asked the people to lend the Government $70 billion of this war cost. Even including the high war taxes and the increased living costs, surveys showed that the money sought for the Drive was there. War taxes at the time were estimated by the Treasury to be $30 billion.

The types of Federal Securities offered by the Treasury during the war were those that were non-marketable and those that were marketable. The first could not be transferred, but, with limitations, could be redeemed on demand. These included U.S. Savings Bonds, U.S. Savings Stamps, and Treasury Tax Saving Notes. The second category included Bills, Certificates of Indebtedness, notes, and bonds.

A war bond was actually a loan by a citizen to the government to help pay for the cost of the war. The purchase cost was $18.75, and 10 years later, at maturity, it was worth $25. If not cashed in, the interest would continue to accrue. In December 1985 the Miracle of America Museum purchased the uncashed bond pictured here from James F. Fleming Jr. for $111.54, its accrued value. MOA

The chief non-marketable securities (Savings Bonds and Tax-saving Notes) were sold continuously and given steady promotion, particularly in the big War Loan Drives. Treasury Bills and Certificates of Indebtedness were offered all through the war. The marketable bonds were likewise offered steadily until November 1942. At that time, the Treasury Department found that too large a portion of the sales was being made to commercial banks. As a result, the great War Loan Drives, eight of them in all, were organized and set in motion. They lasted from November 1942 to the close of 1945.

The War Loan Drives were characterized by sales goals set by types of purchasers as well as by geographic areas. The early drives lasted from three to four weeks; the later ones from six to seven weeks. Sales were, as much as possible, concentrated on individuals, since commercial banks were limited as to amount of purchases. A nationwide organization was formed to promote these sales, consisting of bank representatives, as well as representatives of the Treasury, the Federal Reserve System, and other organizations. The several War Loan Drives and their dates were as follows:

First - Nov. 30 to Dec. 23, 1942
Second - April 12 to May 1, 1943
Third - Sept. 9 to Oct. 16, 1943
Fourth - Jan. 18 to Feb. 29, 1944
Fifth - June 12 to July 8, 1944
Sixth - Nov. 20 to Dec. 16, 1944
Seventh - May 14 to June 30, 1945
Eighth (Victory) - Oct. 29 to Dec. 31, 1945

*Taken from *Delaware's Role in World War II* by Public Archives Commission, 1955.

It Takes Both—
WAR BONDS
AND
TAXES

HELP AVENGE PEARL HARBOR
★ BUY WAR BONDS & STAMPS ★

2-man Jap sub—captured at Pearl Harbor—on nation-wide Treasury War Savings Tour

The Most You Can Save Is the Least You Can Do

BOND POSTERS

Don't Let That Shadow Touch Them
WAR BONDS

BUY War Savings Stamps and lick "the other side!"

SEW, SERVE and SAVE
...Put Your Savings in **WAR BONDS**
ENROLL NOW WITH **AWVS**
AMERICAN WOMEN'S VOLUNTARY SERVICES

PUBLISHED IN COOPERATION WITH THE TREASURY DEPT.,
WAR PRODUCTION BOARD and A.W.V.S. by SPOOL COTTON CO.
J. & P. COATS and CLARK'S O.N.T. THREADS

The U.S. Treasury Department selected this Norman Rockwell painting as its official poster for the 8th War Loan Drive. It originally appeared as the Saturday Evening Post cover for May 26, 1945.

Hasten the Homecoming
BUY VICTORY BONDS

WE CAN...
WE WILL..
WE MUST !
..Franklin D. Roosevelt
BUY U.S. WAR SAVINGS BONDS & STAMPS NOW

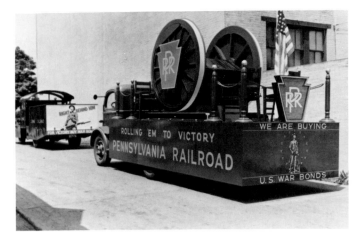

CALIFORNIA STATE RAILROAD MUSEUM

Christmas promotion and curbside service in Wilmington, Del., for the 6th War Loan Drive which ran from Nov. 20 to Dec. 16, 1944. DSA

An unusual mode of transportation used to promote the 7th War Loan Drive, which lasted from May 14 to June 30, 1945. DSA

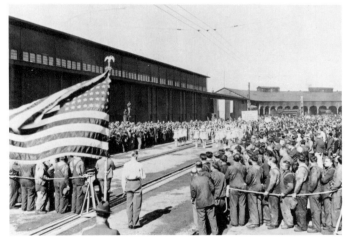

A bond rally at the Southern Pacific Railroad shops in Sacramento, Calif., Oct. 28, 1942. CALIFORNIA STATE RAILROAD MUSEUM

The winning war bond booth at Maryhurst College, Portland, Ore., during the 4th War Loan Drive, 1943. OHS

Movie actor John Payne visits Duke University to promote war bonds. DUKE UNIVERSITY ARCHIVES

The *Hobo News'* slogan was: "A little fun to match the sorrow," but even this unusual New York newspaper helped promote bond sales, as this June 1943 picture shows. LC-USW-3-31117-C

SELLING AND SAVING BONDS AND STAMPS

WAVES at a midwestern Naval Air Station sell bonds from this firecracker-shaped booth. They were successful in their drive to sell enough to pay for two PT-boats. NA 80-G-K-14170

TABLE OF REDEMPTION VALUES OF UNITED STATES SAVINGS BONDS

ISSUE PRICE	$18.75	$37.50	$75.00	$375.00	$750.00
Redemption values after the issue date:					
First year ...	$18.75	$37.50	$75.00	$375.00	$750.00
1 to 1½ years .	19.00	38.00	76.00	380.00	760.00
1½ to 2 years .	19.25	38.50	77.00	385.00	770.00
2 to 2½ years .	19.50	39.00	78.00	390.00	780.00
2½ to 3 years .	19.75	39.50	79.00	395.00	790.00
3 to 3½ years .	20.00	40.00	80.00	400.00	800.00
3½ to 4 years .	20.25	40.50	81.00	405.00	810.00
4 to 4½ years .	20.50	41.00	82.00	410.00	820.00
4½ to 5 years .	20.75	41.50	83.00	415.00	830.00
5 to 5½ years .	21.00	42.00	84.00	420.00	840.00
5½ to 6 years .	21.25	42.50	85.00	425.00	850.00
6 to 6½ years .	21.50	43.00	86.00	430.00	860.00
6½ to 7 years .	21.75	43.50	87.00	435.00	870.00
7 to 7½ years .	22.00	44.00	88.00	440.00	880.00
7½ to 8 years .	22.50	45.00	90.00	450.00	900.00
8 to 8½ years .	23.00	46.00	92.00	460.00	920.00
8½ to 9 years .	23.50	47.00	94.00	470.00	940.00
9 to 9½ years .	24.00	48.00	96.00	480.00	960.00
9½ to 10 years .	24.50	49.00	98.00	490.00	980.00
Maturity value .	25.00	50.00	100.00	500.00	1,000.00

DO YOUR PART TO WIN THE WAR
BUY MORE WAR SAVINGS STAMPS

HELP WIN THE WAR—
WITH THE MONEY YOU SAVE

Join the Payroll War Savings Plan today. If you have already enrolled, step up your savings to at least 10% of your pay.

WE CAN...
WE WILL...
WE MUST!

BUY WAR SAVINGS BONDS
"A DIME FROM EVERY DOLLAR EVERY PAYDAY"

An unusual oil bottle promoting war bond sales. The oil was bottled by the Rio Grande Valley Oil Co., of Albuquerque, N.M.

World War II helped the economy. In 1940, despite eight years of the New Deal, the U.S. economy was still in depression, with an unemployment rate of 14.6 percent. Then, military orders started a rapid recovery. After Dec. 7, 1941, the economy went into overdrive, with real GNP growing at a 12.5 percent annual rate from 1941 to 1944, and emerged from the war stronger than it had been before.

Barnum and Bailey Circus clowns attend a bond rally in Pittsburgh, Pa. FDR

Movie actress, Irene Dunne at a Washington, D.C., bond caravan, Aug. 31, 1942. FDR

The famous comedy duo Abbott and Costello takes part in a "Stars Over America" bond caravan in Washington, D.C., September 1942. LIFE PICTURE SERVICE

School kids buying war stamps in an Institute, W.Va., school. WEST VIRGINIA STATE COLLEGE LIBRARY

Bonds and stamps being sold from a victory booth at West Virginia State College, an all-black college until 1954, in Institute, W.Va. WEST VIRGINIA STATE COLLEGE LIBRARY

DSA

Music students of the National Institute of Music and Arts in Bremerton, Wash., show their bonds and savings stamps. FDR

Another stamp or bond sale is made. BETTMANN ARCHIVE

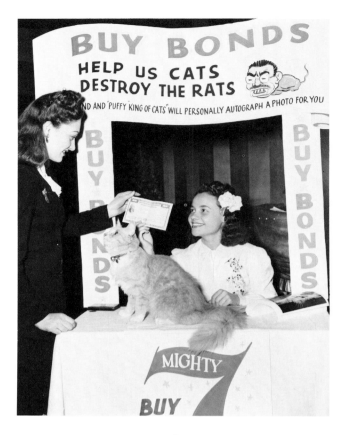

"Puffy" the cat does his part for the war effort at the Cafe Zanzibar in New York City, May 1945. BETTMANN ARCHIVE

"Antique" cars line up to promote bond sales. More than likely they were destined for the scrap yard, Salt Lake City, October 1943. UTAH STATE HISTORICAL SOCIETY, *SLC TRIBUNE*

A huge "United for Victory" rally in Buffalo, N.Y., Feb. 21, 1943. FDR

Bond booth set up at a local movie theater in Huntington, W.Va. MARSHALL UNIVERSITY ARCHIVES, CATHERINE ONSLOW PAPERS

A Victory House for the sale of war bonds erected in front of the Harrison County Courthouse, Clarksburg, W.Va., gets a cleaning in May 1943. CLARKSBURG ENGRAVING CO.

Pearl Harbor Day two years later at the Pearl Harbor Navy Yard. U.S. ARMY MUSEUM HAWAII

Every means possible was used to promote the sale of war bonds, such as this freight car in San Bernardino, Calif. LC-USW3-21603-E

Crowds gather for a bond drive sponsored by the *Salt Lake Tribune*/KDYL Radio in Salt Lake City, Utah, 1942. UTAH STATE HISTORICAL SOCIETY, *SLC TRIBUNE*

MISSOURI HISTORICAL SOCIETY

A Safeway Food Store in Payette, Idaho, advertises the defense stamps that it sells, November 1941. LC-USF34-70936-D

Bank of America billboard, San Francisco, Calif., May 1943. LC-USW3-24539-D

REMEMBER!
That M-1 Garand Rifle Your
Soldier Needs Costs
$80
★
BUY MORE BONDS
AND STAMPS

Coach Edwin Firiera, holding the ball, gives a pep talk
to his team, one of many
composed of workers at the
Pearl Harbor Navy Yard in
Hawaii. People went to
great lengths to promote
war bond sales. O.W.I.
COLLECTION VIA VMI

The Denver Women's Bond and Stamp
Division was an important division of the
Denver Defense Council. It was established at the request of the Treasury
Department to assist in the sale of
defense stamps and war bonds. The office
started under the sponsorship of the
American Women's Voluntary Services,
and was staffed largely by the Rotary
Club Auxiliary. Booths were installed in
the larger stores, theaters and restaurants, and volunteers trained to sell
bonds. People who did not believe in
banks, but instead carried money around
in their pockets, bought bonds at the
booths, and many stated that they were
glad to have the opportunity but would
not trust their funds to regular channels.
The volunteers in the division also
assisted in special events which the
Treasury Department promoted. From its
inception in November 1942 until Dec. 11,
1944, the organization raised
$4,827,133.30. In addition, it sold bonds
for special purposes such as a bomber
called "City of Denver." COLORADO
HISTORICAL SOCIETY

WHY THE CANVASS HERE IS THE ANSWER!

"Everyone agrees that we must win this war. Everyone agrees that no personal need or want must interfere with victory. Everyone agrees that all Americans must pitch in and help in every way they can. Buying Defense Savings Bonds and Stamps is the one way in which each one of us can do his part. Signing pledges to buy them regularly will help even more, for like you and your neighbor and your boss, the Government would like to know how much income it can expect when it is figuring how to meet the costs of war. It can estimate needed taxes. It can estimate bank credit. Until now, however, it has not been able to estimate how much the people themselves are willing to lend. The pledges will tell that story. This knowledge will help the Government speed up orders and production for our armed forces. It will help to build our home defenses and our ramparts overseas. It may help to keep down taxes, if enough of us sign pledges--and keep our word."

It has come to our attention that there have recently been some occasions where uninformed Defense Savings Bond speakers have been carried away with enthusiastic ardor and have made statements which are contrary to the principles underlying the Defense Savings Bond campaign. We feel it is highly important that we be thoroughly familiar with these fundamental principles and that all those cooperating in the campaign and, particularly, all those who are making public appearances and who are publishing articles or stories be accurately informed.

Our attention has been called to one case where an enthusiastic speaker urged his audience to withdraw all savings accounts being held as reserves and to transfer that money and all other investments to Defense Savings Bonds.

Let us have every member of our County Committees and everyone engaged in this program definitely understand the principles which have been so clearly and so frequently stated by the Treasury Department and the National Defense Savings Bond Staff - that the objective in this campaign is to have Defense Savings Stamps and Bonds purchased out of current income. One of the great objectives in this campaign is to provide an effective weapon against inflation and to reduce competition for a limited amount of consumer goods, and to have every possible one of the thirty five million people in America who receive salary, wages or income from other sources use a substantial part of that income for the regular purchase of Defense Savings Bonds and Stamps and to do that not as a token participation but to the point of real personal sacrifice.

The Treasury Department is not asking people to withdraw savings accounts to discontinue building and loan association payments, to discontinue other investment programs, to withdraw life insurance or annuity funds, or discontinue such payments, to convert other investments, to collect mortgages or notes for the investment of such funds in Defense Savings Bonds and, as a matter of fact, it is definitely unwise to do so. It is obvious that if there were any mass movements on the part of the people in America, stirred up by patriotic enthusiasm or war hysteria, in doing this financial and economic chaos would result throughout the country.

Let us, therefore, be sure that all our people are impressed with the need of having Bonds and Stamps purchased out of current income.

Respectfully
Defense Savings Committee

A budget is more important now than ever before! See that yours provides for regular purchases of United States War Savings Bonds!

War bond rally at a Pittsburgh, Pa., theater. FDR

THIS LITTLE PIG HELPS AMERICA
FOR ALL GRADES
RUTH EVELYN HORN
Teacher, Third and Fourth Grades, Public School, Papillion, Nebraska

This Little Pig Went to Market to buy WAR BONDS and STAMPS

Most of us know that the purchase of War Bonds and War Stamps is still the patriotic duty of every American, but we need to be reminded about it occasionally. "This little pig" of the nursery rhyme, scampering off to market, is ready to make his contribution to help win the war. He will serve as an incentive to your pupils to do likewise. Suggest that other animal characters from storybooks be featured in War Stamp posters. Also display the rabbit poster from THE INSTRUCTOR for April 1943.

THE INSTRUCTOR, November 1943

YOU CAN EARN THIS SHOULDER EMBLEM

U. S. WAR STAMP AGENT
WATER WEASEL

MADE OF FELT IN COLORS

JOIN THE DRIVE TO BUY WATER-WEASELS FOR THE ARMY
★ YOUR SUPERVISOR HAS THE DOPE—ASK HIM!
NEWSPAPER BOYS' SECTION—WAR FINANCE DIVISION—U. S. TREASURY DEPT.

OFFICIAL U. S. TREASURY POSTER   WTD 988

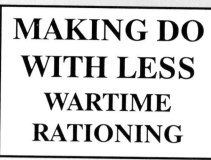

SUGAR IS BEING RATIONED

We furnish this envelope to *Insure Cleanliness*

YOUR COOPERATION IS VITAL TO VICTORY

Thank You!

MAKING DO WITH LESS
WARTIME RATIONING

EXCLUSIVELY YOURS

VICTORY
HAIR PIN KIT

A. AUCOIN
LIQUORS & WINE

DRINK
Coca-Cola

WINE

FISH

CLOSED
FOR
DURATION

VIRGINIA A. B. C. BOARD
THIS COUPON PERMITS THE PURCHASE OF
28 ONE UNIT OF DISTILLED SPIRITS
OR
ONE UNIT OF WINES IN EXCESS OF 14% ALCOHOL BY VOLUME
½ UNIT

VIRGINIA A. B. C. BOARD
VOID IF DETACHED
OR
PRESENTED AFTER EXPIRATION DATE
½ UNIT
28

O.P.A. R-1708 SPECIAL SHOE STAMP
GOOD FOR ONE PAIR OF SHOES
DATE ISSUED
1
WAR RATION BOOK NUMBER

A roadside stand in the vicinity of Lake Charles, La., is closed for the duration of the war. LC-USW3-33981-D

RATIONING

Goods-rationing was one of the consequences of war and one of the most often remembered facets of the conflict. Once America entered the war, the military had first priority on supplies. As the steel, aluminum and other mineral-processing industries strained to expand to meet wartime needs, acute metal shortages resulted. Civilian needs took a back seat to the thousands of ships, tanks and airplanes rolling off the ways and assembly lines of the great war industries.

The Office of Price Administration (OPA) was established in April 1941 to try and regulate inflation and to institute rationing procedures. After America's entry into the war, ration boards were set up in every county in the country, and more than 30,000 volunteers were recruited to handle the paper work. Prices were controlled on 90 percent of the civilian goods sold, and a series of ration books was issued to every man, woman and, child in the country. As the war drew on, nearly every item was rationed or regulated.

Rubber, a critical war material, was the first item rationed; this resulted in the rationing of gasoline. Black markets sprang up around the country, especially in the gas and rubber areas, and criminals even counterfeited ration coupons for resale.

The rationing of food struck every American equally hard. Sugar was the first item to become scarce and was rationed until 1946. Coffee was rationed in November 1942, but was taken off the ration list in July 1943. Similar measures of careful distribution became necessary for most other food items until the end of the war. In addition, non-food items, such as firewood in the Northwest and coal in certain areas of the country, also had to be rationed.

War Ration Book One was issued in May 1942 through local schools, and several more were issued over the next three years. Rationing, or the looming threat of it, sparked a tendency toward hoarding, despite the fact that such practices were looked on as being unpatriotic. A contemporary book called *Consumer Problems in Wartime* addressed this problem:

What was right for the consumer yesterday, even a virtue, is wrong today. The woman who rails at strikes in industry or red tape and incompetence in public officials may have closets stored with canned goods or sugar or coffee. Once that would have meant foresight and good management. Today, however, it means that ugly thing - hoarding.

Thirty percent of all cigarettes went to the Armed Forces. In 1944 they became scarce throughout the United States. Whiskey disappeared in 1944 as distilleries had converted plants to industrial alcohol production in 1942.

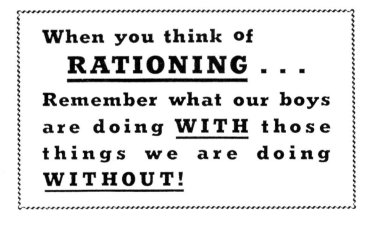

When you think of **RATIONING . . .** Remember what our boys are doing **WITH** those things we are doing **WITHOUT!**

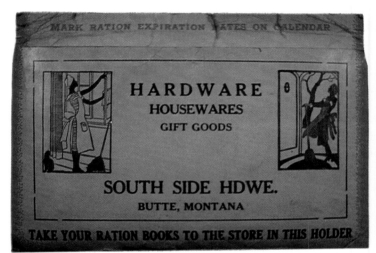

MARK RATION EXPIRATION DATES ON CALENDAR

HARDWARE
HOUSEWARES
GIFT GOODS

SOUTH SIDE HDWE.
BUTTE, MONTANA

TAKE YOUR RATION BOOKS TO THE STORE IN THIS HOLDER

★ WAR PRICE AND RATIONING BOARD ★

★ OFFICE OF PRICE ADMINISTRATION ★

COURTESY SHARON HINSHAW, MISSOULA, MONT.

HOW TO USE YOUR WAR RATION BOOK

IMPORTANT.—Before the stamps of the War Ration Book may be used, the person for whom it was issued must sign it as indicated in the book. The name of a person under 18 years of age may be signed either by such person or by his father, mother, or guardian.

For future reference, make and keep a record of the serial number of your book and the number of your issuing Ration Board, as indicated in your book.

Your first War Ration Book has been issued to you, originally containing 28 War Ration Stamps. Other books may be issued at later dates. The following instructions apply to your first book and will apply to any later books, unless otherwise ordered by the Office of Price Administration. In order to obtain a later book, the first book must be turned in. You should preserve War Ration Books with the greatest possible care.

1. From time to time the Office of Price Administration may issue Orders rationing certain products. After the dates indicated by such Orders, these products can be purchased only through the use of War Ration Books containing valid War Ration Stamps.

2. The Orders of the Office of Price Administration will designate the stamps to be used for the purchase of a particular rationed product, the period during which each of these stamps may be used, and the amounts which may be bought with each stamp.

3. Stamps become valid for use only when and as directed by the Orders of the Office of Price Administration.

4. Unless otherwise announced, the Ration Week is from Saturday midnight to the following Saturday midnight.
16—26649-1

5. War Ration Stamps may be used in any retail store in the United States.

6. War Ration Stamps may be used only by or for the person named and described in the War Ration Book.

7. Every person must see that his War Ration Book is kept in a safe place and properly used. Parents are responsible for the safekeeping and use of their children's War Ration Books.

8. When you buy any rationed product, the proper stamp must be detached in the presence of the storekeeper, his employee, or the person making delivery on his behalf. If a stamp is torn out of the War Ration Book in any other way than above indicated, it becomes void. If a stamp is partly torn or mutilated and more than one-half of it remains in the book, it is valid. Otherwise it becomes void.

9. If your War Ration Book is lost, destroyed, stolen, or mutilated, you should report that fact to the local Ration Board.

10. If you enter a hospital, or other institution, and expect to be there for more than 10 days, you must turn your War Ration Book over to the person in charge. It will be returned to you upon your request when you leave.

11. When a person dies, his War Ration Book must be returned to the local Ration Board, in accordance with the Regulations.

12. If you have any complaints, questions, or difficulties regarding your War Ration Book, consult your local Ration Board.

NOTE

The first stamps in War Ration Book One will be used for the purchase of sugar. When this book was issued, the registrar asked you, or the person who applied for your book, how much sugar you owned on that date. If you had any sugar, you were allowed to keep it, but stamps representing this quantity were torn from your book (except for a small amount which you were allowed to keep without losing any stamps). If your War Ration Book One was issued to you on application by a member of your family, the number of stamps torn from the books of the family was based on the amount of sugar owned by the family, and was divided as equally as possible among all these books.

☆ U. S. GOVERNMENT PRINTING OFFICE 16—26649-1

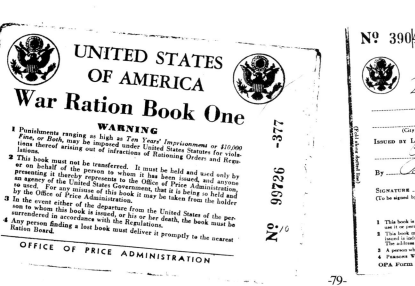

NOTICE. Customary use of metal for your lunch kit has been forbidden by the War Production Board, as steel is needed for war materials. THIS "VICTORY KIT" is provided to take the place of your metal kit. Made of durable fibre board, it is sturdily constructed to give you good service. Pyroxylin coated both inside and out, this kit is water repellent and can be cleaned easily with a damp cloth.

BECAUSE of the nature of the material this kit should not be left or stored in damp or wet locations.

MAGAZINES

are rationed too!

Your dinner table and your automobile are no longer alone in feeling the pinch of war. Paper for your magazines is rationed too.

As a magazine reader, this is extremely important to you. Paper rationing, in many cases, means that fewer copies will be printed. Magazines are falling into line with beans and butter and beefsteaks—into the ranks of the hard-to-find.

Subscriptions too are likely to feel the pinch. The man-power shortage means that the sales-people who used to take care of your magazines may not be calling on you this year.

But you can still order by mail. And be sure of your copies every week or every month, unfailingly delivered to your door by Uncle Sam's mailman.

And at this time, until February 15th, you can secure for yourself the best bargain the mails are likely to offer you in many a day—14 months (not just a year) of The American Magazine, Woman's Home Companion and Collier's Weekly, all three for only $5.00. And payable, if you prefer, at $1.00 a month.

This very special offer saves you $6.60 from the regular newsstand value— $3.16 from the regular yearly subscription price.

So, be sure to order now—definitely before February 15th—and avoid a blackout of your entertainment for the coming fourteen months.

THE CROWELL-COLLIER PUBLISHING CO.
Springfield, Ohio

COF COF

RATION DEPOSIT SLIP

THE UNITED STATES OF AMERICA
OFFICE OF PRICE ADMINISTRATION

ROASTED COFFEE CREDITS

DEPOSITED IN

**THE SECURITY TRUST &
SAVINGS BANK**
SHENANDOAH, IOWA

FOR THE RATION ACCOUNT OF

_____

_____

DATE_____194____

The depositor agrees that this bank will maintain all his ration bank accounts as an agency of and under the direction of the Office of Price Administration and will be responsible only to the Office of Price Administration as provided in General Ration Order No. 3; that the depositor waives all recourse against this bank except for wilful acts or omissions; and that all deposits are accepted subject to count and verification.

ITEMS DEPOSITED	LB. EACH STAMP	QUANTITY OF STAMPS	NO. OF CARDS	POUNDS	
Stamp No._____					
Stamp No._____					
1. List separately the amount of each item deposited other than stamps.					
2. Indicate beside each amount the type of item deposited.					
3. The bank number, which appears on the ration check under the bank name to the right, must be written in beside the amount of each ration check deposited.					
TOTAL					

PREPARE IN DUPLICATE AND HAVE BANK STAMP
OR INITIAL COPY FOR YOUR RECORDS.

RED & BLUE OPA COINS
Shopkeepers will save $35,000,000.

RETAIL TRADE

Something Simple

OPA felt that at last it was about to give the nation's grocers and housewives something really & truly simple. Date of the gift is Feb. 27, but last week, well in advance, OPA was proudly explaining about its new change-making food tokens. The fiber tokens (*see cut*) will be red for meats and fats, blue for processed foods. Each token will be worth one ration point. All red and blue food stamps will be worth ten points, no matter what the figures already printed on them. Stamps will remain valid for twelve weeks instead of the current four. Use of the tokens will mean no more brown stamps.

OPA's Food Rationer Walter Straub figures that the tokens will save shopkeepers an annual $35 million worth of time otherwise spent sorting stamps. The American taxpayer, he judges, will save $1.5 million every time a new ration book is not issued.

The point system at work. Meat and other food items had to be purchased with ration points to divide the limited supplies fairly.

FDR

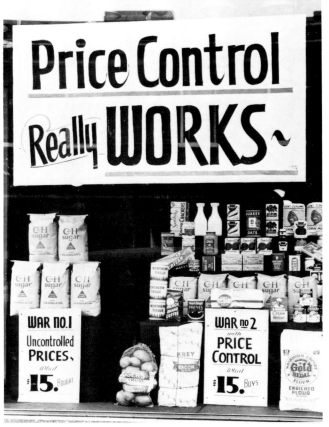

Many retail stores throughout the country indicated support of the government's price control order by displaying this poster. FDR

Lucy Knox, a teacher at McKinley High School in Washington, D.C., instructs a nutrition class on the effects of point rationing on a balanced diet. FDR

A clerk tears off point stamps to cover the food purchase. FDR

As the newspaper headline makes clear, cheating the ration system and even racketeering schemes were not unknown during the war years. In any situation there are always unscrupulous people.

Ceiling prices for tobacco products and razor blades are posted at the counter. FDR

SUGAR RATIONING

The first table food item to become scarce was sugar, which was rationed beginning in April 1942. Memories of rationing during World War I led the American public to runs on sugar just after the Pearl Harbor attack. Imports were halted from the Philippines, and the shortage of shipping curtailed deliveries from the Caribbean area. Sugar rationing even continued after the war, well into 1946.

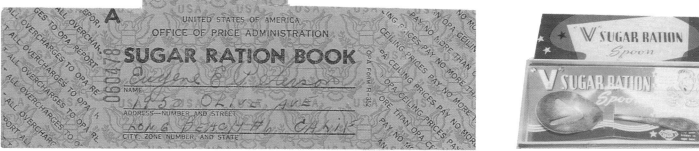

WE MUST GET ALONG WITH LESS SUGAR THIS YEAR BECAUSE—

1. Military needs are high. Each soldier actually consumes twice as much sugar a year as the average civilian now receives.
2. Ships which otherwise might be bringing sugar into the United States are hauling supplies to the battle fronts.
3. Manpower is scarce at sugar refineries and shipping ports.
4. Beet sugar production last year was 500,000 tons short, making the stock of sugar smaller for this year.
5. Last year many people over-applied for canning sugar. We used so much sugar that stocks at the beginning of this year were abnormally low.

DO NOT APPLY FOR MORE SUGAR THAN YOU ACTUALLY NEED FOR HOME CANNING — HELP MAKE OUR WAR SHORT SUGAR SUPPLIES LAST ALL YEAR

READ BEFORE USING 5-POUND HOME CANNING SUGAR COUPONS

Before the attached coupons are used for the purchase of sugar *for home canning*, you or any member of your "family unit" listed on the application must sign each home canning coupon (OPA Form R-312). The person signing must enter the serial number of his War Ration Book Four thereon.

For the purpose of identification, it will be necessary for the signer to take his War Ration Book Four with him when he purchases the sugar.

These coupons are not transferable.

Applicant will print or type below his full name and complete mailing address

NAME *Audrey E. Schneider*

ADDRESS *1728 - 32nd Ave.*
(Number)　　　　　(Street, R. F. D., or Gen. Delivery)

CITY, POSTAL ZONE, STATE *Seattle, 22, Washington*

(Do not detach)

AMOUNT OF SUGAR ALLOWED FOR HOME CANNING

A—A *maximum* of one pound of sugar will be allowed per four quarts of finished canned fruit or fruit juice.

B—A *maximum* of five pounds of sugar will be allowed per person for use in making any or all of the following: jams, jellies, preserves, marmalades, and fruit butters from fruits; for canning vegetables; making pickles, relishes, catsup, mince meat, etc., and for curing meat. However, no more than ~~forty (40)~~ pounds per "family unit" will be allowed.

ANSWER ALL THE FOLLOWING QUESTIONS		DO NOT WRITE IN SPACE WITHIN HEAVY LINES		
		DATE	BOARD NO.	COUNTY AND STATE

1　Have you or any other member of your "family unit" applied for sugar for home canning since January 1, 1945, for any of the persons for whom this application is made?　YES ☐　NO ☑

If answer is "Yes," state name of person who made the application

☐ Disapproved.

Approved for _____ Pounds for Preserving,

for _____ Pounds for Canning,

TOTAL APPROVED _____ Pounds.

2　How many pounds of sugar did you use in 1944 for making jams, jellies, etc., listed in B above?　*10* lb.

2a　How many pounds of sugar will you use in 1945 for making jams, jellies, etc.? (See B above)　*5* lb.

SIGNATURE OF BOARD OR PANEL MEMBER

SIGNATURE OF BOARD CLERK

DATE ISSUED

3　How many quarts (or equivalent) of finished canned fruit did you can with sugar in 1944?　*30* qt.

3a　How many quarts (or equivalent) of finished canned fruit will you can in 1945?　*160* qt.
Divide by 4 (See A above)　*40* lb.

The following estimates may be used as a basis in determining the approximate number of quarts of finished product obtainable from a stated amount of raw fruit.

FRESH FRUIT	UNIT OF MEASURE	APPROXIMATE CANNING YIELD IN QUARTS PER UNIT OF MEASURE
Apples	48 lb. to bushel	20 quarts
Peaches	48 lb. to bushel	20 quarts
Pears	50 lb. to bushel	24 quarts
Plums	56 lb. to bushel	28 quarts
Apricots	48 lb. to bushel	18 quarts
Grapes (for juice)	48 lb. to bushel	18 quarts
Cherries	32 qt. to bushel	20 quarts
Blackberries	24-quart crate	16 quarts
Red raspberries	24-quart crate	15 quarts
Black raspberries	24-quart crate	16 quarts
Strawberries	24-quart crate	12 quarts

4　How many pounds of sugar did you use for canning fruit in 1944?　*80* lb.

5　How many pounds of sugar did the Board grant you for home canning and preserving in 1944?　*80* lb.

6　Do you grow your own fruit?　*Part.*　YES ☒　NO ☐

OPA Form R-341 (2-45) BACK

16—43250-1　☆ U. S. GOVERNMENT PRINTING OFFICE

FAT IN THE RIGHT PLACES

YOU'VE heard the story in part before. At least, your ears have heard it. But has your heart and mind grasped its true significance? This is your job—not someone else's. Your war contribution—not the woman's in the next block. And here is a place where procrastination is doubly bad. Someone may die—someone may suffer needlessly—if you are indifferent.

It all boils down—and perhaps that expression should be expanded to include fries down and roasts down—to the contribution of your waste fats and greases. Not just *saving*, but *getting it to the butcher* and *getting it there now*. These waste fats can be finished munitions of war in twenty-one days from the time you take them to the butcher. But no depth charges will be released if that fat remains in your ice box. Medical and surgical treatment requiring glycerine can't be administered if the waste fats from which that glycerine is obtained remain home.

Which one of these three are you? One housewife in every three saves all her waste fats and takes them promptly to the butcher when she has saved a pound (31 tablespoonfuls). Another one of the three saves, but neglects making that necessary trip to the meat dealer to start her waste fats to the front. And, sad to relate, the third woman seems not to have realized the serious need for her contribution—even though in size it may be like the widow's mite—seems not to visualize the catastrophe which might result if all women did as she.

Every drop is valuable. If each housewife saved one tablespoonful a day, one pound a month, we should have gone a long way toward solving the problem. Two hundred million pounds are needed from the households of the nation annually.

"I mold all my salvage fats into bullets **before** I turn it in. . . . I figure this way, it'll save time."

Fats and oils include animal, vegetable and fish oils. You are not asked to give edible fats that you can make use of in your kitchen in providing for the nutrition of your family. You are asked to give that which is in excess of your needs and that which can no longer be useful.

Remember to fry out trimmings cut from your meats. Chunks of fat should be fried out and strained. Remember, too, that odors do not affect the glycerine properties. The fact that onions or fish have been cooked in the fat makes no difference. Pour into any clean tin can, keep it cool and take it to your meat dealer when a pound or more has been accumulated.

Here is what that one pound which you are turning in this month can do. It can provide glycerine used to manufacture one-third pound of gunpowder, one-half pound of dynamite for demolition work or fabricate three gas mask bags of cellophane.

But all of us must work together all the time, for at the rate of one pound a month, think how long it would take any one of us to fire even one shell from a 12-inch Naval gun (350 pounds of fat needed) or to camouflage even one medium tank (50 pounds needed to manufacture the synthetic resin used).

So let's become determined that, first, each member of the American Legion Auxiliary shall be the one of the three who saves and turns in her waste kitchen fats regularly, and, second, let's get in touch with the salvage committee and help insure that every household in our community shall become conscious of the vital uses of glycerine. Help make the record three out of three. Fats and oils are vital to the continuation of war operations.

Women are the ones upon whom the success or loss of this battle of the war depends.

— RATION CHECK —

THE UNITED STATES OF AMERICA
OFFICE OF PRICE ADMINISTRATION

DATE *Oct 15* 1945

CHECK No. _____

TRANSFER TO THE
MEAT FATS, FISH CHEESE

RATION BANK ACCOUNT OF *Hormel Packing co*
(NAME OF SELLER)

AMOUNT IN FIGURES
16 33
POINTS OF MEAT, FATS, FISH CHEESE

Sixteen Hundred + Thirty-Three Points
(AMOUNT IN WORDS)

HAROLD T ANDERSON
(PRINT OR TYPE NAME OF YOUR ACCOUNT)

Harold T Anderson
(AUTHORIZED SIGNATURE)

BANK OF JAMESTOWN
FR-21   JAMESTOWN, N. Y.   50-129

Buying groceries with ration stamps. NA 171-G-3H-1

University of Wisconsin students registering for ration book number two, Madison, Wisc., February 1943. LC-USW3-18344-D

Prewar and wartime oil containers. Left to right: metal oil can, fiber container with metal ends, all-fiber container, model of a proposed glass container and glass container with metal cap, September 1942. FDR

Metal beer cans were introduced prior to the war, but glass took over as the metal supply dwindled. FDR

Wartime tobacco containers. Left to right: a one-pound paper container, a two-ounce paper container and a two-ounce metal can. Metal containers practically disappeared until the war was over. FDR

A prewar and wartime rayon outfit before and after restrictions. The prewar blouse has French cuffs, balloon sleeves, matching sash and is 24 inches long. The slacks have cuffs and the legs are 24 inches wide. Material used: 6-1/4 yards. The wartime blouse has a tiny band cuff, a modified sleeve, no sash and is 22 inches long. The slacks have no cuffs and the legs are 18 inches wide. Material used: 4-3/8 yards. FDR

No ration stamps were needed for dairy products and eggs. FDR

This display window used two-color price tickets to show what prices of merchandise might have been had the government not established a system of price control. The upper part gave the possible 10-fold inflation price and the lower part showed the actual price under the OPA ceiling, September 1942. FDR

A bread shortage makes shopping more difficult. DENVER PUBLIC LIBRARY, WESTERN HISTORY DEPARTMENT

Line at a rationing board in New Orleans, La., March 1943. LC-USW3-22899-E

HOW TO KEEP YOUR
FARM EQUIPMENT
IN THE FIGHT

John Deere Handbook on Care and Operation

**Make the JOHN DEERE Store
Your Repair Parts Headquarters**

YOU HAVE but one dependable source for John Deere parts—your JOHN DEERE DEALER. He can supply them with the least delay. Make his store your headquarters for expert mechanical service and repair parts—parts which are exact duplicates of those they replace—parts which fit and wear like new. And remember—it pays to ORDER EARLY.

Look for the symbol 'JD' or the name
'DEERE'... They identify the Genuine

JAP PRIMER

1. The Jap worker toils **12 to 16** hours a day... with only **2** days off a month.

2. The Jap worker cannot leave his job or change it. There are no strikes or stoppages in Jap war plants.

3. The average Jap factory wage is **47** cents per day. The average Jap worker is also poorly housed and poorly fed.

4. Japan has some **10,000,000** such workers in war plants. She can draw on **400,000,000** more from among her enslaved peoples.

5. This huge force of cheap labor is turning out vast quantities of weapons to keep fanatical Jap troops fighting.

6. On your job, it's YOU versus the Jap worker.

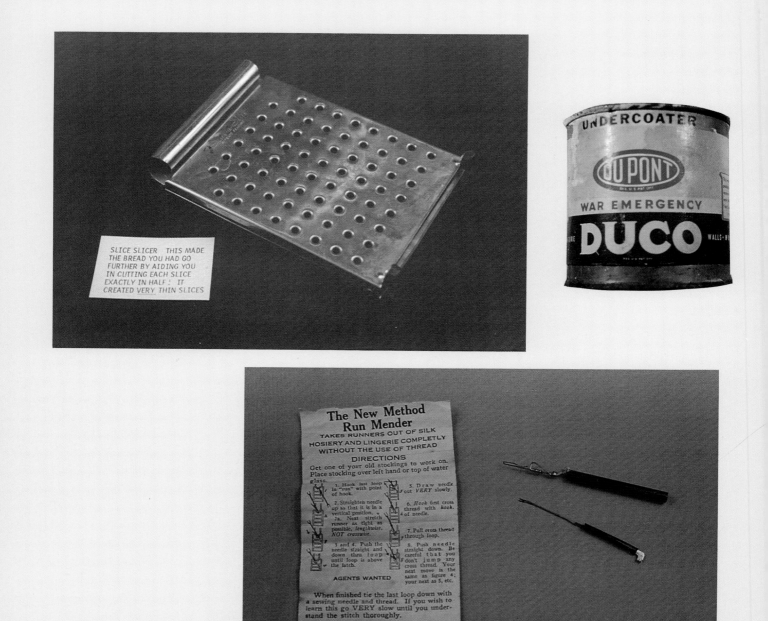

SLICE SLICER THIS MADE
THE BREAD YOU HAD GO
FURTHER BY AIDING YOU
IN CUTTING EACH SLICE
EXACTLY IN HALF! IT
CREATED VERY THIN SLICES

UNDERCOATER
DUPONT
WAR EMERGENCY
DUCO WALLS·W

The New Method
Run Mender

TAKES RUNNERS OUT OF SILK
HOSIERY AND LINGERIE COMPLETLY
WITHOUT THE USE OF THREAD

DIRECTIONS

Get one of your old stockings to work on.
Place stocking over left hand or top of water
glass.

1. Hook last loop in "run" with point of hook.

2. Straighten needle up so that it is in a vertical position.

2a. Next stretch runner as tight as possible, *lengthwise*, NOT *crosswise*.

3 and 4. Push the needle straight and down thru loop until loop is above the latch.

5. Draw needle out VERY slowly.

6. Hook first cross thread with hook of needle.

7. Pull cross thread through loop.

8. Push needle straight down. Be careful that you don't jump any cross thread. Your next move is the same as figure 4; your next as 5, etc.

AGENTS WANTED

When finished tie the last loop down with
a sewing needle and thread. If you wish to
learn this go VERY slow until you understand the stitch thoroughly.

C. BRANNIN
3920½ BOYCE AVE.   LOS ANGELES, CALIF.

RATION STAMPS

| COLOR | GOOD THIS PERIOD | EXPIRES |

MEAT POINTS

PROCESSED FOODS POINTS

SUGAR POINTS

BONUS POINTS

When you Bake ·Bake with Maca

KRAFT AMERICAN PASTEURIZED PROCESS CHEESE

KRAFT CHEESE COMPANY MANUFACTURER·CHICAGO,ILL.

75

KRAFT AMERICAN PASTEURIZED PROCESS CHEESE

THIS NEW CARTON SAVES ESSENTIAL MATERIAL FOR THE WAR EFFORT

2 POUNDS NET WGT.

GASOLINE RATIONING

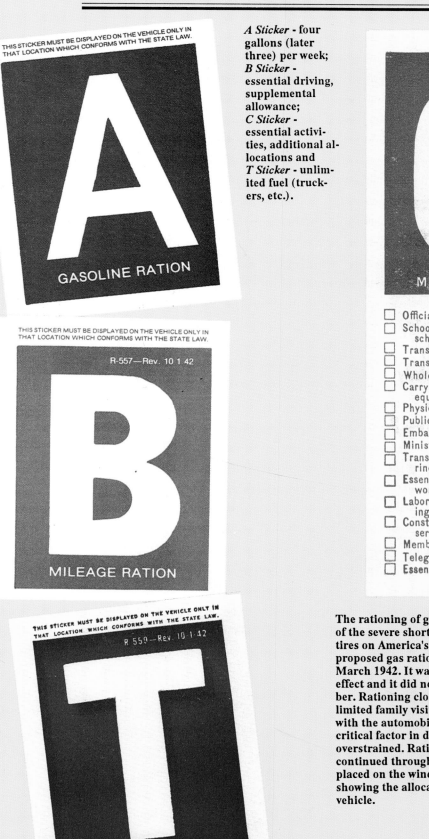

THIS STICKER MUST BE DISPLAYED ON THE VEHICLE ONLY IN THAT LOCATION WHICH CONFORMS WITH THE STATE LAW.

A

GASOLINE RATION

THIS STICKER MUST BE DISPLAYED ON THE VEHICLE ONLY IN THAT LOCATION WHICH CONFORMS WITH THE STATE LAW.

R-557—Rev. 10 1 42

B

MILEAGE RATION

THIS STICKER MUST BE DISPLAYED ON THE VEHICLE ONLY IN THAT LOCATION WHICH CONFORMS WITH THE STATE LAW.

R-559—Rev. 10-1-42

T

MILEAGE RATION

A Sticker - four gallons (later three) per week; *B Sticker* - essential driving, supplemental allowance; *C Sticker* - essential activities, additional allocations and *T Sticker* - unlimited fuel (truckers, etc.).

R-558—Rev. 10-1-42

C

MILEAGE RATION

☐ Official Gov't or Red Cross business.
☐ School official traveling school to school.
☐ Transportation 4 or more to school.
☐ Transportation of United States mail.
☐ Wholesale newspaper delivery.
☐ Carrying newsreel photographic equipment.
☐ Physician, surgeon, veterinarian.
☐ Public Health nurse or interne.
☐ Embalmer.
☐ Minister, priest, or rabbi.
☐ Transportation of farm workers, marine workers, or farm materials.
☐ Essential hospital, utility, or war worker.
☐ Labor conciliation, recruiting, training workers.
☐ Construction, repair, maintenance services or production specialist.
☐ Members of Armed force to duty.
☐ Telegram delivery.
☐ Essential scrap agent.

The rationing of gasoline for domestic use was a result of the severe shortage of rubber. To preserve existing tires on America's automobiles, government officials proposed gas rationing and a 35 mph speed limit in March 1942. It was May before rationing went into effect and it did not become nationwide until December. Rationing closed parks and tourist attractions, limited family visits and halted America's love affair with the automobile. Public transportation became a critical factor in daily life but it too was severely overstrained. Rationing, in some form or other, was continued throughout the war. Stickers had to be placed on the windshield of every American vehicle showing the allocation of gasoline allowed for that vehicle.

(Top) **Christmas shoppers and cars crowd Fifth Avenue at 38th Street, New York City, in December 1941.** (Bottom) **The same scene after gas rationing.** NA 171-G-11F-3 and NA 171-G-11D-2

This gas station, like many others, shortened its hours because of the shortage of gasoline. MINNESOTA HISTORICAL SOCIETY

Inequity is apparent in this sign at a gas station in the Midwest in September 1942 when there was already gas rationing in the East. Before long, however, gas was rationed nationwide. FDR

A busy spot on the Pennsylvania Turnpike. Since gas was rationed up ahead, this was a good reason to fill up. FDR

This gas station in Williamsburg, Virginia's first capitol, is shut up tight in April 1943. LC-USW3-24602-C

No gas from these pumps at a station in the automobile capitol, Detroit, Mich., April 1943. LC-USW3-21613-C

The sign says it all in this closed gas station which has been converted to a home, between Columbus and Cincinnati, Ohio, September 1943. LC-USW3-37468-E

This prewar sign on the once-busy Pennsylvania Turnpike seems hardly necessary during a wartime weekday. FDR

One Armco Steel Company employee finds a way around the gasoline shortage by riding his horse to work at the Norton Blast Furnace in Ashland, Ky. FRANK B. ELAM PHOTO

A MESSAGE TO OUR TENANTS FROM THE GOVERNMENT

Help stop fuel waste

1. **Use less hot water.**
2. **Turn off radiators to prevent over-heating.**
3. **Don't demand heat 24 hours a day.**
4. **Keep windows closed as much as possible.**
5. **Don't leave lights burning.**

SAVING FUEL SAVES TRANSPORTATION FOR AMERICA'S WAR EFFORT

The Mississippi Travelers Association, like other groups around the country, set up a system for sharing rides. It was very difficult to get around with the compounded problems of little gasoline, no new tires available and old cars. NA 171-G10C-12

"Penny A Mile"
REQUEST for RIDE

RIDER   RIDER

DATE _____

AREAS DESIRE TO COVER - NO. _____

   ROUTE DESIRES

   _____ _____ _____

   _____ _____ _____

   _____ _____ _____

FINAL DESTINATION DESIRED _____

RIDER _____   ADDRESS _____

HOME PHONE _____   BUSINESS PHONE _____

TIME START _____   TIME FINISH _____

WILL YOU SHARE YOUR CAR WHEN POSSIBLE? _____

MAKE OF CAR OWNED _____ YEAR _____ BODY TYPE _____

SPONSORED BY MISSISSIPPI TRAVELER'S ASSOCIATION

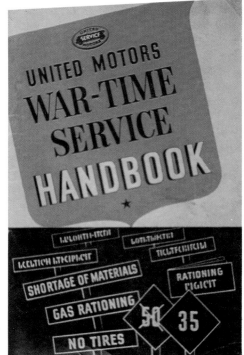

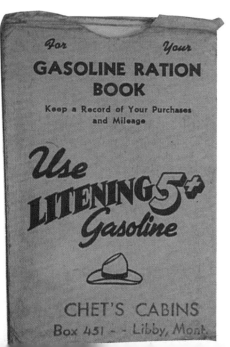

Al Pierson (right), owner of Pierson Motor Company in Lititz, Pa., shows his one remaining used car to a local farmer in November 1942. Before the war there were always three new cars in the showroom, but civilian automobile production stopped in early 1942. The supply of new and used cars dried up in the nation, and repairing autos became the chief business of the dealerships. LC-USW3-11105-D

Orphans of the Storm—By Hungerford

THE GREAT RUBBER SHORTAGE

The military needs two basic elements to fight - gasoline to power its engines and rubber to run its vehicles and fly its planes. The oil to make gasoline was available from domestic sources and from South America. Natural rubber, the source of most of the country's rubber, was mainly obtained from Africa, and the Dutch East Indies. Both of these sources were virtually closed down by enemy occupation or the lack of transport and submarine activity.

One way of keeping a supply of rubber on hand was to recycle used rubber. The government had instituted a used rubber drive before the war but results were disappointing. While the one-war stockpile of natural rubber was rather high, it didn't help when five huge mills in Falls River, Mass., belonging to Firestone Tire and Rubber Company, burned to the ground, reducing the stockpile by one-eighth.

The military was using rubber at an unprecedented rate and synthetic rubber plants were just coming online. Something had to be done quickly, especially after the Pearl Harbor attack.

President Roosevelt appointed a committee to examine ways of alleviating the shortage. It was headed by Bernard M. Baruch, Harvard president James B. Corant and MIT president Karl T. Compton.

Their report came directly to the point: "We find the existing situation to be as dangerous that unless corrective means are taken immediately this country will face both military and civilian collapse."

Three steps were recommended:

1. Nationwide gas rationing to reduce tire use.
2. A 35 mile-an-hour national speed limit.
3. An increase in synthetic rubber production.

A nationwide intensive rubber scrap drive was promoted. Collection centers were set up throughout the country and huge piles of old tires sprung up. Rubber for civilian products soon dried up and manufacturers had to switch to other products like wood and some types of metal. Automobile tires were driven far beyond their normal life expectancy; civilians had to make due the best they could. Tires became more precious than gold if one could even find any to buy. Most of the domestic rubber for tires had to go to public transportation vehicles and to essential needs of wartime industries.

As the war dragged on through the years, the supply of rubber was always a problem. Synthetic rubber production eventually eased the problem with many plants built around the country.

THE RUBBER SITUATION

We need 842,000 tons:

WAR NEEDS JULY '42 TO JAN. '44

We have 631,000 tons we can count on:

CRUDE SUPPLY JULY '42 TO JAN. '44 ▢SHORTAGE

We hope to fill the shortage with:

SYNTHETIC

We have some reclaimed rubber, but our priceless reserve is on our cars:

If we drive "as usual" this will happen by April 1943:

And this will happen by 1944:

"We will keep our armed forces fighting and our essential civilian wheels turning."
—BARUCH REPORT

TO MAKE TIRES LAST

Gasoline is rationed:

Tires must be inspected:

Speed limit is set:

You must sell all unmounted tires to the Government:

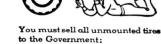

THIS IS WHY YOUR MILEAGE IS RATIONED

When the Japs seized Malaya and the Dutch East Indies they seized the source of 90 percent of our rubber supply. This was a blow at our war production and our transportation system, for our country depends on its 27 million passenger autos and 5 million trucks for more than 80 percent of its essential transportation.

The Baruch Committee, appointed by the President, reported:

"In rubber we are a 'have not' nation!

"If the present rate of tire wear continues, by far the largest number of cars will be off the road next year and in 1944 there will be an all but complete collapse of the passenger cars in America."

We are seriously short of rubber for military and other essential purposes. We simply do not have the rubber to do as much driving as in the past. We must save our rubber supply for bomber tires, pneumatic rafts, and hundreds of other articles of war.

We must save the rubber on our cars. The surest and fairest way to make our tires last is rationing of mileage through rationing of gasoline all over the Nation. We must drive slowly and carefully, so a national speed limit of 35 miles per hour has been set. We must take care of our tires, so a compulsory Tire Inspection Plan has been organized.

Only by doing these things can we "keep our armed forces fighting and our essential civilian wheels turning."

OFFICE OF PRICE ADMINISTRATION, Washington, D. C., November, 1942

WHAT YOU MUST DO
to qualify for gasoline and tires

Since mileage rationing is designed to keep your car rolling by making your tires last, a vital part of the mileage rationing plan is regular inspection of everybody's tires.

You must have your tires inspected regularly by an official OPA inspector. He will be found at OPA Official Inspection Stations. Inquire at your Local Rationing Board for locations.

This is how The Tire Inspection Plan works:

1 **Your Tire Inspection Record** is attached to The Tire Record and Application for Basic Mileage Ration. On it you fill in serial numbers of all tires you own, whether mounted on your vehicle or not.

2 **You will be denied Mileage Rations** if you or anyone in your household[1] owns any passenger tires (including scrap tires) not mounted on motor vehicles or equipment. You must sell or give such tires to the Government under the Idle Tire Purchase Plan.[2] Mounted tires means tires on running wheels including one spare per motor vehicle.

3 **The Tire Inspection Record** will be signed and returned to you if you have complied with the provisions above. You must keep the Tire Inspection Record in your car at all times.

4 **First Tire Inspection Period** is between December 1, 1942, and January 31, 1943, during which time all vehicles must have their tires inspected by an authorized OPA inspector. He may charge up to 25¢ per vehicle if no tires are removed. If he removes tires, he may charge 50¢ per tire. After January 31, A and basic-D drivers must have tires inspected every 4 months with inspections at least 60 days apart. B, C, and supplemental-D drivers must have tires inspected every 2 months with inspections at least 30 days apart.

5 **The inspector will check** the condition of your tires and the serial numbers. If serial numbers differ from those on your Record, he will inform the Local Rationing Board, unless you have been authorized to purchase another tire and you have Part D of a Tire Certificate showing any tire serial number not shown on the Record. If tires are O. K., he will sign your Record. If he finds repairs to tires, tubes, or vehicle necessary for tire conservation, he will not sign the Record until you carry out his recommendations. If a tire is worn smooth, he may recommend a recap. In that case he must remove the tire from the wheel to complete the inspection. If your tire is not fit for recapping, he may recommend replacement. In all cases, he will report any evidence of tire abuse to the Local Board.

6 **You apply to your Local Board** for a Rationing Certificate if the inspector recommends a recapping service for your tire, or a new or used tire or tube. These cannot be obtained, however, without a Rationing Certificate. If you have complied with all tire and gasoline regulations and the Rationing Board finds you are eligible, it may issue a Certificate for recapping service or for the grade of tire to which you are entitled.

Rationing Boards may deny you rubber and gasoline:

If you do not have your Tire Inspection Record signed during every inspection period.

WHAT YOU CAN DO
to make your tires last

1. Drive, start, and stop slowly.

2. Take curves slowly.

3. Look out for bumps, including curbs.

4. Inflate tires properly at least once a week.

5. Keep wheels aligned.

6. Keep brakes adjusted.

7. Shift all tires every 5,000 miles.

8. Repair breaks, cuts, and leaks promptly.

9. Straighten or replace bent rims.

and

10. SHARE YOUR RIDES!

If you need a recap or another tire or tube, go to an OPA Inspector promptly—then take his recommendation to your Local Rationing Board. Do not go to the Board first.

Inspector signs your record if tires are O. K.

He recommends repairs if they are needed.

He recommends recap or replacement if needed.

If you abuse your tires and tubes.

If you violate the 35 miles-per-hour speed limit.

If the serial numbers on your tires are not the same as those on your Tire Inspection Record, unless you have been authorized to buy another tire and have Part D of a Tire Certificate showing any serial number not listed.

---

* Different regulations apply to fleet, commercial, and Government cars.
[1] This means only members of your household related to you by blood, marriage, or adoption.
[2] Sell or give scrap tires to a scrap dealer.

OPA FORM NO. R-2
(REV 4-1-43)

REPLENISHMENT PART

UNITED STATES OF AMERICA
OFFICE OF PRICE ADMINISTRATION
OF MILEAGE-RATIONING
PROGRAM CERTIFICATE

No. 872940 X

GRADE

TYPE   # 3

QUANTITY   SIZE

Pass

Four   600x16

TIRE, TUBE, RECAP,
PING SERVICE, ETC   **Tires**

This Part B may be used for replenishment
of the above.

ISSUE
DATE   5-19-44

10570640
10070645
11170287
10770478

Turn in four

Baldwin Tire Co.

2317 S. Quannah

WAR PRICE AND RATIONING BOARD No.

CERTIFICATE-HOLDER'S
NAME   Charles M. Cortore

1412 N. 24th

Tulsa, Oklahoma.

PART

B

(CITY) TULSA   OKLA (STATE)

BY _Bailey_
NOT VALID unless signed by Issuing Officer.

OPA FORM R-605 (REV. 4-44)

UNITED STATES OF AMERICA • OFFICE OF PRICE ADMINISTRATION

RUBBER FOOTWEAR

PURCHASE CERTIFICATE

PAIRS   TYPE

IN FIGURES

(DATE ISSUED)

G 205657

NAME   ADDRESS

IS AUTHORIZED TO ACQUIRE   PAIRS OF TYPE No.
                          (IN WORDS)   (IN WORDS)

MEMBERS OF THE TRADE MUST ENDORSE
NAME AND ADDRESS ON BACK

INVALID IF ALTERED OR ERASED

(LOCAL BOARD NUMBER OR OTHER ISSUING OFFICE)

CITY   STATE

BY

☆ U. S. GOVERNMENT PRINTING OFFICE   619038

Tires became more precious
as the days went by,
Imperial County, Calif.,
March 1942. LC-USF34-72184-D

The share-the-ride committee in Highland Park, Ill., shows how it's done at the train station. NA 171-G-10C-7

Prewar and wartime baseballs. Left: cork-centered prewar ball; right: new ball with rubber center. Cork-cushioned centers in baseballs, official in the major leagues for more than a decade, were banned during the war. Rubber that had been used in the now-curtailed manufacturing of golf balls was substituted. OWI, VIA GEORGE C. MARSHALL FUND

This John Deere tractor owned by Warren Thompson of Missoula, Mont., was built during the war when the shortage of rubber forced the company to replace the rubber tires with steel wheels.

"Use it up, wear it out, make it do or do without."

Newspaper and magazine cartoonists poked unabashed
fun at the home front chaos of shortages and rationing.

AMERICA WILL MARCH TO VICTORY
ON THE LEATHER YOU SAVE

Today it is all important to get the last mile of wear out of the
Florsheim Shoes you own and the pair you buy. If you follow
these simple instructions for the preservation of shoes, you will be
helping the leather conservation program to the fullest extent.

Most Styles $10⁵⁰ and $11

THE FLORSHEIM SHOE SHOP
884 MARKET STREET
CALIFORNIA

Follow
THE FLORSHEIM SHOE
Conservation Plan

It's good judgment and your
patriotic duty to conserve leather. You
can increase the wear of your
Florsheim Shoes by giving them extra care.

1 Clean shoes with Saddle Soap, and shine with a good cream polish.

2 Alternate shoes from day to day and use a shoe horn to slip on shoes.

3 If shoes are damp, insert shoe trees, and let them dry at room temperature.

4 Never allow wet shoes to dry near direct heat.

5 Have run-over heels and thin soles re-placed immediately.

OPA FORM R-1703

FORM APPROVED
BUDGET BUREAU NO. 08-R323

UNITED STATES OF AMERICA
OFFICE OF PRICE ADMINISTRATION

APPLICATION FOR A SPECIAL SHOE STAMP

IMPORTANT

Read these instructions before filling in this form

This application is to be used only by a person who would suffer serious hardship if he were unable to buy a pair of shoes in addition to his regular ration.

There are not enough shoes to give everyone all the shoes he wants, but there are enough for all who really need them. Stop and think, before you complete this form. Have you any shoes that will meet your needs? Do not make this application unless you can qualify under all four of the following rules:

(1) You do not have a valid War Ration Shoe Stamp (or Special Shoe Stamp) and no member of your family has a War Ration Shoe Stamp that you can use.

(2) No employer or institution furnishes you with shoes that will meet your needs.

(3) The shoes are needed for occupational or general wear—not merely for maintaining personal appearance or for sportswear.

(4) You have no more than one pair of shoes in wearable or repairable condition that will meet your needs.

1. YOUR NAME (PLEASE PRINT OR TYPEWRITE)

ADDRESS (STREET AND NUMBER);

CITY AND STATE

OCCUPATION | YOUR WAR RATION BOOK NO.

2. DESCRIBE THE KIND OF SHOES YOU NEED TO BUY:

3. STATE THE SPECIAL PURPOSE FOR WHICH THE SHOES ARE REQUIRED AND WHY YOU NEED ANOTHER PAIR AT THIS TIME:

---

4. How many pairs of shoes do you own? Include all street, dress, sport, work, athletic, evening, and play shoes that you can wear or that can be repaired. (Include only shoes made in whole or in part of leather or with rubber soles.)

TYPE OF SHOES (a)	TOTAL NUMBER OF PAIRS OWNED (b)	HOW MANY PAIRS CAN BE WORN FOR THE SAME PURPOSE AS SHOES YOU NOW REQUEST (c)

I HEREBY CERTIFY THAT:

1. I do not have a valid War Ration Shoe Stamp or Special Shoe Stamp and no member of my immediate family (related to me by blood, marriage, or adoption and living in the same household) has a War Ration Shoe Stamp that I can use.

2. No employer or institution furnishes me with the shoes for which I am applying, and that all the statements and answers I have made on this application are true and complete. I understand that I am to use the requested shoe stamp to buy shoes only of the type and for the purpose stated in this application.

Any person who makes any false statement or false representation in this application is subject to criminal prosecution under the laws of the United States.

SIGNATURE OF OR NAME OF APPLICANT | DATE

SIGNATURE OF PERSON ACTING FOR APPLICANT | RELATIONSHIP (CHECK ONE)
☐ PARENT ☐ GUARDIAN ☐ OTHER AGENT

The Local Board will decide on the merits of each application and will satisfy itself that the applicant will suffer serious hardship if not permitted to buy a pair of shoes before a new War Ration Shoe Stamp becomes valid.

ACTION TAKEN (FOR LOCAL BOARD USE ONLY)

CHECK ONE
☐ SPECIAL SHOE STAMP ISSUED
☐ SPECIAL SHOE STAMP DENIED

LOCAL BOARD NUMBER | DATE

IF DENIED, GIVE REASON

CITY AND STATE

SIGNATURE OF BOARD MEMBER

A boy tosses a rubber ball onto a pile of salvaged rubber at a Georgia Avenue filling station in Washington, D.C., June 1942. LC-USF-34-100173-E

SALVAGE FOR VICTORY

WE SERVE

SAL**V**AGE
WILL WIN THE WAR !
THROW *YOUR* SCRAP INTO THE FIGHT!

DON'T BURN IT—SAVE IT
WASTE PAPER
IS NEEDED FOR DEFENSE

SCRAP DRIVES

THE WHITE HOUSE

August 27, 1942.

The boys and girls of America can perform a great patriotic service for their country by helping our National Salvage effort. Millions of young Americans, turning their energies to collecting all sorts of scrap metals, rubber, and rags, can help the tide in our ever-increasing war effort.

They will earn the gratitude of every one of our fighting men by helping to get them the weapons they need—now. I know they will do their part.

Franklin D. Roosevelt

FRANK B. ELAM PHOTO

COURTESY JOHN DEERE CO.

NEWSPAPER COLLECTIONS

Boy Scouts sort collected newspapers at a railroad siding in Clarksburg, W.Va. CLARKSBURG ENGRAVING CO.

Jimmy Hargis, of Portland, Ore., who won $150 in 1942 for the most paper collected in the state. OHS; *OREGON JOURNAL* PHOTO

The American Legion collecting scrap paper in Chillicothe, Ohio, January 1942. LC-USF-33-16196-M5

During the war newsprint was a major focus for recycling, just as it is today. Schoolchildren, who were at the forefront of the collecting activity, are shown here working on a paper drive. MINNESOTA HISTORICAL SOCIETY

Save those waste fats!

BRING WASTE FATS HERE

OFFICIAL FAT COLLECTING STATION

Prepared by Glycerine Producers and Associated Industries with Approval of the

WAR PRODUCTION BOARD

TEAR OFF

Hang this up in your kitchen!

Save your WASTE FATS to make explosives!

1. The Need Is Urgent. War in the Pacific has greatly reduced our supply of vegetable fats from the Far East. It is necessary to find substitutes for them. Moreover, fats make glycerine. And glycerine makes explosives for us and our allies—explosives to down Axis planes, stop their tanks, sink their ships. We need millions of pounds of glycerine and you housewives can help supply them.

2. Don't throw away a single drop of used cooking fat—bacon grease, meat drippings, frying fats—every kind you use. After you've got all the cooking good from them, pour them through a kitchen strainer into a clean, wide-mouthed can. Keep in a cool, dark place. Please don't use glass containers or paper bags.

3. Take Them to your meat dealer when you've saved a pound or more. He is cooperating patriotically. He will pay you for your waste fats and get them started on their way to the war industries. It will help him if you can deliver your fats early in the week.

SEE FURTHER INSTRUCTIONS ON THE REVERSE SIDE OF THIS SHEET

Housewives!

SAVE WASTE FATS FOR EXPLOSIVES!

Bring Them Here

2 RED RATION POINTS

FOR EVERY POUND OF

USED FATS

SAVE USED FATS TO MAKE GUNPOWDER!

Cans filled with reclaimed household grease are dumped into pressure cookers at a rendering plant. The cooker melts the grease, and the empty cans are removed for detinning. Other types of cookers remove grease from cans by steam plates and hot coils, eliminating the necessity for putting the cans into the cooler. FDR

TINFOIL SALVAGE

Tins by the thousands are about to be reclaimed at the Newark, N.J., plant of the Tin Salvage Institute. They were melted down and cast into pigs of solid metal for reuse in war industries. FDR

Students at the City College of New York collect tinfoil from chewing gum and cigarette packages for the defense effort. NA 171-G-12A-8

RUBBER SALVAGE

John L. Rogers, director of the Division of Defense Transportation, displays a truck tire which has been driven for 146,000 miles and is still considered usable. It will be retrod to run for another 70,000 miles. Americans had to go to extraordinary lengths to conserve their tires and to drive on tires which today would be considered very unsafe. They had no choice during the war years. FDR

The need for rubber was critical after supplies were cut off from the Dutch East Indies, and the military demand increased greatly. But this 100-acre collection area at a Midwest recovery plant would signal a massive superfund cleanup project in today's environmentally sensitive world. NA 171-G11M-1

The Gilmore Oil Company was one of dozens that has closed or been bought up by larger companies. Here an independent Gilmore dealer shows off this old car rigged out for a rubber drive in 1942. FDR

Another Gilmore car plugs the scrap drive. FDR

Stage and screen star Judy Canova opens her personal salvage drive for scrap rubber by aiming a well-placed shot at the Axis - she's donating her trusty slingshot to the drive. FDR

Even locks were salvaged for the war effort.

Even golf balls were salvaged for their rubber content, and we have to wonder whether this didn't reduce the playing time for avid golfers like Bing Crosby, shown here with a bin full of balls. FDR

Huge piles of salvaged material feed a large Midwest rubber plant. In the making of many essential products, reclaimed stock was preferred to pure, raw rubber. FDR

NYLON and SILK SALVAGE

"Here's where your parachute came from," Deena Clark, Civilian Defense Volunteer, tells Tech. Sgt. Leo Matkins of the Army Air Corps. The worn-out nylon and silk stockings in this barrel would be reprocessed and made into parachutes, towropes for glider planes, powder bags for artillery pieces and other war material. In one three-month period nationwide, 626,127 pounds of old silk and nylon stockings were collected. FDR

The Salvation Army used its extensive facilities nationwide for collecting salvage material. These boxes contain laundered silk stockings given up by women in a Minnesota city. Silk was used for a variety of war material, including parachutes and medical supplies. MINNESOTA HISTORICAL SOCIETY

SCRAP METAL DRIVE

War brought more serious concerns than rooting for local ball teams. Here Uncle Sam implores citizens to recycle scrap for the war effort, October 1942. COURTESY MARSHALL UNIVERSITY, MORROW LIBRARY

William Steig's "Kid Salvage" was produced for the OWI to stimulate scrap collections.

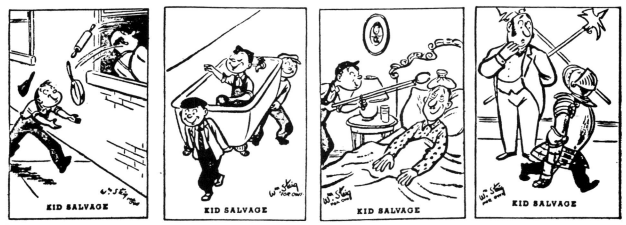

William Steig's Kid Salvage is a regular feature, supplied in one column spots. These are intended to stimulate scrap collections.

A mass of scrap that was dumped in a vacant lot in Lancaster, Pa., prior to salvage, November 1942. LC-USW-3-10910-D

Scrap metal at Fort Kent,
Maine, August 1942. LC-USF-
34-83771-C

Scenes of a scrap drive conducted in Ashland, Ky., in 1941 before America entered the war. The drive was
sponsored by Armco Steel Company. FRANK B. ELAM PHOTOS

An obsolete barber's chair and doctor's chair get one
last tryout before going to the scrap drive. FRANK B.
ELAM PHOTO

Even a moonshine still is donated to the scrap drive.
FRANK B. ELAM PHOTO

In this eastern scrap yard, scrap compressed into cubes waits to be fed to the hungry furnaces of the steel mills. At least 50 percent of scrap had to be used in the open-hearth process. FDR

A gigantic scrap drive in Akron, Ohio. FDR

Boy Scouts shove pots and pans into the path of a steamroller in Tillamook, Ore. OHS

Even abandoned trolley tracks were dug up for the war effort. A local inventor demonstrates his "railjerk" in Asheville, N.C., in 1942. He claimed it could pry loose a mile of track a day using three men. FDR

Farmers throughout the nation contributed to scrap drives. Here a WPA weighmaster weighs scrap from a farm in Dexter, Mich. FDR

School children in Butte, Mont., flash the "V" for Victory sign as they pose in October 1942 on a pile of scrap that they collected. LC-USW-3-9700-D

Scrap drive parades were held in most American cities, large and small. This parade in Hattiesburg, Miss., was reviewed by the governor of Mississippi and the mayor of Hattiesburg in April 1942. FDR

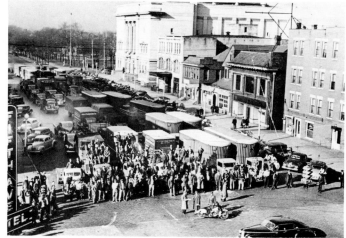

Scrap drive on 5th Avenue in Huntington, W.Va. The Cabell County Courthouse is in the far background, and the City Hall is the large building in the background. MARSHALL UNIVERSITY ARCHIVES, CATHERINE ONSLOW PAPERS

Boy Scouts of Troop 121, United Church of Van Nest, Bronx, N.Y., push an old car into a Bronx wrecking yard where it probably was sold for scrap. NA 171-G-11M-1

Scrap was collected from every corner of the country. Here Tom Boles, superintendent of Carlsbad Caverns National Park in New Mexico, donates an old lawnmower to a drive in the park. The Park Service gathered a total of 10 tons of metal during this drive. CARLSBAD CAVERNS NATIONAL PARK

Salvage collection in this Region with its widely scattered population required the development of unusual procedures.

In the standard type of state salvage organization, each Washington Salvage Division (Scrap Processors, Industrial, Special Projects, and General Salvage) had its own representative working independently. This form of organization was top heavy for the states in this region and led to confusion and duplication of effort. This cumbersome organization was replaced by a single state salvage manager having responsibility for all phases of salvage. The various voluntary state, county and local committees were merged with one chairman in each community having charge of all types of salvage activities in that community.

A program or "drive" chairman was then appointed to organize special collection campaigns, such as for scrap iron and steel, paper, tin and household fats.

Volunteer committees were flexible enough to enlist the support of individual organizations or groups, such as schools, Scouts, service clubs and Chambers of Commerce. Each group invariably brought new ideas and enthusiasm into a drive.

Early in our salvage program many committees donated to charity the entire proceeds from their salvage activities, and then found themselves devoid of funds to meet preliminary expenses of future campaigns. This weakness soon became obvious, and corrective measures were taken.

It was necessary to have our War Production Board personnel contact volunteer committees at regular intervals to prevent loss of interest and disintegration. It was impossible to keep an effective committee together merely through correspondence or infrequent personal calls. Approximately 576 county and local chairmen and from 8,000 to 12,000 individual volunteers participated in various programs in this Region. The chairman of these committees were contacted every 30 to 60 days, depending on the salvage potential of their communities.

More extensive use of established agencies and organizations for volunteer work was necessary in this region than elsewhere. For example, the Extension Service of agricultural colleges, through their numerous extension agents, distributed literature to every farmer during the rubber dirve, the scrap iron and steel drive, and many others. Also enlisted to aid in iron and steel scrap drives were service clubs, farm granges, co-operatives, schools, churches, county commissioners, implement dealers, and industry itself.

Of particular interest was the use of personnel of various military posts in this Region. The Army trained men for the collection of battlefield scrap, and through the efforts of our salvage personnel, consented to detail the trainees to civilian scrap collection programs for their final training. This permitted the salvage of much scrap in remote locations by military men and equipment. This program was so successful in Region IX, where it was originated, that other regions adopted it. The use of military aid not only secured much scrap which could not otherwise have been recovered, but also had a psychological effect in the communities canvassed, and stimulated the public in their salvage work.

A unique plan for collecting tin cans was developed by designating grocery stores as local collection depots for prepared cans. Through the cooperation of wholesale bakers, grocers, and bottlers, the cans were picked up daily and trucked to the loading docks of commercial trucking companies. These trucking companies agreed to haul the cans without cost to a central depot in Denver. Cans were moved as far as 600 miles in this way. Cooperation of wholesalers and retailers was excellent. By enlisting the aid of the Denver Advertising Club and securing donations, art work for newspaper advertising, and signs for collection depots were prepared. Press releases and radio script were written by volunteers. Even though this Region's program for salvaging tin cans was successful, it was hindered by (1) lack of organized national sponsorship, and (2) lack of sufficient remunerative incentive for the work of volunteer committees.

Scrap drives as well as bond drives were promoted throughout the country during the war years. This is a street scene in St. Paul, Minn. MINNESOTA HISTORICAL SOCIETY

Every category of American citizen from young children to older folks, male and female, collected or gave up personal items or things from their homes for the war effort. MINNESOTA HISTORICAL SOCIETY

Students at Lincoln High School, Portland, Ore., hold a banner expressing sentiments of the day over scrap-filled jalopies. OHS

Age was no deterrent when it came to scrap. Many valuable antiques (at today's prices) were made into war materials. These antique fire engines, donated by the city of Griffin, Ga., stand ready to end their days as scrap. They dated from 1867 to 1913. FDR

Scrap metal drive in Ashland, Ky. FRANK B. ELAM PHOTOS

This World War I howitzer that sat on the grounds of the old Capitol lawn in Frankfort, Ky., was given up in a World War II scrap drive. Many war artifacts that today would be considered important or historically valuable were consumed by these intensive scrap drives. KENTUCKY HISTORICAL SOCIETY

In 1920 this German cannon was sent to Charleston, W.Va., as a World War I trophy. When America entered World War II, it was decided by members of John Brawley American Legion Post 20, posing here by the cannon, to return the artillery piece to the Germans in the form of shells or part of a tank. Johnnie Andre sits on the cannon. RICHARD ANDRE

ALUMINUM AND TIN CAN COLLECTION

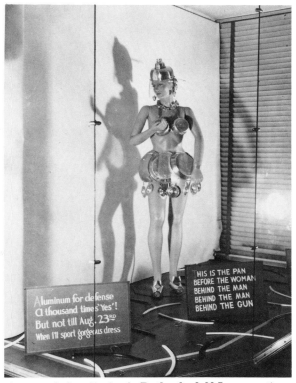

Aluminum for defense a thousand times 'Yes'! But not till Aug. 23rd When I'll sport gorgeous dress

HIS IS THE PAN BEFORE THE WOMAN BEHIND THE MAN BEHIND THE MAN BEHIND THE GUN

A store window display in Rutherford, N.J., promoting the National Defense Aluminum Collection (July 21-29, 1941). This collection was conducted by the office of Civilian Defense, and some of the aluminum obtained was used in defense industries. Much of the lower-grade aluminum collected, which could not be put to use directly for defense, was employed to replace new aluminum in the manufacture of consumer goods, thus releasing new aluminum for use in defense production. FDR

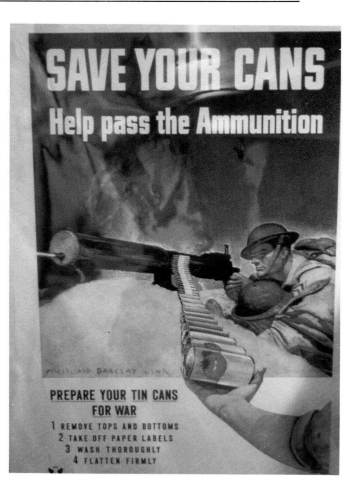

SAVE YOUR CANS
Help pass the Ammunition

PREPARE YOUR TIN CANS FOR WAR
1 REMOVE TOPS AND BOTTOMS
2 TAKE OFF PAPER LABELS
3 WASH THOROUGHLY
4 FLATTEN FIRMLY

Even before America got into the war, scrap was being collected for the new defense effort. This drive took place in the remote northern Idaho community of Orofino in July 1941.
LC-USF-34-70028-D

Boy Scouts in St. Paul, Minn., add to the thousands of aluminum pots deposited on the grounds of Franklin School, 1941.
MINNESOTA HISTORICAL SOCIETY

A mound of salvaged aluminum in Los Angeles six months before Pearl Harbor.
FDR

Today this lot would be an antique car collector's dream, but these cars are all about to be melted down at a Great Lakes steel mill to be used against the Axis. The sign on the car in the center reads: "My running days are over. My duty now is to lick the Japs." FDR

Wooden bumpers replaced metal ones donated to the scrap drive in Wilmington, Del., October 1943. DSA

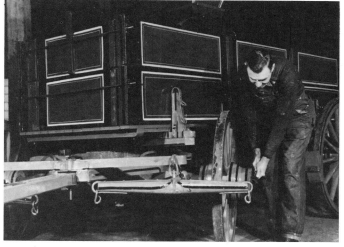

As a result of the rubber shortage, these once-familiar vehicles were again produced during the war at a southern wagon plant. FDR

Old jewelry collected by the city of Kerrville, Texas, in honor of Adm. Chester W. Nimitz, commander-in-chief in the Pacific campaign and a Texan, and the servicemen fighting in the Pacific. Kerrville had a population of 5,000 at the time. USN

AWVS (American Women Volunteer Service) junk jewelry drive in Wilmington, Del., October 1943. DSA

FOOD FOR VICTORY

Students at Jane Addams High School in Portland, Ore., work in the school victory garden for physical culture credit, 1943. oHS

A victory garden window flower box gets watered at Roosevelt Field, Long Island, N.Y., 1943. NA 80-G-K-15108

A 1943 poster. U.S. ARMY MUSEUM, HONOLULU

At their peak there were more than 20,000,000 Victory Gardens in the country, producing 40 percent of all vegetables grown in the country.

Plan Your Victory Garden NOW!

BUY WISELY – COOK CAREFULLY – STORE CAREFULLY – USE LEFTOVERS

A Farm Security Administration poster. LC

WARTIME-RATION RECIPES
FOR DELICIOUS MEALS

FOR 2 AND 4 AND 6

HEALTH-FOR-VICTORY CLUB
Meal Planning Guide

Featured this Month:

THE MORE WOMEN AT WORK
...THE SOONER WE'LL WIN!

OUR DAILY BREAD AND BUTTER
76 Recipes not in the August Issue

Contributed in the interest of the National Wartime Nutrition Program
PREPARED BY HOME ECONOMICS INSTITUTE
Westinghouse Electric & Manufacturing Co. • Mansfield, Ohio

15¢

September 1943

"DOGGONE IT, FELLOWS!
THESE GUYS KNOW
THERE'S A WAR ON!"

FOOD IS AMMUNITION
DON'T WASTE IT

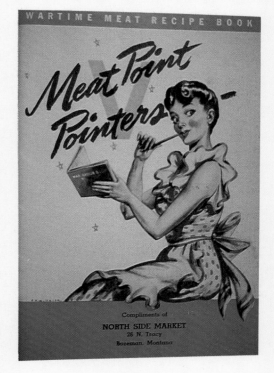

WARTIME MEAT RECIPE BOOK

Meat Point Pointers

Compliments of
NORTH SIDE MARKET
26 N. Tracy
Bozeman, Montana

With little space and plenty of ingenuity, these enterprising city dwellers have created a thriving garden in the narrow strip of ground between their driveway and fence. FDR

A victory garden campaign in Minnesota, 1944. MINNESOTA HISTORICAL SOCIETY

No place was too small, too isolated or too ritzy to have a victory garden. This plot is on Wilshire Boulevard in Los Angeles, February 1943. LC-USW3-35296-D

OO VICTORY GARDENS *in* 1944
,000 HOME CANNERS

OBJECTIVES

A Garden on Every Farm
More Urban Gardens
Better-Balanced Gardens
More Productive Gardens
Improved Utilization

These youngsters are carefully selecting seeds for the vegetables they will plant in their victory garden. FDR

Young and old alike worked their victory gardens. This gardener is raking the soil to pulverize it to prepare it for seed. FDR

Victory Farm volunteers in Clarkfield, Minn., receive T-shirts, **July 18, 1943.** MINNESOTA HISTORICAL SOCIETY, *MINNEAPOLIS TRIBUNE*

Plowing a victory garden on Boston Common, April 1944. FDR

The shortage of farm workers was critical during the war years. German prisoners of war, interned Japanese-Americans, kids, senior citizens and thousands of Mexican farm workers were used to harvest the millions of acres of crops throughout the country. These Mexicans, brought north by the Farm Security Administration in May 1943 to harvest and process sugar beets in Colorado, Nebraska and Minnesota, worked under contract with the Inter-mountain Agricultural Improvement Association.
LC-USW33-31868-ZC

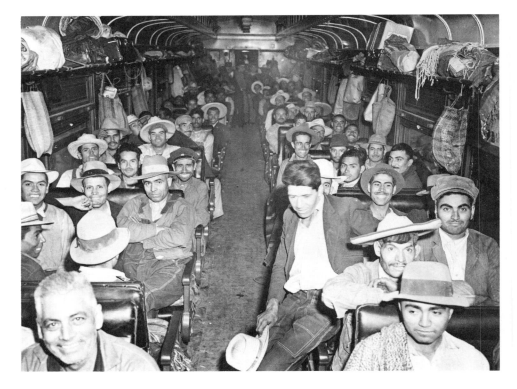

A victory garden in Hawaii in 1942. U.S. ARMY MUSEUM HAWAII

A gas station in Twin Falls, Idaho, sells gasoline for essential use only - just for farmers who feed the country. LC-USF 34-73807-D

"Take care of it brother, you may not get another."

MEAT RECIPE BOOK

VICTORY MEAT EXTENDERS

Compliments

NATIONAL LIVE STOCK AND MEAT BOARD

KEEP YOUR WAR EQUIPMENT
FIT AND FIGHTING
FOOD FIGHTS for freedom

VICTORY COOK BOOK
How to
EAT WELL...LIVE WELL...
PLAN BALANCED MEALS...
under
FOOD RATIONING

FREE with purchase of LYSOL

MINUTE
PLAIN UNFLAVORED
GELATIN
WARTIME DESSERT RECIPES!

Victory Pack
Extra Heavy
WAXED PAPER
FOR SANDWICHES, CUT IN TWO
FOR PRESERVING FOOD
Clean · Fresh
24 SHEETS   12 x 18

Lunch BAGS
36 FOR 10¢
DESIGNED FOR WAR WORKERS
AND SCHOOL CHILDREN
· CLEAN AND SANITARY
· ECONOMICAL AND CONVENIENT
· ELIMINATES LUNCH BOXES
· EASILY DISPOSABLE

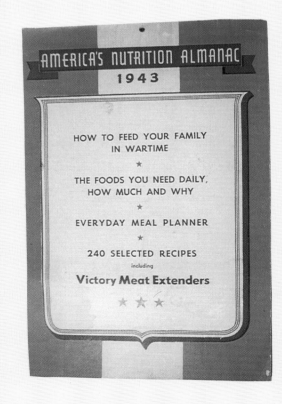

The Sinews Of War

Day by day the prime place of *food* in total war is becoming increasingly apparent. Long before Pearl Harbor Secretary of Agriculture, Claude R. Wickard, said:

"Food will win the war and write the peace."

As the war pace quickens, we are all beginning to realize how true and how all-important that slogan is.

Making advance announcement of canned goods rationing, Elmer Davis, Director of War Information, said:

"Food is a weapon in all wars, but in this one more than usual. . . . We are using our food supply as a weapon, positively; so distributing it that the American army and navy and the American people will be well nourished; yes, and so that the armies of our allies will be kept strong too."

At the same time, Mr. Wickard said:

"Food is a weapon — a most powerful weapon. And the food we consume here at home is just as much a material of war as the food we send abroad to our soldiers and fighting allies."

Most recently, the vital necessity for food has been emphasized by Major General Lewis B. Hershey, Selective Service Director, and Paul V. McNutt, War Manpower Commissioner, in their recent radio addresses.

Pointing out that workers in war jobs must do *everything* that must be done in total war, General Hershey continued:

"They must grow and process food and fibers.

"They must process the consumer goods necessary to maintain a healthy nation.

"They must do everything necessary to make our fighting forces invincible on the battlefronts and our nation healthy and efficient on the home front."

Later, in the same address, General Hershey said:

"The selective service system must always recognize the responsibility of procuring the men our armed forces need with the least possible disturbance to our national health and efficiency."

War Manpower Commissioner McNutt said:

"No nation at war, particularly a democracy, can suspend everything on the home front while it fights on the battlefront. We must grow food. We must process that food, put it into containers, transport it to the point of consumption . . . and do the thousand and one things needed to keep our home economy functioning. We could not possibly do away with all civilian activity, even if any one were foolish enough to wish to."

Food, like bullets, and planes and tanks, is ammunition. Men and women who work to produce, to process, to distribute that food are putting weapons in the hands of our fighting men as surely as the men and women producing guns.

Let this knowledge make every individual in the food industry proud of his share in the winning of this total war. Let every member of the Kraft organization redouble his energies, proud in the thought that, though others may be building the guns, he is helping to build the strong sinews of the strong arms which will carry those guns to victory.

Don't let 'em get you down, Oswald.

I NEED EVERY CHEESEMAKER MORE THAN EVER NOW!

★ ★ ★ ★ ★ ★ ★ ★ ★ ★

The time has come . . .

In 1941 we all heard that the government would need a tremendous increase in cheese production "for defense." Thousands of dairy farmers and cheesemakers responded wholeheartedly.

★

In 1942, after Pearl Harbor, the need for increased cheese production was obvious—vital. Cheesemakers and dairy farmers alike got right on the job. And, while final figures for 1942 production are not yet available, it is certain that they will show a production increase far beyond any previous year—a miracle of accomplishment—a big job, well done!

★

But, in 1943 the government asks for the production of over a *billion pounds* of cheddar cheese—cheese needed by our Armed Forces, by our folks at home, and by our fighting allies.

★

To meet that need, every can of milk that goes to a cheese factory, every vat of milk that's mixed with starter, must be made into *clean, quality* cheese. *Now, the time has come when America cannot afford to waste a single pound of milk or a single pound of cheese.*

★ ★ ★ ★ ★ ★ ★ ★ ★

TO ALL GENERAL FOODS EMPLOYES:

During the past twelve months our country has moved along a difficult and dangerous path. But the important thing is that we went *forward*. When 1942 began we were still stunned by the shock of Pearl Harbor. By the end of the year we were not only supplying our allies, but we were launched on a powerful offensive.

In 1942 our main problem was to gather military strength. We needed planes, tanks, guns and ships -- and we needed them in a hurry. The results of our effort along these lines are now being tested on the battle fields of the world.

We have entered 1943 faced with another crisis -- food production and processing. America is not only the arsenal of the democracies, it is the breadbasket as well. Without food there can be neither a fighting nor a home front. Without food there can be neither victory for us nor peace.

You and I, as members of the food industry, are part of that army behind the army. Last year we grew, processed and transported more food than ever before. We need to do even more in the year ahead. Some of us have forgotten, in the excitement of the moment, that our work -- so essential for our country's welfare in peacetime -- becomes vital in time of war.

Recently many important men, including President Roosevelt, ex-President Hoover, Food Administrator Wickard, War Manpower Commissioner McNutt and others, have issued statements on the necessity of maintaining and increasing food production. On September 16, 1942, Director of Selective Service Hershey, putting words into action, issued Bulletin No. 20 which began, "The War Manpower Commission has certified that Food Processing is an activity essential to the support of the war effort."

This tells us where we stand. The rest is up to us.

Sincerely yours,

Clarence Francis

PRESIDENT

January 15, 1943

FOR DEFENSE
BUY
UNITED
STATES
SAVINGS
BONDS
AND STAMPS

CHEESEKRAFT

Give!
RED CROSS
WAR FUND

MAY, 1942

CHICAGO, ILLINOIS

VOL. 22, NO. 5

KRAFT MOBILIZES FOR VICTORY!

FREEDOM'S FIGHT UNITES KRAFTMEN ON ALL FRONTS

J. L. Kraft Keynotes Wartime Faith For Ultimate Victory

We At Home Must Match Spirit of Boys In Service

By J. L. KRAFT

We are at war!

We hear these four words many times a day. Hearing them often, the unthinking man or woman interprets the phrase to mean "The nation is at war" —or "The other fellow is at war" without any personal conviction of responsibility.

J. L. Kraft

But WE—you and I of the Kraft Cheese Company — our neighbors and friends, and the man who lives down the street — we are at war, all of us. And each of us must wage that war with all our might and all our intelligence.

An Outstanding Example

As a corporation, our company has pledged all-out aid to the full limit of our resources, and behind that pledge is the personal pledge of every individual who goes to make up our organization. A recent statement in a national magazine article says that the Kraft Cheese Company

(Continued on Page 21, Col. 3)

Bonds For Bullets!

Let's give our Kraft boys in the front lines the airplanes, guns, and tanks they need, by buying all the War Bonds and Stamps we can. Sign up now to buy regularly — every payday. America will NOT be beaten. Say it with bonds!

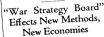

KRAFT

THE NAVY   THE ARMY   THE MARINES

Vancouver Kraftman Makes History With Royal Air Force

A quiet but determined-looking young man is Pitt Clayton, of Vancouver. Up until 1938 he was associated with the Coast Produce Company, Kraft Distributors on the Canadian Pacific Coast, when he joined the Royal Air Force. Since that time his exploits have made one of the most thrilling and inspiring chapters of the war, and have won him advancement to the rank of Squadron Leader, the Distinguished Flying Cross, and a Bar to the D.F.C.

Pitt was in the thick of it at Dunkirk. During this battle one of the men in his plane was shot, and a second man bailed out, leaving Pitt all alone. Then his plane was hit and set on fire, but he managed to stay in the air, put the fire out, and fly his ship back to Croydon.

Later, on a raid over Occupied France in which he had been instructed to bomb a certain objective, he noticed a lot of lights come on at a spot below him, and presently could make out the ground lights of an air field. Pitt brought his plane down to the first level, and found himself among a group of German planes. Being both quick-witted and courageous, Pitt turned on his lights and circled with the enemy planes. One by one they landed, while Pitt kept circling. When they were all down, he unloaded his bombs on top of them and streaked for home. For this

(Continued on Page 25, Col. 3)

ALL DEPARTMENTS GEARED TO WARTIME EFFICIENCY

"War Strategy Board" Effects New Methods, New Economies

Entire Kraft Organization Welded Into Smooth-Working Victory Unit

North, South, East and West, from coast to coast, from border to border, Kraft mobilizes for victory! Kraft men and women everywhere — in plant and office, in production and distribution, from J. L. Kraft to the very newest member of the organization "enlist" for the duration, each contributing his important share to backing up the nation's armed forces with the morale and will-to-win upon which ultimate victory must be based.

Winning War Comes First

The primary business of all industry today — as of every individual American and the nation as a whole — is the winning of a war. Therefore, these days the primary interest of the entire Kraft organization, the focal point of all Kraft planning is the gearing of every phase of the Kraft business to the important part it can play in helping win.

"War Strategy Board"

All Kraft activities are now planned by a central "war strategy board" composed of key men from all departments of the company. This central board is divided into a series

(Continued on Page 23, Col 1)

Through the Red Cross

You may help save the life of YOUR fighting man. Through the Red Cross you can send your dollars, your spare time work, your blood, straight to the front line, where it will do the most good. Give today! Your help is needed!

JUST BY Keeping Well
YOU can help WIN THIS WAR

With nearly one-third of America's physicians in the armed forces, we must save our remaining doctors' time for serious and unavoidable sickness and accidents.

FOLLOW THESE 5 SIMPLE HEALTH RULES

1. EAT RIGHT
These are the key foods: milk, butter, eggs, fish, meat, cheese, beans and peas, fruit, green leafy vegetables and the yellow ones, whole grain or enriched cereals and bread. Eat 3 good meals a day!

2. GET YOUR REST
Regularity counts most. You can't catch up on lost sleep or missed relaxation! Try to keep on a regular schedule every day. Take it easy for a little while after lunch and dinner. Go to bed on time, get up on time.

3. SEE YOUR DOCTOR ONCE A YEAR
You have your car checked and serviced every thousand miles. Do as much for your body. Physicians can prevent many diseases and illnesses for both children and grownups nowadays. Give your doctor a chance now, BEFORE you get sick. Go to see him!

4. KEEP CLEAN
Plenty of baths, lots of soap. Clean hands, clothes, houses, beds! Get fresh air, sunshine. Drink plenty of water.

5. PLAY AND RELAX DAILY
Romp with the family, visit with friends, take walks, play games — or do whatever you like to give your mind and body a rest from the daily grind on the job. "All work and no play makes Jack a dull boy."

YOUR
WAR GARDEN
for 1944
Helpful Information
FROM
Firestone
FARM AND GARDEN
SERVICE BUREAU

SUMMER CARE
of the
WAR GARDEN
Including
INSECT CONTROL

Compliments of
Firestone
FARM AND GARDEN
SERVICE BUREAU

57

FOR DEFENSE
SAVE and SELL
this empty can

HEINZ PURE CIDER VINEGAR

EXHIBITS and PARADES

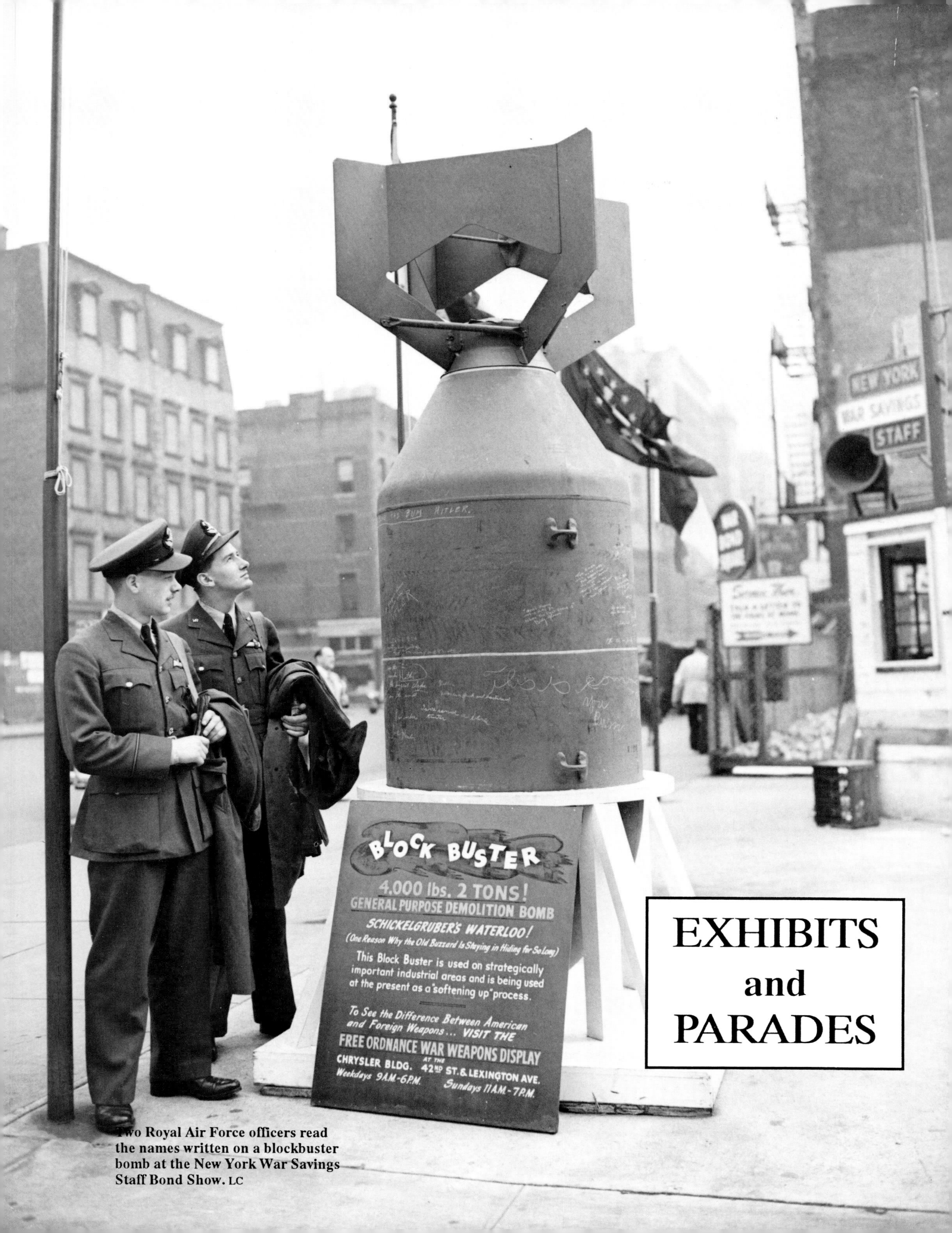
NEW YORK
WAR SAVINGS
STAFF
BLOCK BUSTER
4,000 lbs. 2 TONS!
GENERAL PURPOSE DEMOLITION BOMB
SCHICKELGRUBER'S WATERLOO!
(One Reason Why the Old Buzzard Is Staying in Hiding for So Long)
This Block Buster is used on strategically important industrial areas and is being used at the present as a "softening up" process.
To See the Difference Between American and Foreign Weapons... VISIT THE
FREE ORDNANCE WAR WEAPONS DISPLAY
CHRYSLER BLDG. AT THE 42ND ST. & LEXINGTON AVE.
Weekdays 9A.M.-6P.M. Sundays 11A.M.-7P.M.

Two Royal Air Force officers read the names written on a blockbuster bomb at the New York War Savings Staff Bond Show. LC

The U.S. Navy put on a 6th War Loan exhibition on Chicago's waterfront in November and December 1944. The middle photo shows the interior of the main exhibit hall with an F6F "Hellcat" fighter aircraft in the foreground. USN

Navy war exhibit in New York City, November 1943. Wave PR 3/c Myra Jean Clark, attached to NAS New York (Floyd Bennett Field), poses with a parachute in front of a display of recruiting posters. USN

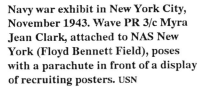

"Nature of the enemy" exhibition, designed by the Office of War Information and installed along the plaza of Rockefeller Center in New York City, June 1943. LC-USW3-31149-C

Viewing a wrecked German Messerschmitt fighter plane in Bakersfield, Calif., February 1942. LC

The Galia County (Gallipolis, Ohio) honor roll, May
1943. LC

A sign erected in Abilene,
Kan., listing all the persons
from Dickinson County,
Kan., in the service during
WWII, including Abilene's
most famous son, Gen.
Dwight David Eisenhower.
P.W. JEFFCOAT, ABILENE, KAN.

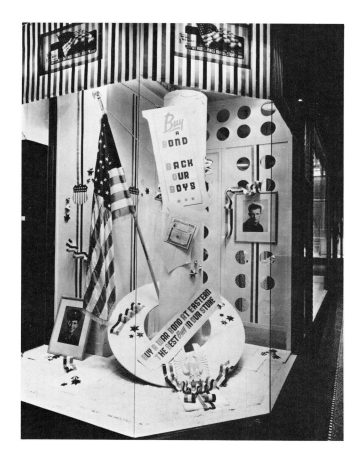

"Buy a Bond" window in Portland, Ore. OHS

A bulletin board, with letters and pictures of Duke University alumni, kept on campus. DUKE UNIVERSITY ARCHIVES

Opening ceremonies for the Victory Center in downtown Portland, Ore., Oct. 20, 1944. The flags of the Allies are hung at the top. OHS

Display windows in Fligel-
man's Department Store in
Helena, Mont., in 1944.
MONTANA HISTORICAL SOCI-
ETY

Window display for the
War Manpower Commis-
sion in Clarksburg, W.Va.,
April 1945. CLARKSBURG EN-
GRAVING CO.

Radio station, KUTA, Salt Lake City, Utah, sponsors a U.S. Navy display promoting naval enlistment, January 1943. UTAH STATE HISTORICAL SOCIETY

"Jinx to the Japs" show sponsored by the El Cerrito, Calif., Chamber of Commerce, Feb. 18, 1942. *OAKLAND TRIBUNE*

Protecting America's natural resources, especially the vast forests of the Pacific Northwest, was a vital part of the war effort. Here a U.S. Forest Service float participates in a parade in Coeur d'Alene, Idaho. U.S. FOREST SERVICE, PANHANDLE NATIONAL FOREST

A Japanese two-man midget submarine which was launched from an I-Class submarine outside Pearl Harbor before the dawn attack on the naval base on Dec. 7, 1941. Five subs were launched but none inflicted any damage on American ships. This one was beached on the opposite side of Oahu from Pearl Harbor and one of the two-man crew was captured. The sub was eventually taken to the mainland and traveled the country promoting war bond sales. It is now on temporary display at the Admiral Nimitz Museum in Fredericksburg, Texas. It will eventually be returned to the Arizona Memorial in Honolulu. USN

On exhibition at Mare Island. U.S. NAVAL INSTITUTE

The Japanese midget submarine now on temporary display at the Admiral Nimitz Museum in Fredericksburg, Texas.

President Roosevelt visiting the Mare Island, Calif., Navy Yard in 1942. In the background is the Japanese midget submarine that was beached on Oahu right after the Pearl Harbor attack. USN

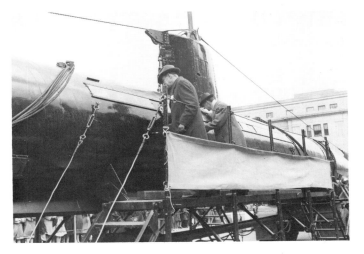

The sub on display in Wilmington, Del., on April 14, 1943. DSA

Sailors view the captured Japanese submarine.

The midget sub in Pittsburgh, Pa. FDR

June 1942, a war
heroes parade in Salt
Lake City, Utah. UTAH
STATE HISTORICAL
SOCIETY, *SLC TRIBUNE*

Patriotic parade on
Winchester Avenue,
Ashland, Ky., in 1944.
FRANK B. ELAM PHOTO

Patriotic parade in Casper, Wyo. NA

Massed colors are carried by John Brawley Post 20, American Legion, marching down Capitol Street, Charleston, W.Va., on Army Day, April 6, 1942 (the author's fourth birthday).
RICHARD ANDRE

A parade starts at St. Louis' Union Station and proceeds downtown on Sept. 19, 1943. A show at Kiel Auditorium the night before raised more than $16 million for the 3rd War Loan. MISSOURI HISTORICAL SOCIETY

Parade of City Patrol Corps in front of the New York Public Library. BETTMANN ARCHIVE

Part of the crowd of 200,000 that lined the streets of St. Louis, Mo., in October 1943 to watch a parade promoting war bond sales. MISSOURI HISTORICAL SOCIETY

A civilian defense parade in Puerto Rico, April 4, 1943.
NA 171-G-14E-1

War heroes parade in Salt Lake City, Utah. UTAH STATE HISTORICAL SOCIETY

Float carrying an Mk. XIII aircraft torpedo in a Navy Day parade at the Naval Torpedo Station in Alexandria, Va. USN

A Marine Corps station apparently located in a small house in Athens, Ohio, in January 1942. Recruiting stations sprang up in every corner of the United States after the Pearl Harbor attack. LC-USF34-64383-D

RECRUITING

JOIN THE U.S. MARINES

U.S. MARINE RECRUITING OFFICE

USMC

HOURS
9-11AM - 7-9 PM

DEFEND YOUR COUNTRY

ENLIST NOW in the UNITED STATES ARMY

FLY WITH THE U.S. MARINES

JOIN THE WAC NOW!
ARMY OF THE UNITED STATES

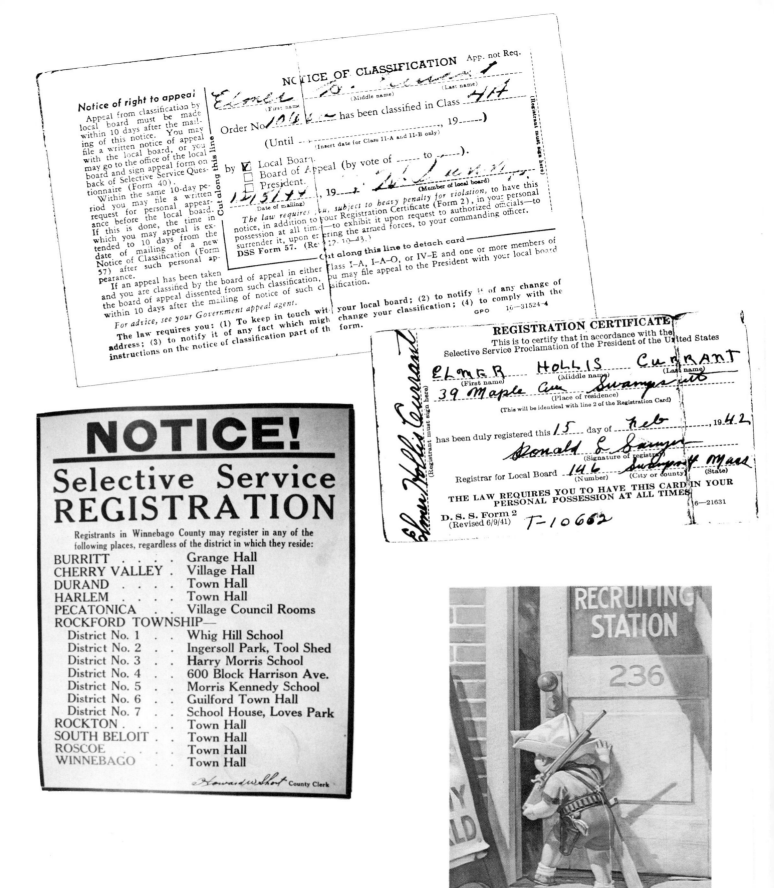

Notice of right to appeal

Appeal from classification by local board must be made within 10 days after the mailing of this notice. You may file a written notice of appeal with the local board, or you may go to the office of the local board and sign appeal form on back of Selective Service Questionnaire (Form 40).

Within the same 10-day period you may file a written request for personal appearance before the local board. If this is done, the time in which you may appeal is extended to 10 days from the date of mailing of a new Notice of Classification (Form 57) after such personal appearance.

If an appeal has been taken and you are classified by the board of appeal in either classification, and one or more members of the board of appeal dissented from such classification, you may file appeal to the President with your local board within 10 days after the mailing of notice of such classification.

For advice, see your Government appeal agent.

The law requires you: (1) To keep in touch with your local board; (2) to notify it of any change of address; (3) to notify it of any fact which might change your classification; (4) to comply with the instructions on the notice of classification part of the form.

GPO 16—31524-4

NOTICE OF CLASSIFICATION App. not Req.

Elmer H. Currant

(First name) (Middle name) (Last name)

Order No. _____ has been classified in Class I-A

(Until _____, 19____)

(Insert date for Class II-A and II-B only)

by ☑ Local Board.
☐ Board of Appeal (by vote of ___ to ___).
☐ President.

12/5/44, 19__ (Date of mailing) (Member of local board)

The law requires you, subject to heavy penalty for violation, to have this notice, in addition to your Registration Certificate (Form 2), in your personal possession at all times—to exhibit it upon request to authorized officials—to surrender it, upon entering the armed forces, to your commanding officer.

DSS Form 57. (Rev. 12.10-43.)

Cut along this line to detach card

REGISTRATION CERTIFICATE

This is to certify that in accordance with the Selective Service Proclamation of the President of the United States

ELMER HOLLIS CURRANT

(First name) (Middle name) (Last name)

39 Maple Ave Swampscott

(Place of residence)

(This will be identical with line 2 of the Registration Card)

has been duly registered this 15 day of Feb, 1942

Ronald L. Sawyer

(Signature of registrar)

Registrar for Local Board 146 Swampscott Mass

(Number) (City or county) (State)

THE LAW REQUIRES YOU TO HAVE THIS CARD IN YOUR PERSONAL POSSESSION AT ALL TIMES

D. S. S. Form 2 (Revised 6/9/41) T-10662

6—21631

Elmer Hollis Currant (Registrant must sign here)

NOTICE!
Selective Service REGISTRATION

Registrants in Winnebago County may register in any of the following places, regardless of the district in which they reside:

BURRITT	Grange Hall
CHERRY VALLEY	Village Hall
DURAND	Town Hall
HARLEM	Town Hall
PECATONICA	Village Council Rooms
ROCKFORD TOWNSHIP—	
District No. 1	Whig Hill School
District No. 2	Ingersoll Park, Tool Shed
District No. 3	Harry Morris School
District No. 4	600 Block Harrison Ave.
District No. 5	Morris Kennedy School
District No. 6	Guilford Town Hall
District No. 7	School House, Loves Park
ROCKTON	Town Hall
SOUTH BELOIT	Town Hall
ROSCOE	Town Hall
WINNEBAGO	Town Hall

Howard W. Short County Clerk

RECRUITING STATION 236

The day after Pearl Harbor, Dec. 8, 1941, these men crowd into a recruiting station in San Francisco. That Monday was a busy day in recruiting stations of all the services as men rushed to join the fight against the new enemy. LC-USF34-81861-E

A sign in Oklahoma City, Okla., in November 1942. LC-USW3-10821-D

Several recruits for the U.S. Marine Corps are welcomed by a recruiting officer in Oakland, Calif., February 1942. *OAKLAND TRIBUNE*

George Camblair reporting to his Selective Service Board in Washington, D.C., after receiving his induction notice, September 1942. LC-USW3-7967-D

Men 45 to 65 in Idaho Falls, Idaho, registering for selective service. In April 1942, all men that age group were required to register, but they were never called up. LC-USF34-65594-D

A lonely soldier next to a recruiting poster in Detroit, Mich., on New Year's eve, December 1941. LC-USW3-16481-C

A Coast Guard recruiting station in Detroit, Mich., in August 1942. The Coast Guard was responsible for water rescues within the United States and offshore, and for helping to protect the coastline against enemy intrusion and saboteurs. Normally a branch of the Department of Treasury, the organization came under U.S. Navy command during the war. LC-USW3-7073-D

High school students being sworn in for some type of volunteer service in a judge's office in Berkeley, Calif., Jan. 30, 1942. *OAKLAND TRIBUNE*

A window display promoting the Mountain Troops, which would become the 10th Mountain Division and would win its laurels in the bloody battles of the Italian campaign. The division trained to ski and climb mountains, and many of America's most famous skiers and mountain climbers joined. After the war, many of them played a leading role in the development of ski areas throughout the nation. DR. FRANK HOWARD, SAN RAFAEL, CALIF.

Form 10A 4.14.43

NATIONAL SKI ASSOCIATION QUESTIONNAIRE

FOR MEN SEEKING ASSIGNMENT OR TRANSFER TO MOUNTAIN TROOPS

TO: THE NATIONAL SKI PATROL SYSTEM
415 LEXINGTON AVENUE
NEW YORK CITY

I desire assignment (or transfer) to mountain troops, and I hereby apply for your assistance. If you approve my application, and there are still openings available,

A. ☐ I will ask my draft board for immediate voluntary induction, with the understanding that you will request my assignment to the Mountain Training Center when I report to my reception center, after induction. (See Instructions, Section 2)

or

B. ☐ I will wait for my regular induction, with the same understanding as above. (See Instructions, Section 2)

or

C. ☐ Having already been inducted, but not having begun basic training, I apply for assignment to the Mountain Training Center for basic training. My ASN is _____, I was inducted on _____, and I have been ordered to report for active duty at _____ (See Instructions, Section 2) on (date) _____ .

or

D. ☐ Having already been inducted, but undergoing basic training and still unassigned, I apply for assignment to a mountain unit upon completion of my present basic training. My ASN is _____, and I was inducted on (date) _____, and I shall complete basic training about (See Instructions, Section 3)

or

E. ☐ Being already in the service, and assigned, I will request transfer to mountain troops through military channels, expecting the National Ski Association to send my questionnaire to the Commanding Officer of the Mountain Training Center, for his information if my request for transfer reaches him for his approval. (See Instruction, Section 4)

I attach the required letters of recommendation.

Date _____ Applicant's Signature _____

1. NAME (Please print) _____

2. ADDRESS _____ (CITY) _____

3. AGE _____ 4. MARRIED? ___ 5. SINGLE? ___ 6. No. of DEPENDENTS _____

7. NATIVE BORN? ___ 8. NATURALIZED? ___ 9. ALIEN? ___ 10. FIRST PAPERS? ___

11. DRAFT BOARD NUMBER AND ADDRESS _____

12. INDUCTION DATE: Probable _____ Definite _____

13. EDUCATIONAL BACKGROUND (Give dates, grades and years completed)
   a. Grade School _____
   b. High School _____
   c. College _____
   d. Post Graduate and Technical _____
   e. Special Studies _____
   f. Languages Spoken and Read _____

14. PREVIOUS OCCUPATION, WITH APPROXIMATE DATES
   _____
   _____
   _____

15. HAVE YOU HAD PREVIOUS MILITARY EXPERIENCE? IF SO, DESCRIBE.

16. SKIING EXPERIENCE
   a. Cross Country ___ years, (where?) _____
   b. Downhill ___ years, (where?) _____
   c. Touring ___ years, (where?) _____
   d. Ski Mountaineering ___ years, (where?) _____
   e. No. years instructing experience ___ Professional? ___ Amateur? ___

17. MOUNTAINEERING AND CAMPING EXPERIENCE (Give locations and length of time engaged)
   a. Snow and Ice Climbing _____
   b. Rock Climbing _____
   c. Forestry Service _____
   d. Timber Cruising _____
   e. Packing horses or mules _____
   f. Mountain or forest guiding _____
   g. Trapping _____
   h. Prospecting _____

18. If you have had no skiing or mountaineering experience, write us what general qualifications for mountain training you think you have - describe camping and athletic experience, etc., and present physical condition. Use separate sheet, and attach to this sheet.

A questionnaire for those wishing assignment or transfer to mountain troops. The National Ski Patrol was responsible for the initial recruitment. DR. FRANK HOWARD, SAN RAFAEL, CALIF.

Inducted men marching to a reception center in Houston, Texas, May 1943. LC-USW3-31019-D

New WAVES and SPARS take the oath of enlistment in a ceremony in front of City Hall in New York City on Feb. 8, 1943. "WAVES" was the acronym for "Women Accepted for Voluntary Emergency Service." This service group, a branch of the U.S. Navy, was established on July 31, 1942, under Lt. Cmdr. Mildred Helen McAfee. The SPARS were women serving in the Coast Guard. NA 80-G-40692

Checking draft numbers in Salt Lake City, Utah, March 1942. UTAH STATE HISTORICAL SOCIETY

New recruits getting their physicals in Huntington, W.Va. MARSHALL UNIVERSITY ARCHIVES, CATHERINE ONSLOW PAPERS

PROTECTING
THE
NATION:
Civilian
Defense

CIVILIAN AND NATIONAL
DEFENSE EXPOSITION
GRAND CENTRAL PALACE
Sept. 20 to Oct. 18, Inclusive
See the Battle of Production

Civilian Defense

America had seen how German bombs destroyed the cities of Europe in 1940 and '41, and it became apparent that some type of defense was necessary for Americans. The need became greater after the fall of France in May 1940 and the possible collapse of British defenses.

President Roosevelt therefore created the Office of Civilian Defense (OCD) in May 1941 with the goal of coordinating the myriad programs and the millions of people who wished to volunteer to defend their homes.

The mayor of New York City, Fiorello H. LaGuardia, was appointed to head the office. He in turn appointed First Lady Eleanor Roosevelt to be his assistant.

After the Pearl Harbor attack, there was a frenzy of activity as the authorities considered the country was in a state of peril. However, except for a few isolated Japanese submarine shellings on the West Coast and a few instances of Japanese balloon bomb raids in the Pacific Northwest, America's cities and rural areas were untouched by enemy attacks.

The OCD, however, became an agency rife with controversy, which eventually led to both LaGuardia's and Roosevelt's resignations in 1942. Nevertheless, the confusion at the top did not dampen the enthusiasm of the volunteers who, at peak strength, numbered more than 10 million.

Every aspect of defense of the civilian population was addressed, from firefighting to air raid drills, first aid instruction, aircraft spotting and message carrying. But by late 1943 the threat of enemy invasion to the country had waned, and some functions of the OCD were dismantled. Most of the blackout restrictions, though, continued until the end of the war, and many of the OCD volunteers helped out in natural disasters that occurred in the country during the war years.

Civilian defense gave the civilian populace a sense of pride and purpose with the idea that even on the home front every man, woman and child could do his or her part for the war effort.

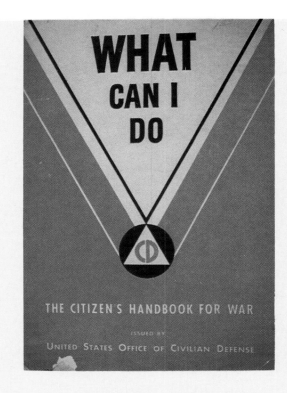

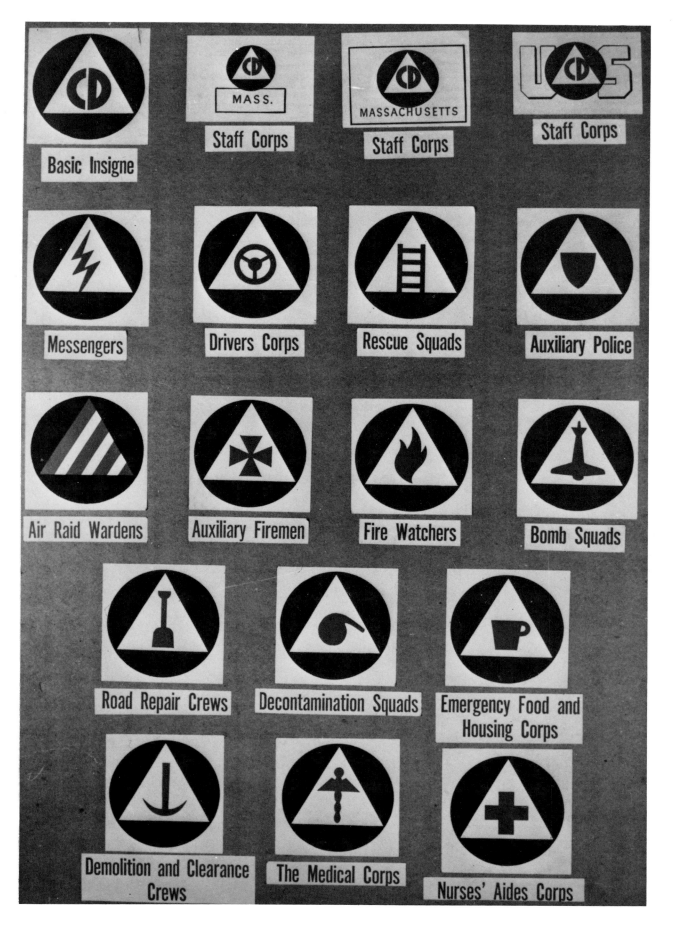

Basic Insigne

Staff Corps

Staff Corps

Staff Corps

Messengers

Drivers Corps

Rescue Squads

Auxiliary Police

Air Raid Wardens

Auxiliary Firemen

Fire Watchers

Bomb Squads

Road Repair Crews

Decontamination Squads

Emergency Food and Housing Corps

Demolition and Clearance Crews

The Medical Corps

Nurses' Aides Corps

Eleanor Roosevelt with Mayor LaGuardia after she was sworn in as assistant in the Office of Civilian Defense. FDR

New York Mayor Fiorello H. LaGuardia, head of the Office of Civilian Defense, autographs an illustration of a cartoon idea he submitted at an exhibition of cartoons concerning lost war production hours, sponsored by the OWI. LC-USW-331134-C

Fiorello La Guardia, mayor of New York City and first head of the Office of Civilian Defense, was an American aviator in Italy during WWI and made propaganda broadcasts to Italy during WWII.

New York Mayor Fiorello H. LaGuardia, head of the nation's Civilian Defense, speaks at a Civilian Defense Volunteer Organization information and recruitment booth at Radio City Music Hall in New York City, May 1943. NA 171-G-10I-1

U.S. ARMY MUSEUM HAWAII

A fire watcher, on the alert for falling incendiary bombs. Watchers and crews were responsible for disposing of the bombs before they could erupt into a major blaze. FDR

Two types of air raid warden helmets. NEW MARKET BATTLEFIELD MILITARY MUSEUM, VA.

An old veteran of the Spanish-American War is sworn in as a civilian defense volunteer in Marietta, Ohio, in January 1942. LC-USF-34-64402-D

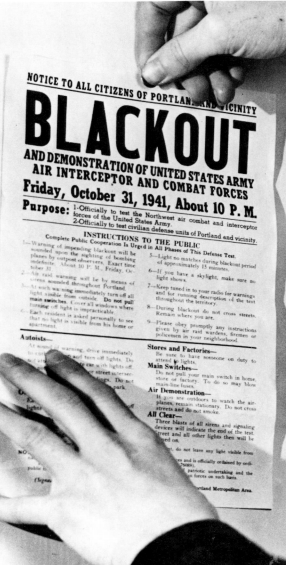

Blackout on Pennsylvania Avenue, Washington, D.C., just after Pearl Harbor. FDR

Even before the Pearl Harbor attack, air raid drills were held throughout the country. This handbill announces a drill in Portland, Ore., in October 1941. OHS

MONTANA HISTORICAL SOCIETY, MELVIN & ALMA RYGG COLLECTION

New War Time Orders

Pull down all shades before lighting any lights. You are subject to arrest by Military authorities for violation of this order. Your cooperation is requested.

The Management

☉ BLACKOUT ☐

READ THIS FOR YOUR PROTECTION AND SAVE IT!

Westinghouse
MAZDA
LAMPS

MORE LIGHT LONGER

The whole purpose of blackouts is to secure the maximum of protection for all citizens and property in a given area.

In time of air raids, the darkening of all buildings and premises wherever possible prevents the enemy from easily finding his objective, and thus minimizes the destruction he can cause.

Providing effective blackouts requires the whole-hearted assistance and cooperation of all citizens, both for their own protection and that of their neighbors.

There will be no general turning off of power circuits. Such a step would be highly detrimental to defense production and hazardous to all persons in the area affected. It will be the rule of the utility companies not to interrupt service to any customer.

It will be the responsibility of each to arrange his own blackout as best suits his needs and conditions. Different types of buildings, premises, and conditions require different methods of treatment to produce blackout. Some methods are comparatively simple, while others are complicated and require much more treatment to secure the proper results.

In all cases it is essential that NO light be allowed to show outside the building.

FOR RESIDENCES: The following instructions are of value. During air raid alarms all occupied rooms in the house will have to be darkened, and lights permanently turned out in others (electric bulbs removed), so they can not be turned on through mistake or carelessness where windows are not covered. All lights near an outside door must be screened so that no light is visible outside when the door is opened.

Outside porch or yard light bulbs must be removed so lights can not be turned on by mistake.

Provision must be made to darken every window, glass door, skylight and exterior opening wherever lights are used after dark, using dark blinds, window shades, thick curtains, special screens, or other heavy material. **Any material which allows a glow to be seen outside will not do.** Other glazed openings can be covered with paint on the outside and paper or other materials pasted on the inside.

Go around the house to see that no lights are visible from outside.

FOR STORES, SHOPS, ETC.: In general, the same methods as used for residences should be followed, but these must be supplemented by additional protection to meet particular conditions. **No night lights must be allowed to show.** Provisions should be made to have these turned off immediately on alarm or not lighted at all.

All sign and window display lighting should be turned off in early evening or not turned on at all.

FOR LARGE BUILDINGS: In cases where at least one employee remains on the premises all night, and where no night lights are absolutely needed, a complete blackout can be made by opening the main switch for the duration of the alarm. If, however, the building is occupied during the night, some lights should be left burning in corridors and at exits. If these are shielded and served from a separate circuit connected ahead of the main switch, the same procedure may be followed.

In cases where there are no employees on the premises after closing hours, all lights may be turned off at closing hours or by a time-switch later. **If it is necessary that some night lights be used, arrangements should be made to have these turned off immediatey on alarm.**

In all cases where **ANY** lights are needed during an alarm, they must be effectively screened so as not to be visible outside. Light-locks should always be used when necessary.

FOR HOSPITALS, FACTORIES, ETC.: For advice on the methods which serve best together with information on screening windows and exits, shielding and dimming necessary lights, light-locks, etc., see or call the nearest **OFFICE OF CIVILIAN DEFENSE.**

The foregoing provisions for your protection are recommended by us. We urge your full cooperation in these and all other defense measures.

VICTORY
LIGHT
The 3 IN 1 Light
WITH *INTERCHANGEABLE* LENSES

LENS FOR
RED DANGER

LENS FOR
WHITE REGULAR USE

AND FOR HOME USE--
LENS FOR
BLUE BLACKOUTS

During Blackouts . . .

COFFEE SHOP and HUNT ROOM will be open but patrons are requested to enter through the main hotel entrance as outside entrances of these rooms will be locked to insure perfect blackouts in them.

HOTEL *Bellevue*

Putting up blackout curtains, which did not have to be black, just heavy or thick enough to keep light from shining through. They were supposed to be big enough for an overlap, so that no outline showed. FDR

A civilian defense worker shows a family how to use a blackout curtain. NA 171-G-1-B-10

Times Square, New York City, a bright-light section that could have provided a tempting target to an enemy bomber. FDR

WHAT WE FOUND IN LAST NIGHT'S BLACKOUT

AC107 ©MWM

A 1942 Chevrolet rigged for blackout driving. U.S. ARMY MUSEUM HAWAII

AWVS HOME BLACKOUT DEMONSTRATION

An AWVS (American Women Volunteer Service) group who instructed people in Wilmington, Del., on how to prepare homes for blackouts. DSA

AIRCRAFT SPOTTERS

During the early days of the war, the U.S. Army established the Aircraft Warning Service (AWS) along the Pacific Coast. Radio posts, manned year-round as a primary mainland defense system, were established using mainly U.S. Forest Service fire lookout towers. Most of these posts were in remote areas of the national forests; some had to be supplied by pack string. To operate the radios of the day, heavy batteries had to be taken and stored at each post. These lookouts, plus many others in the interior forests of the west, were of utmost importance in guarding against forest fires and reporting downed aircraft in the remote areas. When the Japanese balloon bombs began appearing over the forests in late 1944 these lookout towers became even more important.

Fire lookouts throughout the country were part of the Intercepter Command and reported planes seen from their lookouts. Here Barbara Mortensen identifies a high-flying plane from her lookout in the White Mountain National Forest in New Hampshire, June 1943. FDR

One type of air raid siren which could be heard for several miles, and which was usually placed on the roofs of fire houses. Fortunately, they never had to be used except in drills. FDR

Citizens of Gresham, Ore., receive armbands identifying them as observers of the Aircraft Warning Service. OHS

An aircraft spotter in a remote location. NA 171-G-6-I-1

The tower of the elegant La Valencia Hotel in La Jolla, Calif., was used as an aircraft spotting tower during the war. Many of the hotel's guests climbed up into the gold-domed tower to scan the skies for enemy planes. As part of the area's Civilian Defense program, spotters were in the tower 24 hours a day. LA VALENCIA HOTEL

Mrs. E.V. Ricken-
backer, second from
left, watches as a group
of volunteer airplane
plotters at a filter
center push markers
into place. These
volunteers worked
four- to five-hour
shifts, sometimes after
getting off their
regular jobs. FDR

An air raid drill in New
York City, Dec. 15,
1941 - before and
during. NA 171-G-1-C-9 &
10

These students at American University constituted one of the first Civilian Defense Fire Guard brigades to be organized. With a shortage of men on campus, these 12 women students volunteered for the dangerous job of fighting fire bombs, should they be dropped on university buildings. NA 171-G-4A-4

An exterior view of the first big air raid shelter on New York City's Lower East Side, which opened on July 13, 1942. It was half-a-block long and occupied the space formerly used for recreational activities by the tenants of a model tenement, the Lavanburg Homes. The entrance was protected by 4,000 sandbags. Students in the Architecture Department of Pratt Institute of Technology prepared the plans and specifications. BETTMANN ARCHIVE

Hollywood stars sit in a shelter on the Warner Brothers movie lot during a practice air raid drill on Jan. 4, 1942. Left to right: director Michael Curtiz, actor Dennis Morgan, actress Bette Davis, a studio workman, actress Irene Manning and another workman. BETTMANN ARCHIVE

This fancy 1941 air raid shelter was about 45 feet under the Allerton House Hotel in New York City. It proved to be a comfortable place to spend time, and the hotel even installed an auxiliary lighting system in case its own light plant was shut down. BETTMANN ARCHIVE

No, this is not a chicken coop but an air raid shelter for the home. Weighing less than 500 pounds, it was constructed with a steel top and steel slats on the bottom. With this construction and wire mesh sides, it provided protection against flying debris and falling beams and bricks. The 30-inch high posts at each corner could support a 35-ton load. It sold for about $100 and could hold four people or two people for sleeping purposes. BETTMANN ARCHIVE

A scene in the basement of the Capitol building during Washington's first daylight air raid practice, June 2, 1942. Senators in the foreground, left to right, beginning with the third from the left: Sen. Burton K. Wheeler, Montana; Sen. Guy Gillette, Iowa; Sen. Scott Lucas, Illinois; Sen. Joseph Guffey, Pennsylvania; Sen. Kenneth McKellar, Tennessee; and Sen. George W. Norris, Nebraska. BETTMANN ARCHIVE

An air raid shelter in the Bitterroot Valley of Western Montana. This building still stands as the Fort Owen Inn near Stevensville. LC-USF34-65332-D

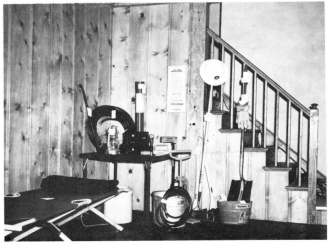

A display of air raid equipment that should be placed in every home. NA 171-G-1-A-4

A family in Hawaii gets their children ready for a possible gas attack. U.S. ARMY MUSEUM HAWAII

The Decontamination Squad is employed for a drill on chemically neutralizing an area which has been subjected to attack with a persistent gas (mustard gas and lewisite are persistent gases and may be either sprayed or dropped from low-flying planes). The volunteers are spreading a mixture of sand and chloride of lime to neutralize the area. NA 171-G-3E-19

Middle right: A civilian defense headquarters in Hawaii. Hawaii was, of course, very sensitive to a possible enemy attack since the Japanese had proven they could do it. But they never attacked the islands again except for a single plane fly over some months after Pearl Harbor. U.S. ARMY MUSEUM HAWAII

A shipyard worker at the Newport News shipyard volunteers as an air raid warden. He's carrying what appears to be a hand-held siren. LC-USW-3-1926-E

A first aid class in a tenement area of southwest Washington, D.C. LC-USW-3-11405-C

NA 171-G-1-A-3

Raymond Runk, an accountant at the Animal Trap Company, Lititz, Pa., and a civil defense fire captain, gives a lecture on German bombs to Boy Scouts who are learning to be messengers. In emergencies their duty would be to report fire bombs to the authorities. LC-USW3-11700-E

Guy Davenport, 11, and Maynard Clark, 14, read the air raid instructions posted in the Gilbert S. Hastings post office and general store in West Danville, Vt., July 1942. This would hardly have been a prime target, had they even been able to get their planes across the Atlantic. LC-USW-3-53814-E

A WERS (War Emergency Radio Service) transmitter-receiver keeps this Air Raid Warden Post in direct communication with the community Civilian Defense control center. The set was built from old home receivers by civilian radio volunteers. After brief instructions, it could be operated by anyone who could use a telephone. NA 171-G-8B-1

Famous actress Helen Hayes and helpers put a fire truck through its paces at her Nyack, N.Y., home. The girls are her daughter, Mary MacArthur, and her niece, and the boys are her adopted son, Jamie MacArthur, and an English war refugee. NA 171-G-3A-2

Scenes like this one in Portland, Ore., were familiar to Civilian Defense volunteers. Here a "victim" is treated for "electric shock" at the scene of a "bomb attack." The volunteers wanted to be ready for any emergency involving an enemy attack - which fortunately never came. OHS

This class at Benjamin Franklin High School in New York City learn the basic principles of first aid along with their English courses. Their teacher was certified in both subjects. FDR

Another one of the realistic "rescues" of "bombing victims" practiced throughout the country, this one in Scranton, Pa. Smoke was used in some of them. Luckily, the United States, except for Honolulu and Dutch Harbor, Alaska, never had to experience the horrors of the real thing, as did other countries. NA 171-G-4E-1

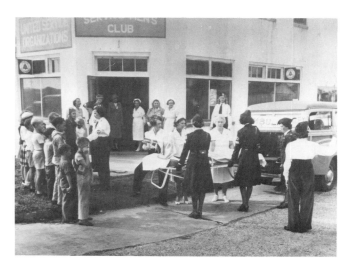

Women's Auxiliary Police practice first aid at a USO club in Jacksonville, Fla. NA 171-G-3C-1

Local children and adults
gather inside the shelter.
FRANK B. ELAM PHOTO

The municipal office building in Baltimore prepares for
possible air raids with sandbags, April 1943. Because
Baltimore was a vital seaport, bustling with war
industries, it was considered a prime target for enemy
air raids. LC-USW-3-22114-E

Students at Alexis I. Dupont School in Wilmington,
Del., put the final sandbag on one of the protective
walls around the school on Jan. 24, 1942. DSA

MODEL MAKERS

Students at Roosevelt High School, Los Angeles, Calif., make model airplanes to Navy specifications for distribution to military and civilian groups. FDR

Students in a basic aviation course at Weequahic High School, Newark, N.J., test model airplanes for accuracy of specification. The models were used by civilians and the military to help identify high-flying planes. FDR

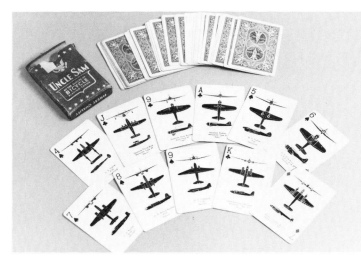

Even playing cards were used to teach the public to recognize Allied and enemy planes. U.S. ARMY MUSEUM HAWAII

Aircraft identification models were cast for the Army Air Force by the thousands using a black, hard plastic-rubber composition similar to that used in phonograph records. They were produced for practically every significant U.S. or foreign aircraft of the period and were hung from the ceilings of operations offices, aircrew ready rooms and lounges, and briefing rooms at airfields throughout the world where U.S. flyers were stationed. On the home front, they were valuable aids for training volunteer civilian observers.

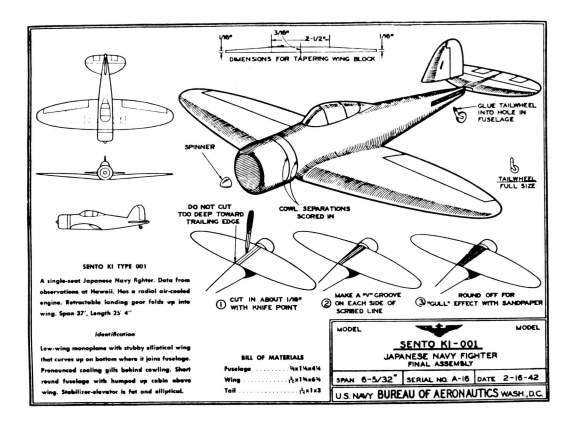

DIMENSIONS FOR TAPERING WING BLOCK

SPINNER

GLUE TAILWHEEL INTO HOLE IN FUSELAGE

TAILWHEEL FULL SIZE

DO NOT CUT TOO DEEP TOWARD TRAILING EDGE

COWL SEPARATIONS SCORED IN

① CUT IN ABOUT 1/16" WITH KNIFE POINT

② MAKE A "V" GROOVE ON EACH SIDE OF SCRIBED LINE

③ "GULL" EFFECT WITH SANDPAPER ROUND OFF FOR

SENTO KI TYPE 001

A single-seat Japanese Navy fighter. Data from observations at Hawaii. Has a radial air-cooled engine. Retractable landing gear folds up into wing. Span 37', Length 25' 4"

Identification

Low-wing monoplane with stubby elliptical wing that curves up on bottom where it joins fuselage. Pronounced cooling gills behind cowling. Short round fuselage with humped up cabin above wing. Stabilizer-elevator is fat and elliptical.

BILL OF MATERIALS

Fuselage . . . . ⅝ x 1¼ x 4¼
Wing . . . . 3/16 x 1¼ x 6¼
Tail . . . . 1/16 x 1 x 3

MODEL		MODEL
SENTO KI - 001		
JAPANESE NAVY FIGHTER		
FINAL ASSEMBLY		
SPAN 6-5/32"	SERIAL NO. A-16	DATE 2-16-42
U.S. NAVY BUREAU OF AERONAUTICS WASH., D.C.		

Instructions for the construction of a wooden Sento KI-001 recognition model. In addition to the cast mass-produced models, many others used for training were donated by clubs and amateur modelers. It was quite an honor for a person to have a model accepted since the specifications and accuracy requirements were very precise.

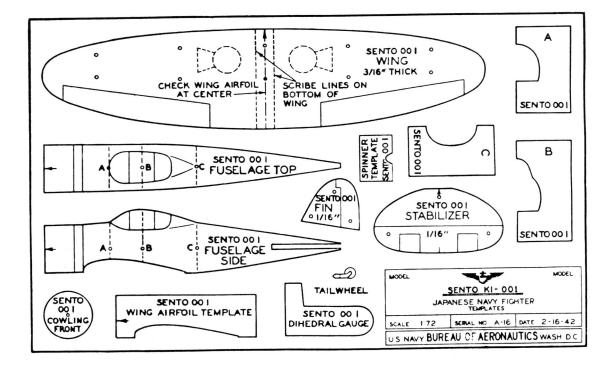

SENTO 001 WING 3/16" THICK

CHECK WING AIRFOIL AT CENTER

SCRIBE LINES ON BOTTOM OF WING

A

SENTO 001

C

SENTO 001

B

SENTO 001

SPINNER TEMPLATE SENTO 001

SENTO 001 FUSELAGE TOP

SENTO 001 FIN 1/16"

SENTO 001 STABILIZER 1/16"

SENTO 001 FUSELAGE SIDE

SENTO 001 COWLING FRONT

SENTO 001 WING AIRFOIL TEMPLATE

TAILWHEEL

SENTO 001 DIHEDRAL GAUGE

MODEL		MODEL
SENTO KI - 001		
JAPANESE NAVY FIGHTER		
TEMPLATES		
SCALE 1:72	SERIAL NO A-16	DATE 2-16-42
U.S. NAVY BUREAU OF AERONAUTICS WASH D C		

These women, members of the Utah Council of Defense, are on the scene for mapping, first aid and ski patrol duties. NA 171-G-6-G-1 & 2

This dramatic pose shows what not to do in the event of an air raid - get excited and cause panic. The OWI caption states that one of the enemy's purposes is to create panic and continues: "Getting excited is helping the enemy to achieve this purpose; keeping calm is defeating it. It is difficult to guess whether this girl is attempting to imitate an air raid siren, or even Mussolini proclaiming another victorious retreat. At any rate, here is not a good example to follow during an air raid." FDR

It's not an invasion from Mars but just military personnel and civilians going about their business wearing their infernal gas masks. U.S. ARMY MUSEUM HAWAII

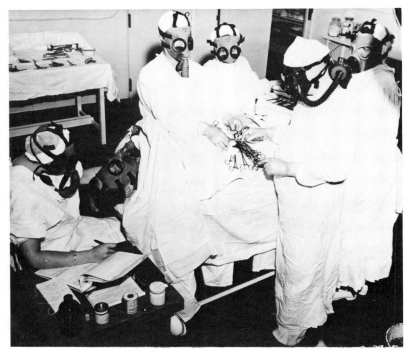

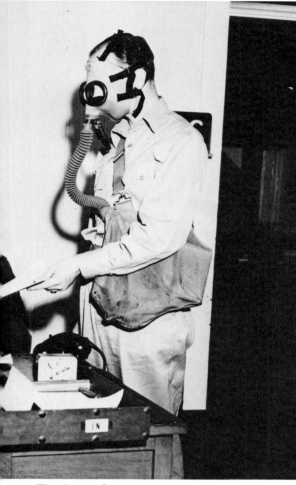

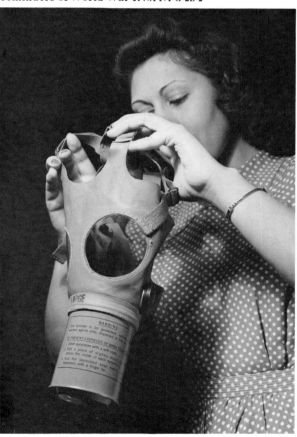

Even children were fitted with gas shields in Hawaii.
U.S. ARMY MUSEUM HAWAII

The threat of a gas attack was real in the early days of the war, and the fear was a holdover from the terrible reminders of World War I. NA 171-G-2B-2

The threat of an enemy gas attack, something that had happened in World War I, was on everyone's mind for the first six months of the war. Here Boy Scout John Toeplitz, with an assist from Donald Hallam, tries out his homemade respirator in readiness for a "poison gas" raid, May 1942. DSA

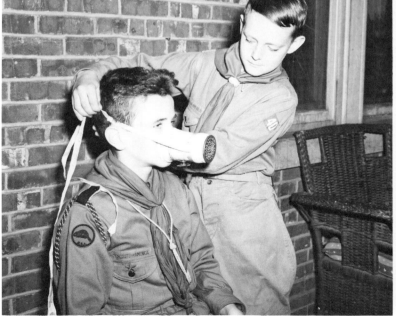

CIVIL AIR PATROL

One of the many World War II civilian volunteer groups was the Civil Air Patrol (CAP), officially created on Dec. 1, 1941, under the Office of Civilian Defense. During the war, CAP members flew anti-sabotage patrols, target towing, border patrols, search and rescue, anti-submarine coastal patrol missions and also aided in recruiting Army Air Force (AAF) trainees. The CAP consisted of more than 75,000 volunteers on April 29, 1943, when it was transferred to the War Department as an auxiliary of the AAF. On anti-sub patrol, CAP crews in light planes ranged as far as 150 miles out to sea. During 18 months of anti-sub patrol in 1942-43, CAP crews flew 244,600 hours, the equivalent of 24 million miles. They reported 173 enemy subs and summoned aid for 91 ships in distress and for 363 survivors of submarine attacks. After some CAP planes began carrying bombs and depth charges, they attacked 57 subs, sinking or damaging at least two. Other subs were destroyed by Air Force or Navy planes and ships called out by CAP pilots by radio. CAP efforts in World War II were not without sacrifice, for during anti-sub patrol operations alone, they lost 90 airplanes and 26 members.

The dusk patrol at Civil Air Patrol base headquarters of Coastal Patrol No. 20, Bar Harbor, Maine, set their watches from a time signal before going to their planes, June 1943. LC-USW-3-32558-C

Sgt. Pat Pate, who worked in a law office in Corpus Christi, Texas, before joining the Civil Air Patrol during the war. LC-USW-3-33953-D

CAP uniforms were the same as the Army's except for distinguishing red shoulder loops. This lieutenant wears Army bars of rank on his shoulders and an Air Corps insignia on his collar. NA 171-G-14A-3

CAP pilots and observers go over the day's flight instructions before taking off in their own planes to patrol coast lines, railroads and other vital installations. Of the 60,000 volunteer members during the war, more than 5,000 were women. NA 171-G-14A-4

Lt. John F. Payne, flight instructor at the Louisiana State University flying school, coaches a CPT (Civilian Pilot Training) student learning to swing a propeller. FDR

Zack Mosley, creator of the nationally syndicated aviation adventure strip, "Smilin' Jack," was one of the volunteer pilots who helped form the Civil Air Patrol, which became an official organization of the U.S. government only six days before Pearl Harbor. He was one of the few hundred CAP Pilots awarded the USAF Air Medal for flying over 300 hours in bomb-loaded civilian planes off the Atlantic coast during the first 18 months of World War II. His "Smilin' Jack" feature first appeared in 1933 and was retired in 1973.

SMILIN' JACK—KEEP THE HOME FIRES OUT

Dr. Cornell Grossman
of Millburn, N.J.,
devised these home-
made guns and shields
to protect against an
enemy air raid or
ground attack. FDR

These sinister-looking
women are members of the
Guardian Angels of New
York, perhaps organized to
ward off potential German
invaders. They were skilled
in marksmanship with their
deadly shotguns, February
1944. BETTMANN ARCHIVE

Students organized at Charlotte Amalie High School, St. Thomas, Virgin Islands, to assist police and fire departments during blackouts and air raids, December 1941. LC-USF-34-47141-D

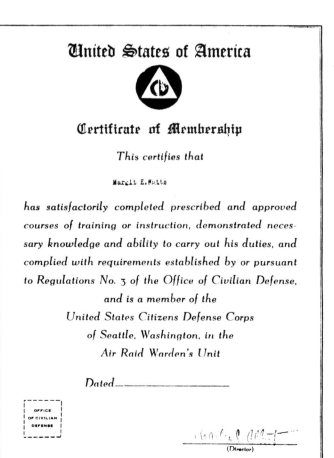

United States of America

Certificate of Membership

This certifies that

Margit E. Watts

has satisfactorily completed prescribed and approved courses of training or instruction, demonstrated necessary knowledge and ability to carry out his duties, and complied with requirements established by or pursuant to Regulations No. 3 of the Office of Civilian Defense, and is a member of the
United States Citizens Defense Corps
of Seattle, Washington, in the
Air Raid Warden's Unit

Dated_____

OFFICE
OF CIVILIAN
DEFENSE

_____
(Director)

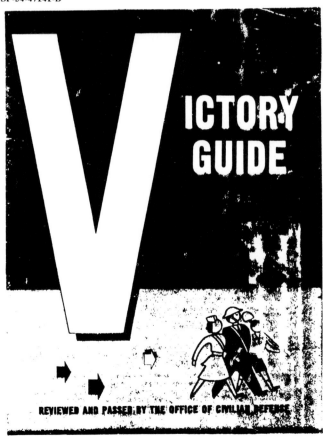

VICTORY GUIDE

REVIEWED AND PASSED BY THE OFFICE OF CIVILIAN DEFENSE

Victory Corps students at Montgomery Blair High School, Silver Springs, Md., stand erect for officers' review. Students wore their uniforms three times a week. To release mothers for war work, Victory Corps girls operated a day nursery. Besides helping the community, the project tied in with the school's home economics course. FDR

Victory Corps girls at Roosevelt High School, Los Angeles, stand at ease. Riflery was one of the many war-training activities offered at the school. FDR

Form One In Your High School~NOW!

BE READY TO JUMP INTO THEIR SHOES !!

PROTECTING
THE
NATION
FROM
FOREIGN
INVASION

LT. THOMAS CUNNINGHAM
ROYAL NAVY
H. M. S. BEDFORDSHIRE
11 MAY 1942 AGE 27

BODY FOUND MAY 14 1942

An air raid spotter at Arden, Del.,
Feb. 21, 1942. DSA

JAPAN and the JAPANESE

日本

A MILITARY POWER WE MUST DEFEAT
A PACIFIC PROBLEM WE MUST SOLVE
BY THE EDITORS OF FORTUNE

FIGHTING
FORCES
SERIES

THE INFANTRY JOURNAL

U.S. ARMY AIR CORPS
OBSERVATION POST

War on the Pacific Coast

by Edwin C. Bearss, chief historian
National Park Service

Japanese Submarines Cruise the Pacific Coast

First Attacks

Japanese submarines operated off the western coast of the United States on several occasions during World War II. When plans were made for the attack on Pearl Harbor, a directive was issued on November 5, 1941, by the Japanese Navy for its *6th Fleet* of submarines to "make reconnaissance of American Fleet in Hawaii and West Coast area, and, by surprise attacks on shipping, destroy lines of communication." After participating in the operations directed against Pearl Harbor, the *6th Fleet* dispatched nine submarines to attack shipping along the coasts of California, Oregon, and Washington. Seven of these vessels were equipped to carry planes for reconnaissance. These submarines began arriving off the coast about December 17 and operated on previously assigned stations from Cape Flattery, Washington, in the north to San Diego in the south.

The submarines remained off our coast for about ten days. Only four of the nine attacked any shipping. The tanker *Agwiworld* was shelled by a submarine off Santa Cruz, California, on December 19, but she escaped. Four other vessels, *S.S. Emidio, Samoa, Larry Doheny,* and *Montebello* were attacked off the California coast before Christmas. Two of these vessels, both tankers, were destroyed.

Claims were voiced at the time that an army B-24 bomber sent a Japanese submarine to the bottom on Christmas Eve, at a point 50 miles off the mouth of the Columbia River. This was an error on the airmen's part, because the submarine assigned to that station, *I-25*, was destined to return to the Pacific coast in the late summer of 1942. The submarine flotilla had planned to engage in simultaneous shelling of coastal cities on Christmas Eve, but at the last moment, Japanese fleet headquarters ordered the submarines to abandon the plan and to return to their base at Kwajalein.

Sinking of *S.S. Emidio*

One of the vessels attacked by the submarines was the General Petroleum Tanker *Emidio*. On Saturday, December 20, she was running down the coast, when at 1 p.m. the lookout sighted a large submarine bearing down. Capt. A.C. Farrow, in an effort to escape conned a zigzag course, which took the 6,912-ton tanker nearer the coast. The submarine, however, was too swift, and she soon drew in range. Her gunners then opened fire with their 5-1/2-inch gun. Six shells were fired, five of them bursting on the target. Several of the lifeboats were damaged, the tanker's radio put out of action, and three sailors knocked overboard. The radioman, however, was able to get off an S.O.S. before his set went dead.

Captain Farrow and most of the crew then abandoned *Emidio*. While they were searching, unsuccessfully, for the men carried overboard, a patrol bomber of the U.S. Navy appeared and the submarine submerged. *Emidio*, with only a skeleton crew aboard, was wallowing and helpless, while Farrow and his people in the two lifeboats looked for the men hurled overboard by the exploding shells. As soon as the bomber disappeared, the submarine surfaced, closed to within 440 yards, and sent a torpedo crashing into the tanker. The torpedo exploded in the after engine room, drowning two of the eleven men remaining aboard. After the submarine had disappeared, the two lifeboats took aboard the nine survivors of the skeleton crew and pulled for the coast. Twelve hours later, they reached Blunts Reef Lightship.

When interviewed by the press Captain Farrow and his crew called the attack, "shameful and ruthless," as they charged the Japanese with deliberately shelling their lifeboats before they could be lowered. "If they had been armed," they boasted, "we would have had a good chance against the submarine," as she was within easy range.

Emidio refused to sink, however. Drifting northward with the current, she came ashore on Steamboat Rock, near the entrance to Crescent City harbor, on the night of December 25. Hundreds of people crowded Battery Point the next day to view the wreck. The tanker's bow was out of the water, and her after portion was submerged. One of the curious reported, "The bridge and forward deck are out of the water, the ship's stack with the letter, G, rising out of the water at the stern, which appears to be riding on the rocky bottom. The bow moves with the rise and fall of the waves."

Emidio drifted free on Wednesday, January 14, and wallowed in the entrance to the harbor, threatening to run down the craft at anchor in Fish Harbor. To prevent the derelict from becoming a "Flying Dutchman," Leo Ward was taken out to the hulk and released its anchor. Although the vessel was in the custody of the United States Coast Guard, Ward was interested in the possibility of salvaging the vessel, and he had contacted officials of General Petroleum in San Pedro. He believed the bow of *Emidio* was sound, and if the after portion could be raised with pontoons or cut away, the craft could be salvaged.

R.C. Porter of San Francisco made a better offer for the hulk than Ward, and he acquired salvage rights to *Emidio*. He hired a crew of local fishermen and boats to carry out the project. Porter, however, failed to notify the Coast Guard of his plan, and he and his men were fired on by the guard as they sought to board the wreck. After identifying themselves, they were allowed to proceed. The anchor chain was cut, and the tides carried the hulk toward Fauntleroy Rock. Nine years were to pass before the rusty bow was finally broken up for scrap, and the forward bollards placed at the foot of H Street in Crescent City, California, as a memorial.

Japanese Submarines Return

Two enemy submarines were off the Pacific coast in February 1942.

First Pacific Coast Torpedoed Ship. "General Petroleum Tanker Emidio Torpedoed by Japanese Dec. 19, 1941 off Eureka Coast, as it appeared after floating to Crescent City, Calif. on Dec. 20, 1941.

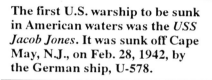

Portions of the hull of the *SS Emidio* on display at Beachfront Park in Crescent City, Calif.

The first to arrive, *I-8*, patrolled northward from the Golden Gate to the Washington coast without encountering any shipping, and then returned to her home port. The second was *I-17*, a large plane-carrying submarine. *I-17* arrived off San Diego about February 19. Four days later, on the 23d, just as President Franklin D. Roosevelt was beginning a "fireside chat," she surfaced off the California coast, near Santa Barbara, and from a range of 2,500 yards pumped 13 rounds of 5-1/2-inch shell into the oil installations. Damage, however, was negligible. She then headed northward and cruised the Humboldt Coast before returning to Japan.

The night after *I-17* shelled the oil installations near Santa Barbara, there occurred the "Battle of Los Angeles."

Tensions had been building up for some time as agitation for removal of resident Japanese from coastal California had mounted. At 2 a.m. word spread that an unidentified plane had appeared on a radarscope bearing in from the Pacific toward Los Angeles. A blackout was ordered and all antiaircraft units alerted. The guns roared into action at 3 a.m., the first shot aimed at a balloon (probably a meteorological balloon over Santa Monica). Within the next hour, the gunners expended over 1,400 rounds of ammunition against a variety of "targets" in the Los Angeles area. Exhaustive hearings led to the conclusion by the army that from one to five unidentified planes had penetrated the area, whereas the navy decided that there had been no excuse for the firing.

Fears were voiced on the Pacific coast, following the Doolittle raid on Tokyo in April 1942, that the Japanese would retaliate. Steps were accordingly taken by the United States to beef up its west coast defenses. Victory over a powerful Japanese task force at Midway on June 4, 1942, with the loss of four enemy aircraft carriers, all but ended the threat of a serious attack on the west coast. In effect the Battle of Midway restored the balance of naval power in the Pacific, which the Japanese had upset at Pearl Harbor.

The Japanese occupation of the western Aleutian Islands (Kiska, Attu, and Agattu) in June 1942 caused some members of the American military to fear a further Japanese thrust toward the Alaskan mainland. Japanese submarine operations helped spark these apprehensions. In conjunction with the air attack on Dutch Harbor and the occupation of the western Aleutians, two of the big plane-carrying submarines, *I-25* and *I-26*, had been sent to reconnoiter to the south of Alaska. *I-26* at the end of May departed from the neighborhood of Kodiak Island and made her way toward the Washington coast. One Japanese source claims that the reconnaissance plane of *I-26* "scouted Seattle Harbor and reported no heavy men-of-war, particularly carriers, there."[1]

On June 20 the Japanese established their presence by torpedoing a Canadian lumber schooner southwest of Cape Flattery and then shelling the Canadian radio compass station at Estevan Point on Vancouver Island. The next night, June 21-22, a submarine sent six to nine 5-1/2-inch shells crashing into the Fort Stevens Military Reservation in Oregon, at the mouth of Columbia, inflicting neither casualties nor damage. This bombardment, insignificant in itself, was the first foreign attack on a continental military installation since the War of 1812. On June 23, two torpedoes missed a tanker off the southern coast of Oregon.

The final Japanese submarine patrol off the Pacific coast was undertaken in reprisal for the Doolittle raid. *I-25*, with its reconnaissance plane equipped for bombing, reached the coast near the California-Oregon boundary at the end of August 1942. On September 9 the plane dropped an incendiary bomb into a heavily wooded area on a mountain slope, near Brookings, Oregon. The bomb started a forest fire, but it was quickly brought under control by firefighters. *I-25*, after staying out of sight of American forces charged with her destruction, attacked with torpedoes and sank two tankers on October 4 and 6 off the coast of southern Oregon. These attacks marked an end to submarine warfare off the west coast.

1. U.S. Strategic Bombing Survey, *Interrogations of Japanese Officials* (2 vols. Washington, 1946), Interview 97, Comdr. Masatake Okumiya, Oct. 10, 1945.

The *Los Angeles Examiner* of Dec. 25, 1941, headlined a story about the torpedo attack on the *Absaroka* off the California coast. DON YOUNG, RANCHO PALOS VERDES, CALIF.

The oil derricks west of Santa Barbara at Goleta and the Ellwood Refinery - scene of the first enemy attack on U.S. soil since the War of 1812.

Capt. Bernard Hagen showing the results of a Japanese shell hitting near the absorption plant at the Ellwood Refinery in California. Hagen was later wounded while trying to defuse an unexploded shell and spent 50 days in a hospital - probably the only American serviceman to receive a Purple Heart for enemy action on U.S. soil.

Near misses at a storage tank at the Ellwood Refinery.

Santa Barbara Fire Chief C.L. Tenney in a hole made by one of the 16 to 25 shells that exploded in the Goleta vicinity on Feb. 23, 1942.

Deputy Fire Chief, Albert Brotherton, inspects holes made in the interior of the corrugated wall pump house.

The "Battle of Los Angeles"

Headline of the *Los Angeles Times* on Feb. 25, 1942, attests to the war jitters on the west coast. Over 1,400 rounds of anti-aircraft ammunition were fired at supposed enemy aircraft by trigger-happy soldiers. Earlier, there had been blips on radar screens and visible reports of unidentified aircraft, but no Japanese planes were ever in the area. Fragments of spent shells dropped all over the Long Beach-Santa Monica area. No one ever figured out what caused all the confusion.

German U-Boat Activity

America faced a serious menace at the beginning of the war from German U-Boats which penetrated to within three miles of the east coast shoreline. The commander of the North Atlantic Naval Coastal Frontier stated on Dec. 22, 1941: "It is submitted that should enemy submarines operate off this coast, this command has no force available to take adequate action against them, either offensive or defensive."

The Eastern Sea Frontier (ESF) which stretched from Maine to Geor-

gia was the battleground that involved thousands of people along the coast. The undersea raiders attacked or sunk over 140 ships from tankers to cargo haulers in 1942. These submarines also strew mines in some of the busy shipping lanes, most notably near the entrance to Chesapeake Bay.

People living along the shore got used to seeing flames on the horizon, aiding shipwrecked sailors and watching blimps, planes and vessels of all descriptions fighting these underwa-

ter menaces.

Gradually the U.S. Navy developed techniques for detecting and sinking the U-Boats. This forced the German navy to shift operations more to the Caribbean area. Only 16 ships were attacked in the ESF in the next two and one-half years.

Ten U-Boats were eventually sunk in the ESF and thousands of lives, both Allied and German, were lost from 1942 to 1945.

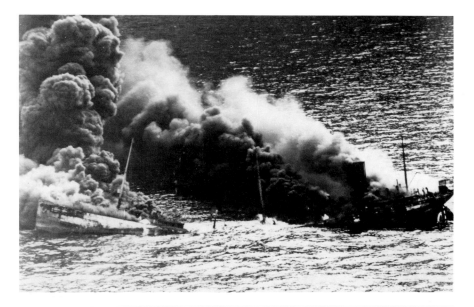

The *Dixie Arrow* was an 8,046-ton United States tanker sunk by U-71 off the east coast on March 26, 1942. The ship burned furiously for an hour before sinking but 22 seamen managed to survive the holocaust. NA 80-G-2183

The tanker Byron T. Benson was bound from Port Arthur, Texas, to Bayonne, N.J., with a cargo of crude oil. She was traveling with another tanker and two armedescorts. But U-552 found its mark on April 4, 1942, and torpedoed her. Twenty-seven seamen were rescued and it took three days for the ship to burn out and finally sink. NA 80-G-63-472

In May 1942, the British ship *HMS Bedfordshire* was torpedoed while on patrol in Allied shipping lanes near Ocracoke Island, one of the barrier islands known as the Outer Banks of North Carolina. Four bodies washed ashore on the island and were buried there. During the 1976 U.S. Bicentennial, the state of North Carolina purchased the property and leased it back to Great Britain as an official piece of English soil. The area is part of the Cape Hatteras National Seashore Recreation Area. PAT GIBSON PHOTOS

Fort Stevens, Oregon
Attack

Fort Stevens, a historic fort near Astoria, Ore., at the mouth of the Columbia River, was attacked by Japanese submarine, I-25, on June 21, 1942.

A hole made by one of the Japanese shells fired at Fort Stevens. Most of the shells fired landed on the beach in front of Battery Russell. They caused no damage, and no one was injured. The fort did not return fire. But the Portland *Oregonian* reported that when the attack subsided, "few if any persons ventured onto the streets of Astoria for some time," apparently expecting the resumption of hostilities. So loud were the blasts from the detonating shells that they were heard as far away as Illwaco, Wash.

Marker at Fort Stevens State Park, Hammond, Ore.
FORT STEVENS STATE PARK

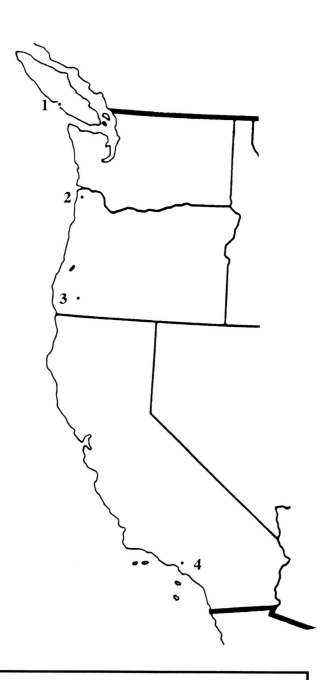

Japanese Attacks Against the West Coast of the United States and Canada

1. Estevan Point, British Columbia

2. Fort Stevens, Oregon

3. Siskiyou National Forest - aerial attack

4. Goleta, California

Examining an incendiary pencil used by saboteurs in Wilmington, Del., June 1941. Left to right: Harry O'Connor, FBI special agent in charge (Baltimore), Supt. Andrew J. Kavanaugh, William Roach, FBI special agent (Baltimore) and Chief Frank Maloney. DSA

Guns, ammunition and radios confiscated in raids on enemy aliens in Delaware, February 1942. DSA

Firearms, ammunition, and a sword belonging to aliens, stored in a vault in Olympia, state capital of Washington. All Japanese and other aliens in Washington had to surrender their radios, cameras and binoculars in addition to weapons and ammunition.

In response to the war hysteria that swept the country in the early months of the war, bridges, such as this one, were guarded and cars were searched for possible saboteurs.

Guns, radios and flags confiscated from Nazi sympathizers soon after America went to war.

An armed guard posted at the Saint Louis-San Francisco Railroad bridge, Tulsa, Okla., October 1942. LC-USW-3-9516-D

This bridge across the Missouri River in Williams County, N.D., was guarded by members of the American Legion from Dec. 8, 1941 to Feb. 1, 1942. Even in the far reaches of North Dakota sites that were presumed vital were guarded after Pearl Harbor. LC-USF-34-64725-D

As in a scene from the Old West, an armed guard stands ready for any approaching trouble at a Phelps Dodge copper mine in Morenci, Ariz., December 1942. Was the trouble expected from enemy saboteurs or from union miners? LC-USW-3-27775-E

A Coast Guard motor lifeboat provides escort to San Francisco's crab fishermen as a wartime precaution. This naval protection included taking the fleet to the fishing grounds at dawn, remaining with it through the fishing hours and finally bringing it home through the Golden Gate in the later afternoon. LC-USE6-D-10158

A guard walking his post at the U.S. Capitol, summer 1943. LC-USE6-D-10158

Members of the Texas Defense Guard assemble in a high school auditorium in San Augustine, Texas, April 1943. LC-USW3-25153-D

Guards at the White House. FDR

The Hawaii Territorial Guard train to repel a possible Japanese invasion. U.S. ARMY MUSEUM HAWAII

The Central Aircraft Spotting Post in Hawaii. These women seem to be having a good time. U.S. ARMY MUSEUM HAWAII

A young soldier with fixed bayonet stands ready for action outside the Iolani Palace in Honolulu. The palace was placed under armed guard after the Pearl Harbor attack. U.S. ARMY MUSEUM HAWAII

This is the patch of the Kauai Volunteers, which was composed almost entirely of Filipino plantation workers, who wanted a role in the war effort since their homeland was occupied by the Japanese.

Hawaii at War

The Territory of Hawaii, 2,300 miles from the mainland, which bore the brunt of the first Japanese attack of the war on Dec. 7, 1941, was placed under strict wartime control. People in nonessential jobs were asked to leave the islands, and defenses were increased in anticipation of another Japanese attack. Soon after the attack, the entire territory was placed under U.S. Military Martial Law which was not lifted until October 1944. Although ruled unconstitutional after the war, martial law was then considered necessary by the military authorities. The thousands of troops who were trained in Hawaii or were on their way to Pacific battlefields brought the war closer to those islands than to any other part of the United States.

Stores in Honolulu prepared for enemy attacks with taped-up windows. Here one store owner fashions "V for Victory" on his windows. U.S. ARMY MUSEUM HAWAII

HAWAII INVASION CURRENCY

The Hilo Minutemen, a volunteer civilian group on the big island of Hawaii, string barbed wire along the coast in the spring of 1942. HAWAII STATE ARCHIVES

The threat of a Japanese invasion was considered a possibility in 1942, even after the decisive battle of Midway. By August the federal government had withdrawn all regular currency used in Hawaii and replaced it with specially printed notes. These had "Hawaii" overprinted in large letters on the back and vertically at each end on the front. The old money was burned in a sugar mill at Aiea, and after Aug. 15, 1942, it became illegal to possess, without a license, the regular notes. The reasoning was that in the event of an invasion, the new notes would automatically become invalid as they were restricted to Hawaii and the South Pacific area. They were free to circulate after October 1944, and were withdrawn by April 1946 when they were replaced with regular, old notes. The $1 notes were overprinted on series 1935A Silver Certificates. The $5, $10 and $20 notes were overprinted on Federal Reserve notes of the 12th (San Francisco) District. $5 and $20 notes were also overprinted on series 1934 and 1934A certificates and the $10 note only on the 1934A certificate. All notes were printed on sheets of 12.

Radar Station B-71
Trinidad Radar Station
California

Courtesy National Park Service

When WWII began, radar was a comparatively new defense development pioneered independently during the 1930s by the British, French, Germans, Japanese and Americans. In the United States, the U.S. Navy and the Army's Signal Corps ran independent development programs.

Earlier aircraft warning systems, relying on sound detection devices and ground spotters, were tested on both the Atlantic and Pacific Coasts in 1937 and 1938, but it was not until the Signal Corps had developed a mobile radar system known as SCR-270 that the War Department in May 1940 directed army commanders to select sites for locating radar stations along the coasts and to adjust the existing Aircraft Warning Service plans to the use of radar. On Aug. 2, 1940, the War Department approved a plan to provide the continental coastal frontiers with 31 mobile detectors, beginning with 11 sites along the northeast Atlantic Coast and 10 along the Pacific Coast. The four Army Air Corps interceptor commands worked feverishly to create a coastal radar net and a supporting corps of ground observers. By Dec. 7, 1941, sites had been picked for 13 radar stations along the East Coast and eight of these were nearing completion; on the West Coast, there were 10 stations to cover 1,200 miles from Canada to Mexico, supplemented by 2,400 ground observers.

The obvious immediate necessity of guarding American coastlines once America entered the war was perhaps even more urgent on the Pacific Coast than on the Atlantic in view of Japan's ability to assault American territory so dramatically demonstrated at Pearl Harbor and again in landings in the Aleutian Islands of Alaska. The threat was further demonstrated when a Japanese submarine shelled an oil refinery north of Santa Barbara, Calif., on Feb. 23, 1942, when another Japanese submarine shelled Estevan Point in British Columbia, Canada, on June 20, 1942, and again when a Japanese submarine shelled Fort Stevens, Wash., on July 21, 1942. With respect to aerial attack, there was early in the war the

possibility of Japanese carriers launching a strike against the Pacific Coast, but even discounting this threat, there was the undoubted ability of Japanese submarines to launch single seaplane strikes, demonstrated on Sept. 9, 1942, when one such submarine-launched aircraft dropped incendiary bombs on Oregon forests a mere 40 miles or so north of the Klamath River.

The radar station south of the Klamath River, in what is now Redwood National Park, was built in late 1942 and early 1943 as the northernmost California station in a network of 72 proposed stations, 65 of which were actually built, stretching from the Canadian border into Mexico. The Klamath station was designated by memorandum dated Nov. 6, 1942, from the Office of the Commanding General, IV Fighter Command, as Station B-71, named "Trinidad." It was also referred to as the "Klamath River" station.

The station appears to have been initially equipped, probably in July 1943, with an SCR-270B portable long-range (120 to 150 mile) radar system moved in from its previous location, probably Station B-38 on Santa Rosa Island (one of two radar stations on that island). Between December 1943 and April 1944, the SCR-270B was replaced with a "permanent" SCR-271 system.

The station consisted of two major buildings, one of which housed the power generating equipment and was disguised to look like a farmhouse, and the operating building, disguised to look like a barn. There was also a two-hole privy. The buildings were erected by a private construction firm under Army contract, and their camouflage features were built-in,

including false wooden siding and false windows over concrete-block construction, and false dormer windows on the power building roof. From the air, the station appeared to be a farm with barn, except for the portable radar located in 1943 in the open and uncamouflaged about 30 feet west of the operating building.

The station was manned by members of the Army Air Corps quartered in barracks near the town of Klamath Falls. It was commanded during part of 1943 by a 2nd Lieutenant Neff, later replaced by one or more 1st lieutenants in succession. One day's operation of the station required a crew of about 35 men to cover the 24 hours in shifts. The station reported by direct phone to an Aircraft Warning Service Filter Officer in Berkeley, Calif. The station was guarded by a detachment of military police, members of which carried rifles and had, in the words of a corporal who served there, "vicious dogs." The station was also protected by three .50 caliber machine guns on anti-aircraft mounts. All of the Army Air Corps men also carried rifles, and the station had one submachine gun always loaded and ready for use.

As the threat of Japanese attack waned towards the end of WWII, the coastal early warning radar stations began to be phased out. But with the need for early warning radar decreasing, the need for air-sea rescue radar increased, and effective July 1, 1944, the Klamath station was converted to emergency rescue service, with the SCR-271 radar replaced with RC-150 IFF equipment. Station B-71 was thus one of only 22 radar stations on the Pacific Coast which remained operational until the end of WWII.

The radar buildings are still intact. REDWOOD NATIONAL PARK

OPERATION PASTORIUS

by Eleanor C. Bishop

Just past midnight on June 13, 1942, U-202 commanded by Lt. Cmdr. Lindner surfaced off the coast of Amagansett, Long Island. Four men dressed in German marine fatigue uniforms were discharged into a rubber raft manned by two sailors. A seabag and four wooden crates were also lowered into the raft and all disappeared into the fog.

Thus began "Operation Pastorius,"* a plan to destroy and cripple the industrial section and transportation facilities of the Northeast and Middle Atlantic States as well as parts of the Ohio Valley. Earmarked for destruction were the following:
1) The Aluminum Company of America plants in Alcoa, Tennessee; East St. Louis, Illinois; and Massena, New York.
2) Cryolite Metals, Philadelphia, Pennsylvania.
3) The locks in the Ohio River between Pittsburgh, Pennsylvania, and Louisville, Kentucky.
4) Hell Gate Bridge, New York City.

*Named for Franz Daniel Pastorious, leader of the first community of immigrant Germans in America - 13 families of Mennonites and Quakers who settled Germantown Pennsylvania, in 1683.

5) The Pennsylvania Railroad Terminal, Newark, New Jersey.

Upon reaching shore, the four men were discharged onto the beach with their "baggage." George J. Dasch (alias George John Davis), Richard Quirin, Heinrich H. Heinck and Ernest Peter Burger. They quickly stripped themselves of their uniforms and donned civilian clothes of a fisherman's type.

At about the same time as the landing, John C. Cullen, 21, Seaman 2nd class, U.S. Coast Guard, left the station at Amagansett on foot to patrol the beach and walked about a half-mile, when he confronted Dasch, the Nazi leader. Seeing Cullen approaching, Dasch told the German sailors to return to the sub at once.

The heavy fog made it possible for them to slip away and paddle the rubber raft back to the sub without being seen and disappear beneath the deep, or so it appeared.

Dasch approached the stranger, and realizing he was wearing a sailor's uniform, and aware that German uniforms and explosives were scattered about on the ground, engaged Cullen in conver-

sation. Realizing that Cullen was a Coast Guardsman, Dasch told him that they were fishermen who had run aground at Southampton. As he was talking to Cullen, Burger started to speak in German and then in English to Dasch, who immediately told him to go back to the others.

Dasch then involved Cullen in a disjointed conversation, first telling him he would meet him in Washington, then threatening his life. When Cullen questioned him about what was in the bags, Dasch answered clams. Cullen, knowing there were no clams in the area, suggested that the strangers accompany him back to the Coast Guard station.

At this point, Dasch reached into a wad of bills totaling $50,000 and offered Cullen $300 to keep quiet about what he had witnessed. Dasch then asked Cullen if he would remember his face. Cullen quickly answered "no" and took off for the station. Burger's interruption had made Cullen nervous, along with the foreign language, the threat, the bribe, the fog-enshrouded indiscernible people and the fact that his

Heinrich Heinck   Herbert Haupt   Werner Thiel   Herman Neubauer

Richard Quirin   Ernest Burger   George Dasch   Edward Kerling

Left to right in top row are Heinrich Heinck, Herbert Haupt, Werner Thiel and Herman Neubauer, electrocuted. Left to right in bottom row are Richard Quirin, electrocuted; Ernest Burger, life imprisonment at hard labor; George Dasch, 30 years in jail, and Edward Kerling, electrocuted. NA 208-N-3418

only weapon was a flashlight.

It took Cullen eight minutes to return to the station, running all the way. He reported to his superior, the acting officer in charge, Boatswain's Mate Carl R. Jennette. After hearing Cullen's story, the station's commander, Warrant Officer Warren Barnes, was contacted at his home nearby.

Jennette, Cullen and three other Coast Guardsmen armed themselves and set out for the spot on the beach in less than five minutes, but there was no sign of a landing on the beach.

Who were these foreigners and how had they been able to accomplish this landing! They were either naturalized American citizens or had been residents of the United States. This "Long Island" group's prior presence in America had prepared them for this mission.

George John Dasch had entered the U.S. illegally in 1922, worked as a waiter in New York and even served in the Army Air Corps prior to his return to Germany in 1941.

Ernest Peter Burger, a member of the Nazi Party, had worked in the U. S. as a machinist, served in the Michigan National Guard and had become a citizen in 1933.

These rare photographs show a U.S. Military commission sitting in judgment in Washington on eight Nazis who confessed they were landed from German submarines with orders to sabotage the U.S. war effort. They were caught by Federal Bureau of Investigation agents a few hours after they had sneaked into the country and thus were not able to carry out their plans. Moreover, their confessions resulted in the arrest of 14 persons, including six women, who were supposed to help them.

Key figures in the trial of the eight Nazis are, left to right in foreground: U.S. Attorney General Francis Biddle, in charge of the prosecution; J. Edgar Hoover, director of the Federal Bureau of Investigation, whose men captured the spies almost as soon as they set foot on U.S. soil, and Col. Carl Ristine, one of the Army lawyers assigned to defend the eight men. NA 208-N-2841

Heinrich Heinck, in the custody of two soldiers, catches a quick glimpse of U.S. Coast Guardsmen whose testimony would probably send him to death as he is led into the courtroom. NA 208-N-2843

Heinrich Heinck, a toolmaker, had lived in America for 13 years, having entered the country illegally in 1926.

Richard Quirin had come to America in 1927, but returned to Germany because of the Reich's offer to finance the return of German nationals qualified as skilled mechanics.

Trained at Quentz Lake, the saboteur school outside of Berlin, these men, familiar with the eastern United States and loyal members of the German-American Bund, lovers of the Fatherland, were natural choices for this expedition.

While the Coast Guardsmen from the Amagansett Station had made their way back to the scene of the landing, the Germans had buried their uniforms and the four waterproof boxes containing explosives, timing devices and detonators, and walked inland. At 5 a.m., a sign announced they were entering Amagansett, New York. They made their way to the train station and took the 6:57 to Jamaica with their heads buried in the morning papers. The fact that they were dressed as fishermen didn't seem to faze the conductor, and upon reaching Jamaica, they transferred to a train which took them into Manhattan and hopefully into obscurity.

Each man received $700, spending it on new clothes, hotel rooms and food, while George Dasch took a train to Washington, checked into the Mayflower Hotel and called the FBI. After telling his story, he was quickly arrested, followed by a speedy apprehension of his co-conspirators.

Four nights after the Amagansett landing, another landing took place 850 miles to the south as German submarine U-584 surfaced 509 yards from the shore at the resort of Ponte Vedra, Florida. Again a rubber boat was inflated and held alongside the sub for Edward Kerling, Werner Thiel, Herbert Hans Haupt and Herman Otto Neubauer to disembark and go ashore.

The men of the "Florida group" had also been trained at the German saboteur school outside Berlin. The leader of the group, Werner Thiel, came to the United States in 1927 and stayed 14 years, even filing first citizenship

A general scene of the entire courtroom on July 15, 1942. The men seated at the rear are the seven U.S. Army generals who comprised the military commission. The prosecutors are at the table at right and the defense counsel, assigned by the court to protect the prisoners' interests, are at the table at left. The Nazi saboteurs are lined up along the left wall. NA 208-N-2839

Four of the eight men who faced possible death as Nazi spies listen to the evidence against them. Left to right are: Werner Thiel, Richard Quirin, an Army officer, Herman Neubauer and Edward J. Kerling. NA 208-N-2840

papers. The others also had been in America before.

Edward Kerling, a dedicated Nazi, had worked as a chauffeur and domestic in the U.S. for 11 years, and Herman Neubauer had been a cook.

Herbert Hans Haupt was brought to America by his parents and received his American citizenship through his father's naturalization.

The "Florida" group was dressed in swimming trunks, navy jackets and work caps upon their arrival. Four boxes of the same size and construction as those landed on Long Island accompanied them. Edward Kerling, the leader instructed the men to dig four holes and deposit the boxes and cover the holes with sand. Upon arriving on shore, the men had tossed their caps and jackets into the boat, and then walked down the beach towards Jacksonville carrying three canvas bags.

At 11 a.m., they changed into the civilian clothes they had been carrying, took a bus to Jacksonville and checked into hotels. Local fishermen found the incriminating evidence - small bombs and incendiary devices. The objectives of the proposed sabotage were found in the papers buried in both New York and Florida.

The "Long Island" group, or Team No. 1 under Dasch's leadership, was to attack the aluminum plant in Tennessee, Illinois and New York; the cryolite works at Philadelphia; and blow up the locks in the Ohio River between Pittsburgh and Louisville. Team No. 2 or the "Florida" group under Kerling's command, scheduled to blow up New York's Hell Gate Bridge in the East River, the Horseshoe Curve of the Pennsylvania Railroad at Altoona, Pennsylvania, and destroy New York's water-supply system, while promoting panic whenever possible. After Dasch revealed the story to the FBI, all saboteurs in New York and Jacksonville were immediately arrested. By June 25, 1942, all Nazi would-be saboteurs had been captured!

A military commission was established to investigate the case and determine the action to be taken. The President of the United States, Franklin D. Roosevelt instructed Attorney General Francis Biddle to direct the investigation and set up a commission of prominent Army generals.

It was revealed that the eight saboteurs who had been trained at Quentz Lake had been trained by Abwehr, the German military intelligence agency run by Adm. Wilhelm Canaris.

The two naturalized Americans, Ernest Peter Burger and Herbert Hans Haupt, and the six other former American residents had been trained to destroy the factories, transportation facilities and communications of the country which had been "home" to all of them at one time or another.

All eight were found guilty! Six were executed by the electric chair at the District of Columbia Jail August 8, 1942, and buried in a potter's field. Dasch, who had exposed the plot, was sentenced to 30 years hard labor, and Burger, one of the naturalized American citizens, was sentenced to life imprisonment at hard labor. Both were deported to Germany in 1948.

America was not secure from landings by enemy aliens intent upon infiltration and destruction. Quite suddenly an internal emergency had arisen. Immediate action was needed and surveys of the coasts were undertaken to determine where the coastlines were most vulnerable, and what type of plan should be put into force to solve the threatening problem.

Two more of the accused awaiting the opening of the trial in the custody of a U.S. Army lieutenant (center). They are Herbert H. Haupt, left, and George Dasch, right. NA 208-N-2844

Organization and Formation of the Coast Guard Beach Patrol

by Eleanor C. Bishop

As witnessed by incidents in New York and Florida, it was obvious that America could be invaded, perhaps not by an armada but certainly by bands of saboteurs who could wreak destruction throughout the country. Although Pearl Harbor and the fall of Bataan and Corregidor had been severe defeats, those incidents seemed so far away from the states until the eight Nazi spies actually landed on our shores.

America's coastline was just as vulnerable as its cities. The danger to her cities lay in the sky - a London-type blitz was always a possibility, though not a probability because of the distance from Europe. Preparations had been made for just such an occurrence.

What was to be done about the three coasts - Atlantic, Pacific and Gulf? Tens of thousands of inhabited and uninhabited shores lay unprotected. They could be invaded by the enemy either in force, such as commando raids, or by saboteurs, as had happened on the East Coast.

The Atlantic Coast appeared to be in the greatest danger because of the strength and successes of Germany's U-boats. Although the United States had been attacked in the Pacific by the Japanese, the danger did not seem so imminent. The distance between Japanese possessions and the Pacific Coast, versus the proximity of Nazi U-boats and Nazi-occupied Europe and North Africa made the likelihood of an Atlantic invasion more of a reality.

The Gulf Coast was particularly fertile for saboteurs because of the oil fields and shipyards in Texas, Louisiana, Mississippi and Alabama. The Nazi and Fascist Fifth Columns had infiltrated many countries in Latin America, making the possibility of landings a fact that could not be overlooked or underestimated.

The Pacific Coast felt threatened and exposed to landings because a midget Japanese sub had been reported off the coast of Santa Barbara, Calif., and a shell reportedly was fired at Ft. Stevens, Oregon. In addition, the hysterical and prejudiced attitude towards the Japanese-Americans, and the strategic naval bases at San Diego, Long Beach and San Francisco, and Seattle in Washington, all contributed to the concern of the populace.

America's coasts were ripe for an invasion of one sort or another. Immediate action was taken to ensure its security. By July 25, 1942, one month after the incidents on the East Coast, a national Beach Patrol Division was organized at Coast Guard Headquarters under the direction of Capt. Raymond J. Mauerman. This action was an instant reaction; but there had been prior organization on a much smaller scale since February 1941, when America's entrance into World War II seemed imminent.

The Coast Guard had helped enforce the Neutrality Act beginning in September 1939, and by General Orders of February 3, 1941, all coast areas had been organized into defense divisions known as Naval Coastal Frontiers. Under Executive Order 8929, the U.S. Coast Guard was transferred from the Treasury Department to the Navy Department on November 1, 1941, for the duration of the war. After February 1942, the Naval Coast Frontiers became known as Sea Frontiers, with the Army and Navy in control of guarding the coasts.

The Army was given the job of defending the land areas, the Navy maintaining inshore and offshore patrols. Because the Coast Guard was now an integral part of the U.S. Navy, it was assigned the task of operating an "information system" by means of beach patrols, picket boat patrols and lookout watchtowers.

The guarding of America's shores became a joint Army-Navy-Coast Guard-FBI operation. The FBI was charged with obtaining evidence of subversive activity (attempted landings by enemy agents) along the coast. This information was to be obtained through Army and Navy intelligence.

It was the job of the Navy to observe marine traffic, enemy activity and movement of suspicious vessels off the coast, while the Coast Guard was given the additional job of surveillance of the local small craft operating in home waters. This included fishing boats and pleasure boats (although some had already been taken over for patrol duty). The Coast Guard was charged with issuing I.D. cards to fishermen and other boatmen. In addition, the Coast Guard still retained its responsibility of rescuing survivors of marine disasters.

Because the Army needed specific information, it was imperative the reports be instantaneous and exact; thus, the beach patrol system was organized as a special agency. It was to be the "eyes and ears" of the Army and Navy - to guard the coast, not to repel invasion.

The directive from headquarters of July 25, 1942, stated:

These beach patrols are not intended as a military protection of our coastline, as this is a function of the Army. The beach patrols are more in the nature of out-posts to report activities along the coastline and are not to repel hostile armed units.

The shock of the German saboteurs' landings prompted the vice chief of naval Operations to inform the commanders of the Sea Frontiers "that the beaches and inlets of the coasts would henceforth be patrolled by the Coast Guard whenever and wherever possible . . . Army and Navy intelligence officers organized a close liaison with Coast Guard Intelligence, which still continued to operate as a separate command but under Navy direction."

All patrol activities were integrated with the work of the FBI, the Immigration Service and the state and local police. Information from lookouts and patrols was quickly relayed to the headquarters of the Naval District, the Sea Frontier and the Defense Command, who in turn relayed it to the FBI, which had the ultimate responsibility for investigation of sabotage.

The Coast Guard, more than any other of America's armed forces, is a part of communities around the nation. Because the stations and lighthouses are distributed in different parts

Coast Guard mounted patrolmen drilling with dogs at the Widener Estate, Elkins Park, Pa. NA

A romp in the surf along the Atlantic Coast for Coast Guard beach patrolmen. U.S. COAST GUARD

of the country, there is no concentration of personnel such as at Army bases and Naval installations. The Coast Guard is a close neighbor who shops at the same grocery store and browses at the same library, takes part in community activities and is always on call to help in distress. Although many patrols were far from town, the men in the patrol knew their neighbors, and the citizens considered them part of their neighborhood.

Each district set up its own beach patrol organization according to the needs of the districts. All three coasts had their particular problems, with many districts having additional problems because of the difficulties presented by the variety of terrain in the area. Sand dunes and swamps, long, sandy beaches and rocky promontories, inlets and rivers were logistically complicated.

There was a special beach patrol officer, who along with his subordinate sections, was under the district Coast Guard officers. The separate beach patrol was divorced from the other activities of the district and operated as part of Port Security until July 1942.

When the Beach Patrol Division was organized under Capt. Mauerman, an entirely new plan was put into effect. By autumn 1942, the beginning of the new system (quickly organized), was in motion. Hundreds of new stations were established, many in temporary dwellings until permanent construction could take place; many sta-

tions remained in private facilities until the patrol was disbanded.

Ten coastal districts maintained a beach patrol organization, and the final count at its peak in personnel was 24,000 officers and men. Excluding the lookout towers, actual beach patrol coverage totaled 50,000 miles.

Boats, jeeps, horses and dogs were utilized by Coast Guardsmen to secure the coastline. By the close of the first fiscal year, 2,000 sentry dogs and 3,000 horses were actively engaged in patrol duty.

The problems of populated and non-populated areas had to be considered along with the topographical ones. As a result, interesting and unusual situations presented themselves.

New England's lobstermen, New Jersey's heavily populated seaside resorts, Palm Beach's "gold coast," shrimpers in the Gulf of Mexico, Greek-American sponge divers at Tarpon Springs, Florida, salmon fishermen in Oregon, surfers in Southern California were all members of a populace which would not be kept off the beaches or off their boats for the duration.

Maine's rocky coast and the Pacific Northwest's remote and heavily forested areas, alligator-infested islands in South Carolina, Georgia and Texas, Louisiana's swampy regions and the isolated off-shore islands of Mississippi and Alabama all contributed to the intricacies of maintaining a viable protection of America's very long and

A dog training school was established at Front Royal, Va., for the Coast Guard Beach Patrol. U.S. ARMY MILITARY HISTORY INSTITUTE

very diverse coastline.

No attempt was ever made to cover the more inaccessible regions. There, only lookout post, inlet boat patrols and aircraft from the Army or Navy were put into service. Where foot or mounted patrols could not cover the areas, motorized patrols were used. It took until the end of 1943 for all the coasts to be under complete surveillance. Patrols were active from Maine to Key West, Panama City, Florida to Brownsville, Texas, and from Seattle, Washington to Coronado, California.

Beach Patrols and Other Defenses

During the first months of World War II, as one allied bastion after another fell to the Japanese in the western and southwest Pacific, the United States greatly strengthened its Western Defense Command. By the end of May and before the victory at Midway, the equivalent of 17 antiaircraft regiments were in position in the three west coast states. Six barrage balloon battalions were deployed in the Seattle, San Francisco, Los Angeles, and San Diego areas. Medium and heavy bombers, long-range patrol craft, and fighters were flown in. Radar stations were built at strategic points and manned. Beach patrols were organized by the Coast Guard. Volunteers assisted the Coast Guard in watching the beaches.

As soon as the extent and significance of the Japanese defeat at Midway became apparent, the army began to reduce the strength of the force assembled for defense of the west coast. First to go were the heavy and medium bombers, to be followed by several of the antiaircraft regiments.

The *Hooligan Navy* was a group of volunteer yachtsmen who worked with the U.S. Navy off the East Coast to hunt for German U-Boats. Ernest Hemingway donated his yacht, *Pilar*, to the "Navy."

One of America's most historic forts, Fort Sumter, guarding the entrance to the harbor at Charleston, S.C., once again was activated for wartime use. This view looks north from #1 searchlight tower, showing Battery Huger's parapet and installations. U.S. ARMY

A camouflaged 90mm gun position on the north side of Battery Huger parapet at Fort Sumter. U.S. ARMY

The Lincoln County Guerrillas, adjacent to Tillamook County, were organized from local volunteers comprised of storekeepers, loggers, farmers, and other everyday citizens, either too old or too young to enter the regular military. OHS

Stewart B. Arnold, a blind veteran of World War I, organized a group of citizen-soldiers in Tillamook County, Ore., in early 1942 to counter a possible Japanese invasion of the Pacific Coast. Although these volunteer guerrilla irregulars would not know it until Portland newspapers broke the story after the war, in the event of a massive Japanese invasion, military strategy would have been to fight a retrograde action and make the stand at the Rocky Mountains. OHS

Two Spies Land in Maine

On Nov. 10, 1944, the German U-boat U-1230 arrived off the Maine coast and waited for more than two weeks for the best tide and weather to proceed into Frenchman Bay. Two men were rowed ashore for an ambitious espionage mission in spite of the fact that Germany's defeat was almost assured. They carried with them $60,000 and 100 diamonds to sell if they needed more money.

William Colepaugh, (26) an American citizen, and Erich Gimpel, (34) a German, were trained to infil-

trate American society, and to gather information about military affairs and the general political reaction to Germany's propaganda efforts. They were to transmit their findings by radio which they would build and by writing letters to American prisoners of war in Germany. The letters would be written in invisible ink and intercepted by Nazi officials.

Once on shore, the spies walked for several miles, then flagged down a taxi to Bangor and proceeded by train to Boston, then to New York

City. For a month they lived it up in New York City eating expensive food, staying in elegant hotels, and entertaining women until Colepaugh got cold feet and gave himself up to the FBI. Both men were caught and tried by military court, found guilty and sentenced to die With the end of the war, however, President Truman commuted their death sentences, Gimpel was deported and Colepaugh was released from prison.

Japanese Balloon Bombs

by Brig. Gen. W.H. Wilbur, chief of staff of the Western Defense Command during World War II

General Doolittle's bombing of Tokyo on April 18, 1942, hit the Japanese right in the middle of their pride. Casting about for a means of reprisal, they conceived the first transoceanic automatic-balloon campaign in history. It took them two years to get ready, but in the six months following Nov. 1, 1944, they turned loose 9,000 ingeniously contrived gas bags, engineered to drop incendiary and fragmentation bombs on American forests, farms and cities.

These new weapons, 33 feet in diameter, were designed to travel across the Pacific at an altitude of 30,000 to 35,000 feet, where prevailing air currents move toward America at the rate of 100 to 200 miles an hour. Although no human exercised any control over the balloons - even by radio - after their release, it is conservatively estimated that 900 to 1,000 of them reached our continent. They showed up all the way from Alaska to Mexico. Nearly 200 more or less complete units were found in the Pacific northwest and western Canada. Fragments of 75 more were picked up on land elsewhere or fished out of the coastal waters of the Pacific, and flashes in the sky indicated to observers that at least 100 exploded in mid-air.

We have tried to belittle this attack. The fact remains that it marked a significant development in the art of war. For the first time missiles were sent overseas without human guidance, and the threat of great damage was very real. We can consider ourselves fortunate that winter snows eliminated the forest fire hazard. If the balloon assault had continued into the dry summer, when our vast western forests were like tinder; if the Japanese had maintained their March 1945 rate of launching an average of 100 balloons a day; and if they had equipped them with hundreds of small incendiaries instead of a few large ones - or with bacterio-

logical agents - they would have wrought havoc.

The Japanese made their first mass balloon tests in the spring of 1944, loosing 200 trial gas bags. None of these reached us. The first successful ocean-spanning balloons were released on Nov. 1, 1944, and on Nov. 4, we received our first report of them. On that day a Navy patrol craft spotted what looked like a large fragment of tattered cloth floating on the sea. A sailor tried to drag the fabric aboard but discovered a heavy mass attached to it. Unable to lift it, he slashed it off with a knife, thus permitting the undercarriage of gadgets and explosives to sink. All that was salvaged was the envelope; it bore Japanese marks, however, and told us that something mysterious had been introduced into the struggle.

From the first we realized the possibilities of this new campaign. Hence the assistance of all government agencies - national, state and local - was immediately enlisted. The Navy was alerted and the FBI was called in. Forest rangers, state and national, were informed that we wanted reports of balloon landings and any portions of balloons or undercarriages that were recovered.

After the finding of the first balloon envelope we had to wait two weeks before a second fragment was salvaged from the ocean. A little later another balloon, burned and partly destroyed, tumbled down in Montana. By mid-December, working from many fragments of information, technicians had figured out the basic principles of the weapon and artists had made drawings of it. We were proud to find, later, that this "mock-up" was correct in all important essentials.

Fragments were sent to the Naval Research Laboratory in Washington, D.C., and to the California Institute of Technology. They found that the envelope was constructed of several layers of heavy parchment stuck together with vegetable glue - and that it was far more effective in retaining hydrogen that our best American rubberized balloon cloth.

Experts who examined sand from

the ballast bags reported the names of five places in Japan from which the sand must have come. The Air Force was asked to check activity at those places. Shortly we had a report, with pictures, of one of the sites. The photos showed a manufacturing plant and outside it several pearl-gray spheres, apparently gas bags being inflated for the flight to America!

Soon one of the pearl-gray bags was spotted in the air near a western U.S. city. The pilot of an Air Force plane, sent up to bring it down undamaged, chaperoned it toward open country by repeated sweeps of air from his propeller. These air blasts caused the balloon undercarriage to tilt so that the hydrogen-control device was released, thus venting the gas and causing the balloon to float gently to the ground. Fortunately the automatic destruction device failed to work. Everything was found intact.

The balloons, we learned later, were constructed at a cost of about $800 each. Each carried about 30 six-pound sandbags, which were released successively by a tripping device actuated by a barometer whenever a balloon dropped below 30,000 feet. Another automatic control opened a valve to let hydrogen escape when the gas bag rose above 35,000 feet. Each balloon carried three or four bombs, at least one of which was an incendiary. The others were 32-pound fragmentation anti-personnel bombs. Both types were controlled by a release mechanism designed to operate after all the ballast bags had been dropped - the Japanese theory being that by that time the balloon would have arrived over the American continent. In addition, there was a device to explode the balloon after all the bombs had been delivered. The fact that this device failed to work on at least ten percent of the balloons which landed enabled us to salvage several practically undamaged.

With each batch of bomb-carrying balloons the Japanese sent along one which gave off radio signals and served as a means of checking on the progress of the flock across the ocean. Because they wanted to be certain of their successful arrival here, the Japanese used

A Japanese balloon that was found in Montana was re-covered and re-inflated for testing purposes. FDR

View of a fuse-timing device suspended from a Japanese balloon recovered eight miles west of Holy Cross, Alaska, on Jan. 21, 1945. The shock absorber device linking the two knotted portions of rope shrouds was made of many light rubber bands. USA

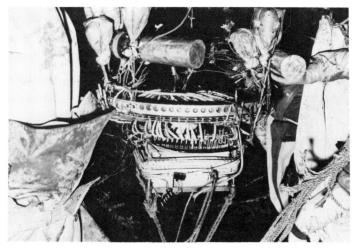

A close-up of the mechanism of a balloon. FDR

Sailors spread out a downed Japanese balloon, location unknown. FDR

rubberized silk instead of paper for the bag of these pilot balloons - apparently believing that rubberized silk was a superior container of hydrogen. But exactly the opposite proved to be true. Only three silk balloons reached the United States.

After a few of the balloons had been recovered we concluded that the danger from explosive bombs was minor, but that incendiaries would be a serious threat during the forest fire season (July through September) on the West Coat. We needed the timber in those forests, so paratroop fire-fighting units were organized to cooperate with the ranger service and civilian forest fire-fighting agencies. At best, however, our blanket of protection would have been very thin.

Meanwhile, to combat the possibility that the balloons would be used to shower down pestilence in the form of plant-disease spores, animal plagues or even human-disease germs, we enlisted state health officers and veterinarians, county agricultural agents, 4-H clubs and agricultural college authorities in the defense program. Decontamination squads were trained; stocks of decontamination chemicals, suits and masks were set up at strategic points. Farmers and ranchers were urged to report the first sign of any strange disease in their cattle, sheep or hogs.

To keep the Japanese from learning what degree of success their campaign was attaining, press and radio both in the United States and Canada accepted a voluntary censorship which proved to be one of the marvels of the war. At the same time, this censorship made it difficult for us to warn our own people. A group of children at a picnic in Oregon found a balloon, apparently tugged at it and exploded the bombs. Five children and a woman were killed.

How were we to advise millions of children of this hazard and also notify farmers and woodsmen in the West of our need for information without permitting a leak to the Japanese? Through superb cooperation from school authorities and teachers, chiefs of police and rangers, we accomplished both ends.

Suddenly, at the end of April, the balloon barrage ceased. Had the Japa-

nese called off the attack, thinking it a failure? Or was it just a deceptive lull before a greater onslaught? Weeks and months passed with no resumption.

The mystery was solved three years later when I visited Japan and conferred with General Kusaba, who had been in charge of the balloon campaign. He told me that altogether 9,000 balloons had been launched and that the Japanese figured at least ten percent should reach the United States and Canada. Word of the initial landing in Montana got away from us and did reach Japan. After that, however, the American press and radio blackout was complete. With only one reported landing on the American continent, the Japanese General Staff began clamping down on General Kusaba. Many times he was told that he was wasting the fast-dwindling resources of his country.

Finally, toward the end of April, General Kusaba was told to cease all operations. The dictum of the staff was, "Your balloons are not reaching America. If they were, reports would be in the newspapers. Americans could not keep their mouths closed this long."

One of only a few actual pieces of a Japanese balloon on display. This one was found in the Yukon, Canada, and is displayed at the MacBride Museum, Whitehorse, Yukon. The Klamath Falls, Ore., museum also displays part of a balloon. COURTESY WAYNE TOWRISS

This monument, dedicated on Aug. 20, 1950, in a pine forest near Bly, Ore., commemorated the death of six people by a Japanese balloon bomb. On May 5, 1945, Elsie Mitchell (26), and five children, Jay Gifford (13), Edward Engen (13), Dick Patzke (14), Joan Patzke (13) and Sherman Shoemaker (11), were killed when one of the fallen bombs blew up as they viewed it. The incident occurred on Weyerhaeuser Timber Company land. COURTESY THE WEYERHAEUSER COMPANY

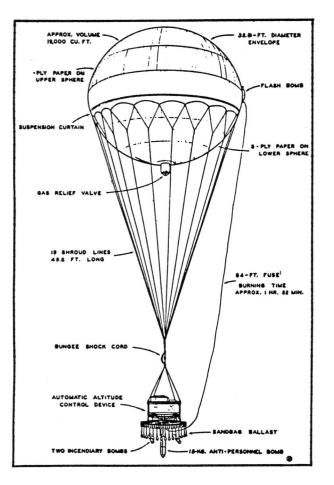

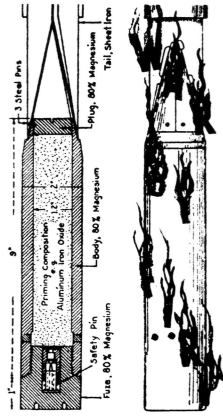

An Interesting Story, If True
by Norman L. Smith, Albion, Neb.

Three armed bombers landed one night at Boeing Field in Seattle, Wash. They were placed in hangars at the south end of the field. Abe Horsham was on a special rework crew and certain emergency modifications were to be made to the planes. At some point in the night the crews were ordered to button up and all three bombers took off. Sometime in the early morning hours the emergency sirens at the field went off. Shortly thereafter one bomber returned and made a crash landing. All crew members were dead except one of the pilots who died soon afterwards. The plane was badly damaged by what appeared to be shrapnel and bullets. Abe's crew worked the rest of the night to remove the wreckage to a nearby hangar. No employee was allowed to go home until the entire group was assembled and had signed an oath of secrecy. If true, was this plane shot at by a Japanese plane or submarine or, more likely, by our own antiaircraft guns?

YOU MUST BE PREPARED TO SAFEGUARD YOUR !!HOME!!

AIR RAIDS!!

Any attempt at invasion spells "AIR RAIDS," and we have learned from England that a single plane can strew incendiary bombs over a large area within a very few seconds. If one should land on YOUR HOME you must know what to do.

CONFLAGRATIONS!!

War and sabotage go hand in hand and fires originating from this source may tax the reserves of your fire department. While your firefighters are engaged in the task of suppressing major conflagrations, you may be forced to extinguish a small fire in your own home.

PRIORITIES!!

It is extremely important that you make every effort to safeguard your home from fire not only because fire protection facilities may be limited in times of emergency, but because it is becoming increasingly difficult to replace many household appliances and materials for home construction.

YOUR RESPONSIBILITY!!

MEN AND MATERIALS MUST NOT BE DIVERTED FROM THE VITAL NEEDS OF NATIONAL DEFENSE.

CHILDREN AT WAR

The caption of this photo states: Sally cuts out the bottoms while Dave flattens out tin cans to turn in to salvage collectors. Cans must be rustless and stripped of paper to be suitable for "de-tinning," which helps keep supplies of the metal available for essential civilian as well as military uses. NA 171-G-120-2

SPIKE KELLY
OF THE
COMMANDOS

What was it like to be a child in America during World War II?

The children of the United States were mercifully spared the misery and fear of bombing, so most memories of that time are not as tramatic as those of the children of perhaps France, Belgium or England.

America was no different from other nations in that considerable propaganda was produced by the government. Youngsters do not have the experience of life common to adults, and while their mothers and fathers knew that a lot of the news was a product of wishful thinking, the children accepted every shred of grandiose allied propaganda as if it were absolutely true and not even subject to question.

Foremost in the propaganda war were the movies. Saturday afternoon would find all the neighborhood kids at the "State" or "Rialto" ready to join in the daring deeds against the "Dirty Nazis" or the "Japs!" The courageous "Yanks" always - without fail - brought forth victory while the miserable Germans or Japanese were forced to crawl into humiliation.

One thing everyone who was a child during World War II will remember is the virtual disappearance of toys. A nation at war had little time to devote to children's playthings, and it was rare indeed for a 1941-45 youngster to receive much for Christmas.

One thing that America had plenty of was wood, and most World War II kids recall having a wooden toy of some kind. Metal was absolutely precious in all forms and dedicated to war use. Rubber was like gold! At one time various manufacturers even went so far as to try to produce entirely wooden scooters.

During World War II, the children of America were brave. It could be argued that they never heard the bombs of war, but they nonetheless all knew what America was fighting for and they all dreamed of the day when Daddy would come home and Adolph Hiterl's head would be served up on a platter!

Most of the kids of 1941-45 will recall the wonderful displays of patriotism - the parades on Memorial Day and Armistice Day. The various patriotic organizations, particularly the America Legion, provided remarkable displays of flags accompanied by drum and bugle corps.

Children's magazines expounded the patriotic fervor of the entire nation. Both of these issues date from 1943 at the height of the war's ferocity.

Schoolchildren line up to buy defense stamps at the post office in New Boston, Ohio, in January 1942. LC-USF34-64390-D

THE·AXIS·CAN'T
GET·OUR·GOAT
BONDS BUY
SMORE STAMPS

Boy Scouts appeal to a crowd of on-
lookers during a 1942 parade in
Ashland, Ky. FRANK B. FRAM PHOTO

These are Junior Commandos of Roanoke, Va., who are preparing, in a heavy rain, to distribute leaflets on their block to inform housewives that the "Scrap for Victory" campaign is on, October 1942. FDR

The charge of the scrap brigade in Roanoke, Va., here includes using a pony cart for collection. FDR

Schoolchildren in Roanoke, Va., are mobilized as home front fighters - to collect scrap for the manufacture of ammunition. FDR

These boys brought scrap rubber to a pile on Sunset Boulevard, Hollywood, Calif. FDR

Delivery vans, 1942 style, line up outside a Greenbelt, Md., grocery store awaiting the customers who placed the orders. Tire scarcity and gasoline rationing curtailed store deliveries, and these youngsters, making deliveries with their wagons, are doing their part for the war effort. FDR

Fat collection day in Roanoke, Va. FDR

Kids even gave up their toys for the scrap drive. Larrie Lou Osterman sits on her front steps in McMinnville, Ore., with her toys. OHS

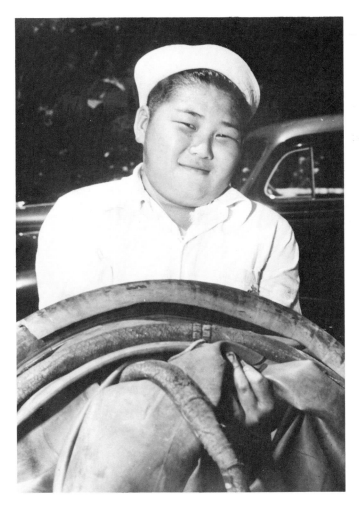

Win Jo helps with the rubber drive in Honolulu, 1942. HAWAII ARCHIVES

Corvallis Junior High School students in Corvallis, Ore., with the 2,000 books they collected for members of the armed forces. OHS

WARTIME TOYS

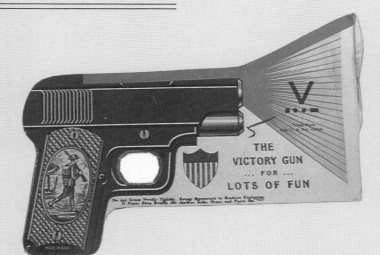

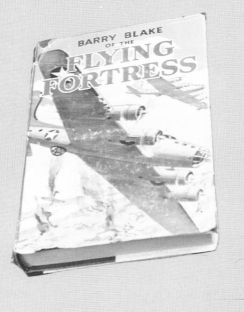

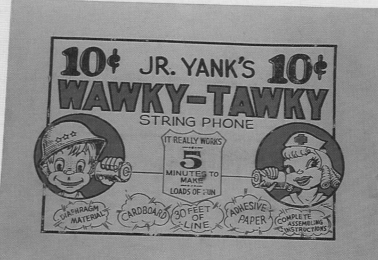

Lionel model trains were other casualties of wartime. They would not appear on the toy shelves again until late 1945.

Modeler's knife in the shape of an American warplane.

RECREATION BULLETIN SERVICE

ISSUED BY

National Recreation Association • 315 Fourth Avenue • New York, N. Y.

File Heading: Recreation in Wartime

WAR AND ADOLESCENTS

　　　　　In an address delivered at the 1942 meeting of the Association for Family Living, George V. Sheviakov in commenting on the effect upon youth of the new conditions which war brings with it states that there is need for careful analysis of what youngsters should do, when they should do what, and what the attitude of adults should be toward their activities. This analysis, he says, should be accompanied by an honest appraisal of the effect of these activities on youth so that errors may be recognized early and corrected. The following quotations are taken from Mr. Sheviakov's address as reported in the January, 1943, issue of The Bookshelf, published by the National Board of the Y.W.C.A.'s:

　　　　　Campaigns are launched to encourage youngsters to collect paper, tinfoil, scrap metal, to buy defense stamps, to make aeroplanes, to join the Junior Red Cross or other newly created clubs for youth. Most of these activities appear to be good and sound although even this is not known for certain, since insufficient observation has been made of their effects on various youngsters. One of the things that should be done is to define exactly the purpose and possible outcome of these new practices. Knowing precisely why we want youngsters to engage in various war activities helps us to understand why certain boys and girls either lose interest or have little to begin with....

　　　　　Some of the dangers inherent in these new activities are outlined briefly below.

　　　　　First, if the activity loses its meaning and becomes boring to children, and, at the same time, children are motivated by external and artificial means to continue it, they are apt to become antagonistic and demoralized.

　　　　　Second, if youngsters are encouraged to engage in too many activities of this kind they may become overstimulated with the result that additional war tensions will be produced.

　　　　　Third, if too much pressure is brought to bear on the youngsters to engage in these jobs, they may break under the strain.

　　　　　Fourth, the competitive element, as a motivating force, involves hazards. Competition as a sole motive is unhealthy to begin with and creates another new pressure. Children...who steal money from one another to buy defense stamps illustrate the point.

　　　　　Fifth, under some circumstances youngsters are urged by adults to participate in war activities as one way for adults to work off their own war jitters. There appears to be a great deal of this emotional exploitation of children at present.

　　　　　Sixth, children's war activities in some cases are encouraged by adults in the interests of their own self-promotion and aggrandizement. This constitutes another kind of exploitation of youth in wartime.

Alan Cole's P-40. As his father, Martin, relates the story: "During the war, substantial toys were almost non-existent. One day, when approaching Riverside, Calif., we saw this pedal plane in a residential yard. As Alan's cousin had a similar one, and his father was a military pilot, naturally Alan wanted one also. For some time we had been in search of such a toy. On the spur of the moment, we stopped and approached the housewife who informed us her son had outgrown it and would sell it for a few dollars. As I was a post engineer at the Victorville Air Force Base, I had our shop fix up the pedal car, painting Alan's name on the side as a general." MARTIN COLE, WHITTIER, CALIF.

These Harlem youngsters, showing an assembly-line approach to the job, salvaged more than 500 pounds of tin cans in one day. They not only collected, but processed, more than half the amount of tin needed to build a fighter plane in just one day. Their headquarters was in a vacant store at 151 East 103rd Street, and, under the auspices of the New York City Salvage Committee, they organized the Tin Can Club of America. FDR

Children wait in line to buy defense stamps at a New York City public school. Mothers staffed the booths and provided other services under the school defense aid program. LC-USW3-13488-E

P.T. PAPER TROOPER
WAR PRODUCTION BOARD

Use the
PAPER TROOPER
Campaign Materials
TO ENERGIZE YOUR
SCHOOL WASTE PAPER COLLECTIONS

Approved by the War Production Board
and Paid for by the Paper and Paperboard Industry

SAVE
A BUNDLE A WEEK
SAVE SOME BOYS LIFE

WAR PRODUCTION BOARD

A MANUAL FOR SCHOOL
ADMINISTRATORS AND COMMUNITY LEADERS

The need for paper was tremendous during the war. The military used paper for over 2,800 items, including draft cards, containers for food rations, protective bands for bombs, targets, shell and cartridge boxes and many, many other products. By April 1942 the supply collected by various methods completely overstocked the market. However by late 1943 the supply was exhausted and another nationwide drive was conducted. Facing another paper shortage in 1945, General Eisenhower himself sponsored a nationwide drive. The Boy Scouts alone collected over 720,000 tons of paper

PAPER TROOPER DISTINGUISHED SERVICE AWARD
WAR PRODUCTION BOARD
2000 POUNDS

The General Eisenhower Waste Paper medal was awarded by the War Production Board to Boy Scouts who collected at least 1,000 pounds of waste paper during the General Eisenhower Waste Paper campaign. During this campaign, which ran in March and April of 1945, 299,936 Scouts earned this award.
MONTANA HISTORICAL SOCIETY

Comic books. COURTESY MICHIGAN STATE UNIVERSITY
LIBRARIES

Winter 1945

July 1943

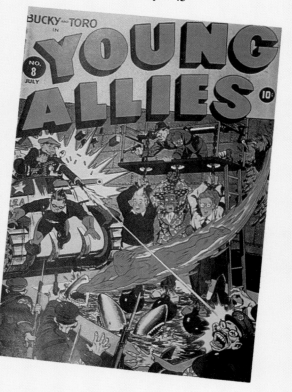

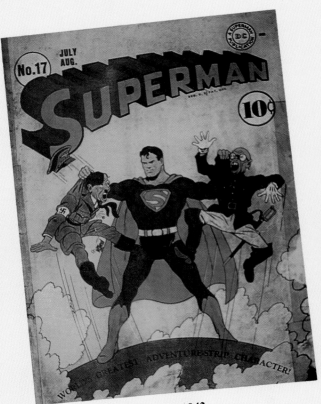

July-August 1942

April 1943

Boy Scouts
• • • • • • • • • • • • •

The day after the bombing of Pearl Harbor, the President of the Boy Scouts, Walter Head, and the Chief Scout Executive, James West, immediately sent a telegram to President Roosevelt reconfirming help from the 1,500,000 active boys and men of the Boy Scouts

Actually the scouts were active before America's involvement in the war by distributing Defense Bond posters and collecting scrap metal.

The contributions by the Boy Scouts to the war effort would fill many pages. They were responsible for selling almost $2 billion worth of war bonds and stamps. They participated in scrap metal, rubber and paper collecting. They also collected milkweed floss which was needed to replace the unobtainable kapok for life jackets.

They collected books, musical instruments, and razors for the troops and clothing for citizens in Europe. In many areas Scouts served as fire watchers and helped with fire prevention campaigns and thousands of Scouts worked hundreds of thousands of hours raising and harvesting food.

Three hundred thousand Scouts served as dispatch bearers distributing posters and war information and participating in various Civilian Defense programs.

In addition over 100,000 model airplanes were built for use by the military to train in aircraft recognition. Scouts helped with the USO, the National Housing Agency, veterans hospitals, the Red Cross, American Legion, VFW, YMCA, Foreign Relief Agencies and many community organizations.

Their total contributions to the war effort are incalculable.

Boy Scouts participated in scrap drives throughout the country both before America's entry into the war and during the wartime years.

These scouts worked on scrap drives in Albuquerque, N.M.

Boy Scouts also participated in promoting the sale of U.S. Savings Bonds.

Scouts collected used rubber tires.

Girl Scouts

In December 1941 Girl Scouts were prepared. Program efforts were focused on skills involving community service. Senior Girl Scouts explored wartime applications of food preparation and preservation, nutrition, child care, shelter, clothing, recreation, transportation, and communications. Girls attended safety workshops, operated bicycle courier services, and promoted the sale of war bonds and stamps.

During this decade, the Girl Scouts also launched three new specialized projects geared to assist the war effort: Hospital Aide, Child Care Aide and Occupational Therapist Aide.

Beginning in 1942, thousands of Girl Scouts worked on tens of thousands of farms through the Farm Aide project. During summer and harvest months, girls were busy weeding, cultivating, spraying, picking, and haying, as well as feeding livestock, repairing small tools, and canning.

An aviation interest project, developed in councils in 1942, was officially adopted as part of the Girl Scout program. The Wing Scouts, as they were called, eventually had use of a Piper Cub training plane presented to the national organization by Mr. Piper himself.

Carrying out these increased wartime activities created a widespread demand for leaders, and a "Volunteers for Victory" leadership drive was launched in 1943. Accelerated leadership training became necessary, both to address the needs of newly recruited leaders and to instruct all leaders, new and seasoned, in conducting wartime community service activities.

By the end of 1944, Girl Scouts had topped the one million mark, logging in 1,006,644 members.

Girl Scouts also contributed to the scrap rubber program and to farm projects. GIRL SCOUTS OF AMERICA

-235-

Wing Scouting was developed for Senior Girl Scouts who were interested in flying and who wanted to learn enough about aviation to be able to serve their country or to be their career. Activities began with the Senior Girl Scout's Mobilist project, which included the study of transportation and operation of bicycles, automobiles, and airplanes. When Wing Girl Scouting was introduced in 1941, there were approximately six aviation troops in the U.S. In May 1942, it was decided that the aviation activities be extended and promoted. A threefold plan was drafted. Its objectives were to make girls air-minded and aware of the importance of air supremacy for the United States, to prepare girls for careers in the field of aviation, and to also prepare them for community service in aviation and allied fields. FDR

These Scouts are packing boxes for shipment to soldiers and civilians overseas.

Girl Scouts did their part for the war effort by manning booths to sell war bonds and stamps in Ashland, Ky.
FRANK B. ELAM PHOTO

Clothing collection for shipment overseas.

Farm work was another wartime activity.

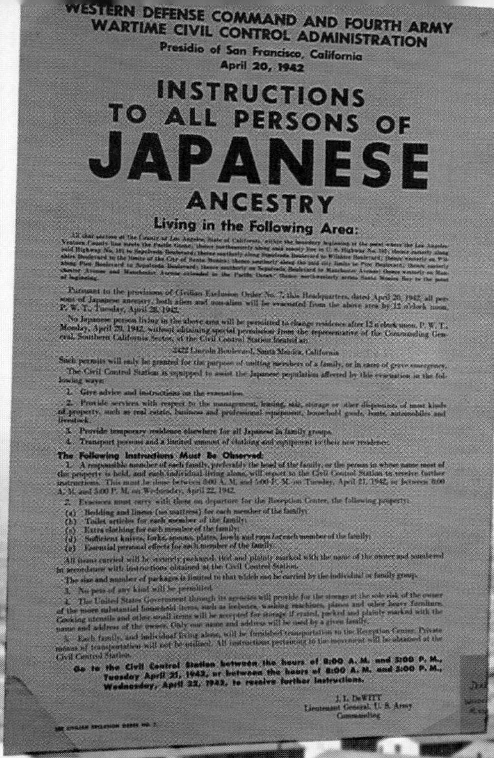

WESTERN DEFENSE COMMAND AND FOURTH ARMY
WARTIME CIVIL CONTROL ADMINISTRATION
Presidio of San Francisco, California
April 20, 1942

INSTRUCTIONS
TO ALL PERSONS OF
JAPANESE
ANCESTRY

Living in the Following Area:

All that portion of the County of Los Angeles, State of California, within the boundary beginning at the point where the Los Angeles-Ventura County line meets the Pacific Ocean; thence northeasterly along said county line to U. S. Highway No. 101; thence easterly along said Highway No. 101 to Sepulveda Boulevard; thence southerly along Sepulveda Boulevard to Wilshire Boulevard; thence westerly on Wilshire Boulevard to the limits of the City of Santa Monica; thence southerly along the said city limits to Pico Boulevard; thence easterly along Pico Boulevard to Sepulveda Boulevard; thence southerly on Sepulveda Boulevard to Manchester Avenue; thence westerly on Manchester Avenue and Manchester Avenue extended to the Pacific Ocean; thence northwesterly across Santa Monica Bay to the point of beginning.

Pursuant to the provisions of Civilian Exclusion Order No. 7, this Headquarters, dated April 20, 1942, all persons of Japanese ancestry, both alien and non-alien will be evacuated from the above area by 12 o'clock noon, P. W. T., Tuesday, April 28, 1942.

No Japanese person living in the above area will be permitted to change residence after 12 o'clock noon, P. W. T., Monday, April 20, 1942, without obtaining special permission from the representative of the Commanding General, Southern California Sector, at the Civil Control Station located at:

2422 Lincoln Boulevard, Santa Monica, California

Such permits will only be granted for the purpose of uniting members of a family, or in cases of grave emergency.

The Civil Control Station is equipped to assist the Japanese population affected by this evacuation in the following ways:

1. Give advice and instructions on the evacuation.
2. Provide services with respect to the management, leasing, sale, storage or other disposition of most kinds of property, such as real estate, business and professional equipment, household goods, boats, automobiles and livestock.
3. Provide temporary residence elsewhere for all Japanese in family groups.
4. Transport persons and a limited amount of clothing and equipment to their new residence.

The Following Instructions Must Be Observed:

1. A responsible member of each family, preferably the head of the family, or the person in whose name most of the property is held, and each individual living alone, will report to the Civil Control Station to receive further instructions. This must be done between 8:00 A. M. and 5:00 P. M. on Tuesday, April 21, 1942, or between 8:00 A. M. and 5:00 P. M. on Wednesday, April 22, 1942.
2. Evacuees must carry with them on departure for the Reception Center, the following property:
(a) Bedding and linens (no mattress) for each member of the family;
(b) Toilet articles for each member of the family;
(c) Extra clothing for each member of the family;
(d) Sufficient knives, forks, spoons, plates, bowls and cups for each member of the family;
(e) Essential personal effects for each member of the family.

All items carried will be securely packaged, tied and plainly marked with the name of the owner and numbered in accordance with instructions obtained at the Civil Control Station.

The size and number of packages is limited to that which can be carried by the individual or family group.

3. No pets of any kind will be permitted.
4. The United States Government through its agencies will provide for the storage at the sole risk of the owner of the more substantial household items, such as iceboxes, washing machines, pianos and other heavy furniture. Cooking utensils and other small items will be accepted for storage if crated, packed and plainly marked with the name and address of the owner. Only one name and address will be used by a given family.
5. Each family, and individual living alone, will be furnished transportation to the Reception Center. Private means of transportation will not be utilized. All instructions pertaining to the movement will be obtained at the Civil Control Station.

Go to the Civil Control Station between the hours of 8:00 A. M. and 5:00 P. M., Tuesday April 21, 1942, or between the hours of 8:00 A. M. and 5:00 P. M., Wednesday, April 22, 1942, to receive further instructions.

J. L. DeWITT
Lieutenant General, U. S. Army
Commanding

SEE CIVILIAN EXCLUSION ORDER NO. 7

JAPANESE-AMERICAN, DIPLOMATIC and ALIEN INTERNEES

View of the barracks at the Manzanar, Calif., WRA camp. FDR

Axis Diplomats

After Dec. 7, 1941, there were hundreds of enemy diplomats and families residing in the United States. Accommodations had to be comfortable yet isolated and secure, and meet the conditions of the Geneva Convention.

Several famous resorts, The Homestead in Hot Springs, Virginia, and The Greenbrier in White Sulphur Springs, West Virginia, were selected because of their isolation and first-rate accommodations.

About 400 Japanese were sent to the Homestead and eventually close to 1,000 German, Italian, Hungarian and Bulgarian citizens were sent to The Greenbrier. Another large resort in Asheville, North Carolina, was used for a short time in 1942.

The following article from Dr. Robert Conte's book, *The Greenbrier, America's Resort* describes the Axis' stay at this famous resort.

Fort Missoula, on the outskirts of Missoula, Mont., was established as an Army post in 1877. The post housed Italian seamen internees from 1940-43; later in the war Japanese-Americans were interned there and finally U.S. Army prisoners were held. The Italians shown in this picture were detained in American ports or were caught on shore at the beginning of the war. These men spent part of the war years working in the woods or on farms in Montana and Idaho. UNIVERSITY OF MONTANA MANSFIELD LIBRARY

Japanese detainees display the creations that they made from stones picked up in their confinement area at Fort Missoula, 1942. MONTANA HISTORICAL SOCIETY

Shortly after lunch on Dec. 17, 1941, The Greenbrier's general manager received a cryptic telephone call from the U.S. State Department. Would the resort be prepared, the caller inquired, to accommodate certain diplomats and citizens from the Washington, D.C., embassies of newly hostile nations? The manager hurriedly called together the hotel staff to consider the unusual proposal, when a second call arrived from the State Department. A decision was urgent, the representative said, because President Roosevelt had ordered the removal of all enemy diplomats from the capital within 48 hours. The staff immediately agreed to notify the government that the entire resort was at its disposal for the duration of this delicate emergency situation. By the end of the specified 48 hours, The Greenbrier was transformed from a private luxury resort into the focal point of international wartime diplomacy.

The State Department was searching for a suitable location to temporarily house diplomats from the Axis powers until exchanges for American diplomats, also trapped in overseas capitals at the outbreak of the war, could be officially negotiated. The Greenbrier fulfilled the government's basic requirements: first, it was relatively isolated and therefore easily guarded; and second, the famous resort offered a kind of first-class accommodations desired, since the State Department hoped to ensure equally fine treatment for interned American diplomats. There was another positive reason for selecting The Greenbrier - two of the key decision-makers in this action, Secretary of State Cordell Hull and Attorney General Francis Biddle, were personally familiar with the resort's quality, facilities and service, as both had frequently vacationed there before the war.

At 5:30 p.m. on Dec. 19, the first contingent of 159 German and Hungarian diplomats arrived in White Sulphur Springs on a secretly scheduled, 11-car Pullman train from Washington, D.C. One Washington newspaper described the departing dignitaries gathered outside the German embassy on Massachusetts Avenue as a "well-dressed throng, abounding in fur coats and smart hair-dos, with dozens and dozens of bags, boxes and bundles, piled picnic-style into their special buses." At the same time, a team of 18 FBI agents was assigned to White Sulphur Springs to enforce the government's strict security regulations controlling all forms of communication into and out of the hotel. Fifty members of the U.S. Border Patrol were transferred to The Greenbrier from their posts along the Canadian and Mexican borders to guard the new guests. The resort was closed to all regular guests, though complying with State Department instructions, The Greenbrier's staff size and quality of service remained unchanged. According to international law set down at the Geneva Convention of 1929, the United States was bound to protect the diplomats and their families, and, as one historian noted, America embraced those accords "with an almost religious fervor." Of course underlying that fervor was the concern for the safety of Americans held overseas. That the Americans were not treated as well in Germany is reflected in the comment of the noted diplomat, George Kennan, who was in charge of 130 Americans at Bad Nauheim near Frankfurt: "most of us were emaciated when we emerged from the experience."

There was, understandably, much apprehension among The Greenbrier's employees as they adjusted to their new role in government service. The FBI thoroughly investigated each employee, especially those who were foreign-born, and all were issued passes and fingerprinted. Everyone was cautioned that the new residents of The Greenbrier were most likely agents of their respective governments and very possibly directing intelligence-gathering operations in this country. The mayor of White Sulphur Springs, Greenbrier employee William Perry, declared to the press, "Our whole tradition here in White Sulphur Springs is one of patriotism and support of our government...We, and I speak for every person in our town, are happy to have this privilege of doing our part during the war crisis."

It was initially understood that the length of The Greenbrier's government service would extend a maximum of three months, with the total number of diplomats and their families amounting to between 400 and 500. But international complications lengthened that time, first from day to day and later from week to week, and swelled the numbers.

By the end of March 1942, the number of diplomatic guests had grown to over 800; by far the largest component were German citizens, but they were joined by 170 Italians, 53 Hungarians, and 11 Bulgarians. The group included all levels of the diplomatic staffs at each embassy as well as businessmen, bankers, newspaper correspondents, military attaches, engineers, servants, and families. Most of these internees were prominent individuals from the highest strata of society in their homelands.

For the most part, the sensitive operation proceeded smoothly. Cable traffic between American officials and adversary nations was carried through neutral representatives of Switzerland, Sweden, and Spain. These cables reported daily menus and living conditions at the various internment locations in order that accommodations for all diplomats were kept precisely parallel. For example, when the Germans complained about the food at The Greenbrier, cables from overseas brought typical menus so that they were served the same fare as that in Bad Nauheim. The activities of the diplomatic guests were restricted by the FBI - the golf courses and riding trails were declared off limits for obvious security purposes - but the tennis courts and indoor pool were in constant use. (For years afterwards many who were children of diplomats at the time returned to The Greenbrier with tales of delightful hours spent frolicking in the pool.) Cottages in Georgia Row were converted into classrooms for the schoolchildren; three weddings were celebrated in the Virginia Room; and six babies, including a set of twins, were born in a nearby hospital in Clifton Forge, Virginia. One of the very few troublesome incidents occurred when the German legation staged a boisterous beer party in the Main Dining Room on Hitler's birthday - cleverly described by one waiter as "a hell of a hail of heils" - but the celebration was quietly quelled by a discreet word from the general manager to the German executive officer. The guests passed much of their time playing chess, backgammon, and ping pong or reading the only available newspaper, *The New York Times.*

On April 1 the Italians, Hungarians, and Bulgarians were transferred to the Grove Park Inn, in Asheville, N.C., making room for nearly 400 Japanese diplomats who had been living at The Homestead, in Hot Springs, Virginia, since December. The game of musical chairs continued the next month, when 400 Germans were repatriated to their homeland and over 500 Germans traveled north to The Greenbrier from Central and South American nations. By mid-May of 1942, the number of diplomats reached its peak of 1,000. From April through June, the hotel was occupied only by Germans and Japanese and an uneasy truce was maintained by the two nationalities. Gwen Terasaki, an American woman married to a Japanese diplomat and interned with him, reported a continual round of wining and dining and cocktail parties among the high ranking members of both embassies. There was some petty squabbling to be sure - each group was careful to sit at opposite ends of the dining room - and the Japanese group endured some pointed heckling from the Germans when news arrived of Jimmy Doolittle's raid over Tokyo. In spite of the good spirits, however, at times there was an undercurrent of tension alternating with boredom among the internees as they coped with the uncertainty of their futures. A few were quite anxious about the wisdom of their government's wartime policies, and Gwen Terasaki noted that there were five American wives of German diplomats, some of whom were very apprehensive about returning to Nazi Germany.

The Japanese diplomats had had their assets frozen by the U.S. government and were therefore pressed for personal funds. Mrs. Terasaki, who had employed several servants while living in Washington, did her own laundry. "I am sure the elegant Greenbrier Hotel has never before or since had washing and ironing going on in so many of its luxurious rooms," she remarked. The Germans, on the other hand, still controlled most of their personal accounts. Because they were not permitted to carry American dollars home with them, they converged on The Greenbrier's shopping arcade spending their soon-to-be worthless dollars on fine art prints and expensive antique silver. All of the shops were rapidly depleted of their entire inventory until one bright entrepreneur produced a stack of department store catalogs and the buying spree began anew. When the Germans departed, two extra railroad baggage cars were required to transport all their newly acquired merchandise.

Arrangements for the international exchange of diplomats were completed in increments through May and June, and The Greenbrier's unusual guests began moving out of the hotel, headed for their homes. The resort had hosted a total of 1,697 persons representing five different nations; the staff had handled 8,519 pieces of baggage. The Japanese diplomats traveled by train to New York, where they boarded the Swedish ocean-liner Gripsholm for the long voyage to Lourenco Marques, the port city now known as Maputo, in the African nation of Mozambique. There they met ships bearing American diplomats from Shanghai and Yokohama for the official exchange directed by the International Red Cross. The German diplomats sailed on the Drottningholm to Lisbon, Portugal, where they were exchanged for Americans who had traveled by train from Berlin. On July 8, 1942, a final group of 151 German aviators left The Greenbrier and the resort's extraordinary 201 days of emergency government service came to an end. There was one interesting footnote: the German, Japanese, and Italian diplomats paid a total of $65,000 in gratuities to The Greenbrier's bellmen, maids, waiters, and porters for excellent services rendered.

Front page of *The New York Times.*
THE GREENBRIER ARCHIVES

-240-

Children of the German Embassy staff at The Greenbrier, where they attended school. Dr. Hans Thompson, German ambassador to the United States, is seen at the top of the steps wearing a white suit and dark tie. THE GREENBRIER ARCHIVES

Japanese diplomats pose for a group photograph at the north entrance to The Greenbrier in May 1942. THE GREENBRIER ARCHIVES

One Japanese diplomat and his family ready for the journey as they are repatriated to Japan by ship in June 1942. THE GREENBRIER ARCHIVES

The Grove Park Inn, Asheville, N.C., which housed Axis diplomats from March to June 1942 before they were repatriated to their own countries. The historic inn opened in 1913 and now has 510 guest rooms, meeting rooms, restaurants, lounges, a nightclub and many recreational facilities. THE GROVE PARK INN

Sun Valley Internee

Sun Valley, located in the Wood River Valley of central Idaho, was the first major ski resort built in the nation. In the 1930s most of the ski instructors at American resorts were imported from Europe.

Sun Valley's ski school was headed by an Austrian named Friedl Pfeifer whose staff was predominantly German or Austrian. Rumor had it that these instructors were listening to shortwave radio and possibly relaying information, but what information or harm they could do from this remote Idaho location is anyone's guess.

Pfeifer grew up in St. Anton, Austria, and escaped from his native country in 1938 after Germany's takeover. Following a stint in Australia, he signed on to coach the United States Women's Olympic Ski Team. In 1939 he traveled to Sun Valley, Idaho, with the team, and at the beginning of the 1939-40 ski season took over as director of the ski school there. He never returned to Australia.

Friedl relates: "I had a staff of seven instructors, all Austrians, and I fired them all. They all had Nazi sympathies."

Things were going along fine at the ski school until Dec. 7, 1941, when the Japanese attacked Pearl Harbor and war hysteria swept the country. As Friedl was still a citizen of Austria, now part of the Third Reich, he and two other aliens from his ski school, Hans Hauser and Sepp Froehlich, were jailed like other German aliens around the country. The *New York Times* reported on Jan. 8, 1942: "Three internationally famous skiers, two of them wed to American heiresses, are being held in Federal custody as enemy aliens."

They were incarcerated in the county jail in Hailey for a week, then transferred to Salt Lake City and finally to an alien camp in Bismarck, N.D.

Three months later Pfeifer had a hearing, was cleared, and went back to Sun Valley to finish up the ski season. After the season he and his family moved to Salt Lake City, and he started the ski school in Alta, Utah, for the 1942-43 season.

In the spring of 1943, Pfeifer joined the ski troops of the famed 10th Mountain Division and wound up in combat in Italy.

AXIS PRISONERS OF WAR

Captured German and Italian military personnel started arriving in the United States for internment in quantity in June 1943. The first prisoners were soldiers captured in the North African campaign. Over 135,000 were shipped from Africa, 142,000 after the D-Day invasion, 40,000 from northern France and 60,000 from Italy. In total approximately 676,000 Axis POWs were held in the United States from 1942 to 1946.

During the earlier stages of war the POWs were housed in abandoned Civilian Conservation Corps camps and existing military camps. Later the War Department constructed special camps, intended to hold from 2,000 to 4,000 POWs, in isolated areas away from the coast lines and international borders.

By the end of the war 155 main POW camps were in operation and over 500 branch camps had been created to house the POWs working in a great variety of industrial and agricultural projects.

Enlisted personnel and officers were generally separated according to the Geneva Convention and there was some segregation according to political beliefs (hard-Nazis, anti-Nazis, etc.).

There were some incidences of prisoner escapes, mainly by individuals or small groups. By 1946 all Axis POWs were repatriated back to Europe.

Major Prisoner of War Internment Camps in the United States

Algoma, Idaho	Croft, S.C.	Indianola, Neb.	Popologen, N.Y.
Aliceville, Ala.	Crossville, Tenn.	Jerome, Ark.	Pryor, Okla.
Alva, Okla.	Crowder, Mo.	Lee, Va.	Reynolds, Pa.
Angel Island, Calif.	David, Md.	Livingston, La.	Jos T Robinson, Ark.
Ashby, Va.	Dermott, Ark.	Lordsburg, N.M.	Roswell, N.M.
Ashford, W.Va.	Douglas, Wyo.	McAlester, Okla.	Rucker, Ala.
Atlanta, Neb.	Edwards, Mass.	McCain, Miss.	Rupert, Idaho
Atterbury, Ind.	Ellis, Ill.	McCoy, Wis.	Ruston, La.
Barkeley, Texas	Evelyn, Mich.	McLean, Texas	Scottsbluff, Neb.
Beale, Calif.	Fannin, Texas	Mackall, N.C.	Shelby, Miss.
Blanding, Fla.	Farragut, Idaho	Maxay, Texas	Sibert, Ala.
Bowie, Texas	Florence, Ariz.	Mexia, Texas	Somerset, Md.
Brady, Texas	Forrest, Tenn.	Monticello, Ark.	Stewart, Ga.
Breckinridge, Ky.	Gordon Johnston, Fla.	New Cumberland, Pa.	Stockton, Calif.
Carson, Colo.	Grant, Ill.	Ogden, Utah	Sutton, N.C.
Chaffee, Ark.	Gruber, Okla.	Opelika, Ala.	Swift, Texas
Clairborne, La.	Hale, Colo.	Papago Park, Ariz.	Tonkawa, Okla.
Clarinda, Iowa	Hearne, Texas	Peary, Va.	Trinidad, Colo.
Clark, Mo.	Hood, Texas	Perry, Ohio	Van Dorn, Miss.
Clinton, Miss.	Houlton, Maine	Phillips, Kansas	Wallace, Texas
Como, Miss.	Howze, Texas	Pickett, Va.	Wheeler, Ga.
Concordia, Kansas	Hulen, Texas	Pima, Ariz.	White, Ore.
Cooke, Calif.	Huntsville, Texas	Polk, La.	Wolters, Texas

The Great Escape

by Lloyd Clark, Phoenix, Ariz.

At about 2 a.m. on Sunday, January 28, 1945, Sgt. Gilbert Brady of the Phoenix Police Department was hailed by a street maintenance foreman at the corner of Central Avenue and Van Buren Street. A tall, lean stranger had just asked for directions to the railroad station. Clarence Cherry was suspicious: "He had a German accent," the foreman said.

Brady caught up with the tall man in the yellow checked shirt at Third Avenue and Van Buren. "Sir, could I see your Selective Service registration?" the police officer asked.

The main replied that he had left it at home.

"Where is home?"

"Glendale."

Glendale, Arizona, or Glendale, California?"

A pause. "Glendale - back east," said the man.

"Come with me to the police station," responded Brady.

Thus quietly ended what has been termed the greatest escape by Axis prisoners of war from a United States compound during World War II.

The man with the accent was Capt. Jurgen Wattenberg, former commander of the German submarine U-162 and more recently the senior prisoner of war at the Papago Park POW Camp just east of Phoenix. Two nights before Christmas, Wattenberg and 24 comrades had undertaken their daring exit through a 180-foot tunnel that led under the camp fence and surfaced on the west bank of the Arizona Crosscut Canal.

Wattenberg had been at large for 35 days. He was the last of the 25 escapees to be recaptured.

The possibility that carefully guarded prisoners could dig an accurately engineered tunnel longer than the width of a football field through desert caliche, all undetected, had never occurred to the camp's officers. The strenuous, surreptitious effort had gone on for three months, despite minimal tools and the constant danger of discovery.

When at last the escape route was completed, the action came quickly.

On the night of December 23, boisterous prisoners using the ruse of celebrating Germany's success in the Battle of the Bulge caused disturbances that distracted guards' attention. In rapid succession, 10 teams of two or three men squeezed into the tunnel and crawled to freedom.

Wattenberg and two of his former U-boat crew, Walter Kozur and Johann Kremer, were the fifth team out. Wading the canal, then quickly changing into dry clothes in the bushes of the canal's each bank, they struck out to the north.

For a plot so successfully executed to this point, the scenario began to fall apart quickly. Within the first day five of the escapees, cold and wet, surrendered to Valley residents.

Puzzled officers and guards started a search for the escape route, but it was not until the day after Christmas that PFC Lawrence Jorgensen discovered the camouflaged exit hatch in the brush alongside the canal. Jorgensen entered the burrow and followed it to a portal under a coal bin beside the bathhouse.

For nearly 40 years after his recapture, Capt. Wattenberg refused to discuss the escape with journalists. Nevertheless, fascinated by the episode, I established a correspondence with him; and at Christmas, 1983, he wrote from his home in Lubeck, West Germany, agreeing to an interview. We met in May 1984, at a vacation retreat in Austria.

At age 83, he remembered in amazing detail the activities of the trio during their absence from the camp. Soon after they left the canal it started to rain, and they took shelter in a shack. Next evening, after a portion of their hoarded rations became Christmas Eve dinner, Kremer took out his harmonica and softly played *Stille Nacht*, "Silent Night."

In the days that followed, they cautiously worked their way into the Phoenix Mountains, finding cover in an eroded alcove near Squaw Peak. On December 28, they celebrated Wattenberg's 44th birthday.

On New Year's Eve, they hiked all the way to Cave Creek Dam impoundment, a distance of at least 12 miles, where they bathed and swam, ate, and drank schnapps to toast the new year and Frau Wattenberg's birthday.

By the end of the first week of January 1945, the men's anxiety about their fellow escapees' fate was intense. Kremer and Kozur ventured into Phoenix after nightfall, returning with several newspapers. Blared one headline, "Two Nazis Apprehended at Mexican Border." Most of the prisoners, it appeared, had by now been caught. In the next two weeks, during forays to replenish their dwindling food supply, Kremer and then Kozur were recaptured.

Wattenberg determined to make his way into the city and somehow quit the Phoenix area, perhaps by freight train. But fate decreed otherwise. On January 28, the tall naval officer once again became a prisoner of war.

Out of my visit with Capt. Wattenberg, a memorable event developed. On January 5, 1985, he and eight other former prisoners of war participated with several of their erstwhile guards in a ceremony of commemoration at the site of the Papago Park camp. On a banner appeared these words: "To renew in friendship an association commenced in anguish."

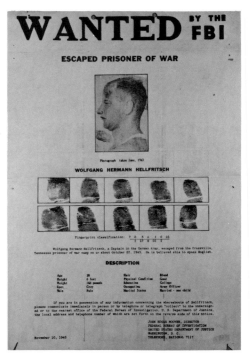

-244-

On Sunday, April 19, 1951, the site of the former Prisoner of War Camp at Papago Park was delineated by the Patrol Road (broken line). A-B marks the Arizona Crosscut Canal. C&D are the City of Phoenix reservoirs. E is the area occupied by the Valley Field Riding & Polo Club. F identifies Barnes Butte, G the amphitheater constructed by the Civilian Conservation Corps, and H is the area of the Desert Botannical Garden. LLOYD CLARK, PHOENIX, ARIZ.

Max Stephan, seen between two U.S. federal officers following his trial in Detroit, is on the way to the gallows. He died for treason against the United States despite his boast that "Germany will not let me hang." His crime was the assistance he gave an escaped Nazi prisoner of war who visited Detroit while trying to flee from Canada to Germany. The prisoner, Lt. Hans Peter Krug, was captured in the U.S. Southwest, and testified at Stephan's trial for the government. In sentencing Stephan, Federal Judge Arthur J. Tuttle declared: "The life of this traitor, Max Stephan, is less valuable than the lives of our loyal sons which are being given to the cause of the United States." NA 208-N-3428

On Saturday, Jan. 5, 1985, a marker was set designating the site of the Papago Park Prisoner of War Camp as an historic site. These men, Jürgen Wattenberg, Wilhelm Günther, and Alfred Hiller, were imprisoned here during World War II. Günter Westphal is behind Wattenberg. They were among nine former POWs who came from Germany for the ceremony. JOHN S. LYNCH PHOTO

Japanese Internment

When war was declared, there were hundreds of thousands of Axis aliens living in the United States. More than 100,000 Japanese issei (first generation immigrants) and nisei (second generation, American citizens by birth) were in the country, most of them living on the West Coast.

There were only minimal restrictions imposed on a few thousand Germans and Italians, but there was a demand for the forced removal of the Japanese-Americans from the coastal areas because of the anger engendered by Japan's surprise attack on Pearl Harbor and because of a general racial and economic animosity directed toward Americans of Japanese descent.

President Roosevelt, under political and military pressure, signed Executive Order 9066 on Feb. 19, 1942, authorizing the placement of more than 110,000 Japanese-Americans in internment camps in the interior of the country. One premise for locating the camps there was to prevent possible sabotage of defense industries and various installations in the coastal areas.

Ten camps were built in mostly desolate, unpopulated areas of several western states and Arkansas. The camps were crowded, and living conditions were uncomfortable. Barbed wire surrounded the camps, and armed guards patrolled the perimeters. There were, however, few instances of violence.

Soon after the internment plan was implemented, thousands of internees were granted leave to join the labor force or to work as farm laborers, since many had owned farms before the war. And the Army recruited several all-nisei units, one of which was the 442nd Regimental Combat Team. Known as "Go for Broke," this team had an outstanding combat record in Europe. The 100th Battalion was composed of Hawaiian nisei, one of whom, now Senator Daniel Inouye, lost an arm in Italy.

By January 1945, those internees still in the camps were allowed to return home. Most had to start over again, as they were forced to sell most of their assets when they were interned. This forced evacuation has been called by the American Civil Liberties Union "the worst single wholesale violation of civil rights of American citizens in our history."

For more than 40 years the internees petitioned the government for compensation for their internment, and finally on Aug. 10, 1988, Congress passed Public Law 100-383 which states the following:

The purposes of this Act are to -

(1) acknowledge the fundamental injustice of the evacuation, relocation, and internment of United States citizens and permanent resident aliens of Japanese ancestry during World War II;

(2) apologize on behalf of the people of the United States for the evacuation, relocation, and internment of such citizens and permanent resident aliens;

(3) provide for a public education fund to finance efforts to inform the public about the internment of such individuals so as to prevent the recurrence of any similar event:

(4) make restitution to those individuals of Japanese ancestry who were interned;

(5) make restitution to Aleut residents of the Pribilof Islands and the Aleutian Islands west of Unimak Island, in settlement of United States obligations in equity and at law, for -

(A) injustices suffered and unreasonable hardships endured while those Aleut residents were under United States control during World War II;

(B) personal property taken or destroyed by United States forces during World War II;

(C) community property, including community church property, taken or destroyed by United States forces during World War II; and

(D) traditional village lands on Attu Island not rehabilitated after World War II for Aleut occupation or other productive use;

(6) discourage the occurrence of similar injustices and violations of civil liberties in the future; and

(7) make more credible and sincere any declaration of concern by the United States over violations of human rights committed by other nations.

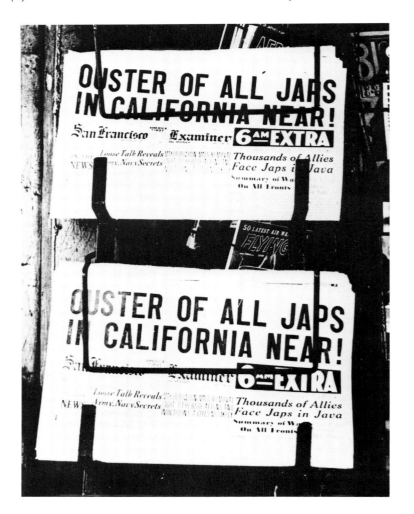

WESTERN DEFENSE COMMAND AND FOURTH ARMY
WARTIME CIVIL CONTROL ADMINISTRATION
Presidio of San Francisco, California
April 1, 1942

INSTRUCTIONS
TO ALL PERSONS OF
JAPANESE
ANCESTRY

Living in the Following Area:

All that portion of the City and County of San Francisco, State of California, lying generally west of the north-south line established by Junipero Serra Boulevard, Worchester Avenue, and Nineteenth Avenue, and lying generally north of the east-west line established by California Street, to the intersection of Market Street, and thence on Market Street to San Francisco Bay.

All Japanese persons, both alien and non-alien, will be evacuated from the above designated area by 12:00 o'clock noon Tuesday, April 7, 1942.

No Japanese person will be permitted to enter or leave the above described area after 8:00 a. m., Thursday, April 2, 1942, without obtaining special permission from the Provost Marshal at the Civil Control Station located at:

1701 Van Ness Avenue
San Francisco, California

The Civil Control Station is equipped to assist the Japanese population affected by this evacuation in the following ways:

1.   Give advice and instructions on the evacuation.

2.   Provide services with respect to the management, leasing, sale, storage or other disposition of most kinds of property including: real estate, business and professional equipment, buildings, household goods, boats, automobiles, livestock, etc.

3.   Provide temporary residence elsewhere for all Japanese in family groups.

4.   Transport persons and a limited amount of clothing and equipment to their new residence, as specified below.

The Following Instructions Must Be Observed:

1.   A responsible member of each family, preferably the head of the family, or the person in whose name most of the property is held, and each individual living alone, will report to the Civil Control Station to receive further instructions. This must be done between 8:00 a. m. and 5:00 p. m., Thursday, April 2, 1942, or between 8:00 a. m. and 5:00 p. m., Friday, April 3, 1942.

Baggage being inspected, a standard procedure before new internees were allowed to enter the Santa Anita Race Track area, an assembly center where Japanese-Americans were held before being sent to a War Relocation Authority internment camp. FDR

Japanese-Americans waiting for buses to take them to a camp somewhere in California. FDR

Members of the Shibuya family pictured at home before their forced evacuation. The father and mother were born in Japan and came to the United States in 1904. The father came with a basket of clothes and $60 in cash, which he built into a prosperous business by raising select varieties of chrysanthemums and shipping them to eastern markets. The six children were born in the United States, and the four oldest ones attended California universities. FDR

Closing sales in shops, as Japanese businessmen were forced to sell out when they were ordered to internment camps. FDR

Loading baggage at the assembly center in Portland. OHS, *OREGON JOURNAL* PHOTO

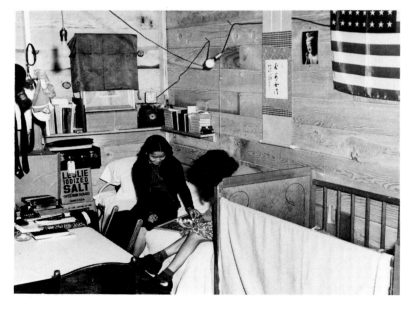

Part of the five-person apartment of the family of the Rev. T. Terakawa in the Pacific International Livestock Exposition Building in Portland, Ore., May 31, 1942. The building was used as an assembly center until internees were moved to permanent camps. OHS, *OREGON JOURNAL* PHOTO

Some of the first 664 people of Japanese ancestry to be evacuated from San Francisco shown waiting to board buses for the trip to an interior relocation camp. LC-USZ62-41601

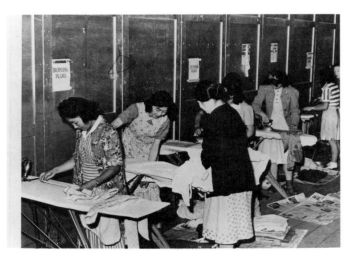

Ironing at the Portland assembly center. OHS, *OREGON JOURNAL* PHOTO

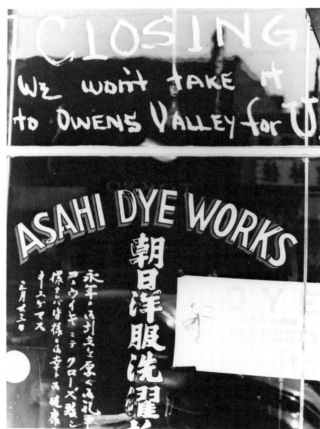

Relocation Camps

A scene at Heart Mountain, Wyo., internment camp.
OHS, *OREGON JOURNAL* PHOTO

Two Japanese mothers at the Heart Mountain internment camp show their stars for sons in the service. OHS,
OREGON JOURNAL PHOTO

Memorial Day services in 1942 at the Manzanar, Calif.,
internment camp. Boy Scouts and American Legion
members participated in the service. FDR

Manzanar, Calif., internment camp, July 1942. FDR

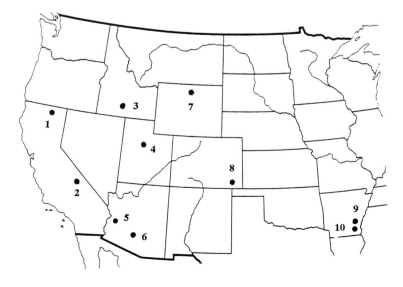

War Relocation Camps

1. Tule Lake, Calif.
2. Manzanar, Calif.
3. Minidoka, Idaho
4. Topaz, Utah
5. Poston, Ariz.
6. Gila River, Ariz.
7. Heart Mountain, Wyo.
8. Granada, Colo.
9. Rohwer, Ark.
10. Jerome, Ark.

Mrs. Harold L. Ickes, wife of the Secretary of the Interior, guides three newly arrived Japanese-Americans who were assigned to work there on a tour of the Ickes' farm near Olney, Md. FDR

A Farm Security Administration camp near Shelley, Idaho, where Japanese-Americans were put to work as farm laborers, July 1942. LC-USF34-73778-D

Scenes at Amache or Granada Relocation Center in Colorado's Arkansas Valley. The first of the approximately 10,000 persons arrived at the 11,000-acre camp in August 1942. Most of the men and some of the women worked in the agricultural fields in the area, harvesting sugar beets and potatoes. At least two-thirds of the residents of the camp were citizens of the United States, and many of the younger men eventually enlisted in the armed forces. The camp evolved into a city, with schools, a newspaper and other amenities of a normal life. In July 1945 the camp was closed and the remaining internees went back to their homes on the West Coast. COLORADO HISTORICAL SOCIETY

Sadao Munemori, a member of the 442nd Regimental Combat Team was the only Japanese-American (Nisei) to win the Medal of Honor during the war for his actions in Italy. The medal was awarded posthumously to his mother who was interned in the Manzanar Camp in California.

Remains of the guard station and warming area at the Minidoka Relocation Center near Twin Falls, Idaho.
COURTESY BETTY ZUCK, TWIN FALLS, IDAHO

THE MINIDOKA RELOCATION CENTER

THIS IS THE SITE OF THE MINIDOKA RELOCATION CENTER, ONE OF TEN AMERICAN CONCENTRATION CAMPS ESTABLISHED IN WORLD WAR II TO INCARCERATE THE 110,000 AMERICANS OF JAPANESE DESCENT LIVING IN COASTAL REGIONS OF OUR PACIFIC STATES. VICTIMS OF WAR TIME HYSTERIA. THESE PEOPLE, TWO-THIRDS OF WHOM WERE UNITED STATES CITIZENS, LIVED A BLEAK HUMILIATING LIFE IN TARPAPER BARRACKS BEHIND BARBED WIRE AND UNDER ARMED GUARD.

MAY THESE CAMPS SERVE TO REMIND US WHAT CAN HAPPEN WHEN OTHER FACTORS SUPERSEDE THE CONSTITUTIONAL RIGHTS GUARANTEED TO ALL CITIZENS AND ALIENS LIVING IN THIS COUNTRY.

HUNT

EXCLUDED FROM THEIR WEST COAST HOMES BY MILITARY AUTHORITIES, MORE THAN 9000 JAPANESE AMERICANS OCCUPIED HUNT RELOCATION CAMP 4 MILES NORTH OF HERE BETWEEN 1942 & 1945.

Until they could resettle in other places, they lived in wartime tarpaper barracks in a dusty desert, where they helped meet a local farm labor crisis, planting and harvesting crops. Finally, a 1945 Supreme Court decision held that United States citizens no longer could be confined that way, and their camp became Idaho's largest ghost town.

25 IDAHO

340

Minidoka Relocation Center
August 16, 1942 to October 26, 1945

You are standing at the entrance area of the Minidoka Relocation Center, one of ten American concentration camps established in World War II to incarcerate the 110,000 Americans of Japanese descent in coastal regions off our Pacific states.

Here 10,000 Japanese American victims of wartime hysteria occupied a 950-acre camp, living a bleak, humiliating life in tarpaper barracks, behind barbed wire and under armed guard.

May these camps serve to remind us what can happen when other factors supersede the constitutional rights guaranteed to all citizens and aliens living in this country.

In front of you stands the waiting room, which was often filled with visitors anxious to see and give support to friends and family restricted to life within the camp. To your left stands the guard station from which all movement in and out of the Minidoka Relocation Center was monitored.

YOU ARE HERE

MINIDOKA RELOCATION CENTER

Plaque on the right has picture and map of the camp. Plaque on the left has names of servicemen from Heart Mountain who died in World War II.

The chimney was part of the hospital heating plant. In 1973 the Heart Mountain Homesteaders asked that the chimney be left as a landmark and it is now included on the National Register of Historic Places with the Memorial.

HEART MOUNTAIN RELOCATION CENTER MEMORIAL
Road 19 - ½ mile off Highway 14A, between Cody and Powell, Wyoming

Camp Construction
June 8 to August 10, 1942

Camp Population: *10,767*

Camp Operation
August 12, 1942 to November 15, 1945

Evacuee Section:
468 barracks, 120' x 20'
20 barracks blocks
Six rooms per barracks from
16' x 20' to 24' x 20'
Two laundry-toilet buildings per block
Two auxiliary buildings 100' x 20' per block,
all with black tar paper exteriors.
High school-frame construction
with Comp.-asphalt shingles
One fire station.

Administrative Section:
Eight office buildings
One recreation hall
One mess hall
150-bed hospital
Sewage treatment plant
Water treatment plant
Power station
Several warehouses
Several staff apartments
Service Honor Roll

Administrative staff:
200 employees
Services offered — legal, financial, relocation, community management, internal operations, camp reports.
Military Police Area:
U.S. 331st Escort Guard
Headquarters for 124 soldiers,
three officers
MP's manned nine guard towers
with high beam search lights,
constructed barbed wire fence
around the camp.

PHOTOS COURTESY OF BONNIE J. BROW, POWELL, WYO.

TRANSPORTATION SYSTEMS

SOUTHWESTERN
GREYHOUND LINES, Inc.
IDENTIFICATION CHECK
Not good for passage or refund
KEEP IN SIGHT
This check will be taken up
by operator at destination
OW–1
BEEVILLE
SAN ANTONIO
SOUTHWESTERN
GREYHOUND LINES, Inc.
OW–1
SAN ANTONIO
201

1778   1943

AMERICANS
will **always** fight for liberty

Summary of
WARTIME INTERNATIONAL
TRAVEL REQUIREMENTS

For departure from
NEW YORK · MIAMI
NEW ORLEANS · BROWNSVILLE
LAREDO · LOS ANGELES
SAN FRANCISCO · SEATTLE

PAA

Via
PAN AMERICAN
WORLD AIRWAYS

THIS INFORMATION IS EXCLUSIVELY FOR PAN AMERICAN PASSENGERS

TAXICABS   RAILROAD TICKETS   COACH TICKETS ONLY   PULLMAN TICKETS   TAXICABS   TELEPHONES

COACH TICKETS ONLY

TRAIN ARRIVALS · TRAIN DEPARTURES · TRACK
TICKET OFFICE   INFORMATION
OPPOSITE SIDE

Servicemen far outnumber civilians as they wait to
board trains in Washington's Union Station. *TIME/LIFE*
PICTURE SERVICE

Railroads at War

In the 1940s most of the nation's railroads had converted or were converting to diesel locomotives. The war brought a vast strain to the railroads, and every locomotive, whether steam, electric or diesel was pressed into service.

Railroads were the lifeblood of America's vast industrial arsenal. Almost everything from the basic raw material to the finished product was moved by rail. Other forms of transportation were also used to capacity, but only railroads could transport large bulky items over long distances.

The railroads, like almost every other American resource, were used to and beyond their capacity. Material for the manufacture of new rolling stock was in short supply, and the manpower drain deprived the railroads of many experienced men. After numerous problems, the government declared the rails essential for war production.

For the first time in history women took over many of the jobs that had been strictly a male-oriented industry.

One of the greatest accomplishments of the rail system was the movement of troops. During the period of December 1941 to August 1945, the railroads moved approximately 43.7 million military personnel, or more than 97 percent of all troops moved during the war. The carriers committed one out of four of their coaches and half of all Pullman cars for troop transport. More than 2,500 troop trains a month operated in the United States. As many as 100,000 troops were on troop trains in a given day.

This was the greatest mass movement of people that ever occurred in the United States, and of course put a great strain on the railroads as well as reducing considerably civilian traffic for the duration.

Not only were troops moved by train, but movements of more than 12 hours' duration were usually made in Pullman sleeping cars. Pullmans caried 66 percent of all the troops, or 30,000 men a night, with a sleeper loaded every two minutes 48 seconds in 1944. This was possible only because the railroads had 2,000 sleeping cars in storage at the start of the war.

Until 1943 the government had banned all new passenger-car construction because of the shortage of steel and aluminum. But with the unprecedented demand for sleepers, 1,200 new troop sleepers were ordered from Pullman-Standard and 400 troop kitchen cars from ACF.

The train terminals on both coasts were clogged with troops going to the battlefields of Europe, Africa, Asia and the Pacific. War materials and foodstuffs were unloaded at the ports for transfer to Liberty ships which would carry them to the armies and to the Allies as lend-lease.

Without the thousands of men and women who ran the nation's railroads, whether from an office, a station or on the trains, who worked long hours in all kinds of weather, the war goods and troops would not have reached their final destination.

Railroads were the vital links that bound together all the country's war industries.

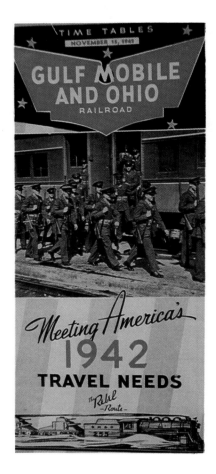

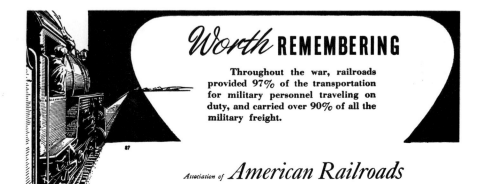

View of locomotive shops at 40th Street, Chicago, Ill., of the Chicago and Northwestern Railroad, December 1942. FDR

His Pin-Up Girl!

TIME and distance separate us from a lot these days—including the kind of travel accommodations the railroads used to be able to give, before they undertook the transport of the largest army and navy in history and the supplies needed to keep that army fed and in trim.

So maybe you'd like something to pin up, too—to remind you that the railroads, when this is all over, will again bring you the safest, most comfortable, most enjoyable transportation that your travel dollar can buy.

Here is the new C & O calendar for 1944. Because of the paper shortage, there may not be enough to go around. So if you'd like one—illustrated with the painting above—better write and reserve one for yourself right away!

CHESAPEAKE AND OHIO LINES

1111 Terminal Tower • Cleveland 1, Ohio

This flag is the trademark symbol of the Wabash Railroad, which has served the "Heart of America" for over a hundred years. Again this time, as in the past, the Wabash is devoting its facilities and its services to the transportation needs of this nation in a struggle to defend and promote freedom, liberty and justice for all.

A train of tank cars transports domestic oil. Although railroads were breaking all-time traffic records, they were still able to provide a vital link in the wartime transportation of domestic oil, hauling it from the Gulf Coast and Texas fields to the East. This service became even more critical when German submarines were sinking tankers hauling oil along the Atlantic and Gulf coasts. FDR

These containers, formerly used to haul cement, were pressed into service to move kerosene from Destrehan, La., to Chelsea, Ma. FDR

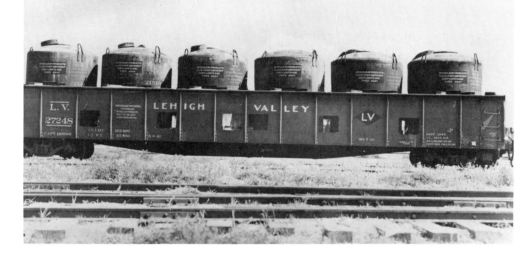

C&O Railway car float #2 loaded with military vehicles and equipment at Newport News, Va., 1943. C&O HISTORICAL SOCIETY

How We Can Help in the Present Emergency

★ ★

To all Southern Pacific Employes:

We are going through a trying period, and every Southern Pacific man and woman has a very personal and vital responsibility in the national defense program.

Production is America's first and greatest need. Efficient transportation is essential to this, in providing a steady, dependable flow of raw materials to plants and establishments and in expediting movement of finished products to destinations. At the same time, troops and their equipment must be transported on dependable schedules and with a minimum of interference with other defense traffic.

This great call upon transportation is a personal challenge to each of us in the railroad service. I am proud of the way Southern Pacific men and women in all branches of the service always meet emergencies, and I am confident that in the present emergency they will gladly accept their responsibilities and will perform every duty assigned to them to the best of their ability, individually and in cooperation with one another, so the full force of our combined strength and skill may be made effective.

A few brief suggestions on how this can best be accomplished are enclosed.

Let us work together as a unit to produce the greatest possible service from our transportation facilities in the present emergency.

San Francisco,
August 25, 1941.

A. T. Mercier
PRESIDENT

"A Christmas without travel will help win the war!"

...Joseph B. Eastman, DIRECTOR, OFFICE OF DEFENSE TRANSPORTATION

Neither your Government nor your railroad *likes* to ask you to give up Christmas travel this year. But we are in the most desperate of all wars. It will take our every resource to win it.

War needs, therefore, have first call on railroad facilities. Because the movement of troops and material is so great—and so vital to America—there will be no extra trains, or even extra cars, for pleasure travel this Christmas.

So we ask you to do one more thing for victory: Don't travel for pleasure during the Holiday season. If you will stay home *this* Christmas, you'll help to win the war. Then, in Christmases to come, we shall all be free to come and go as we please ... and to travel by rail, as in the past, in luxury and comfort.

CHESAPEAKE and OHIO LINES

Geared to the *war* GO of America!

CITY TICKET OFFICE:
809 15th Street, N. W. • Phone: National 0821

THE YANKS ARE COMING—and HOW!

6,500,000 SOLDIERS RODE TRAINS, ON MILITARY ORDERS, DURING THE FIRST 9 MONTHS OF THIS YEAR!

THAT'S THREE TIMES AS MANY AS WERE MOVED DURING THE SAME TIME IN WORLD WAR 1. AND TODAY RAILROADS KEEP 'EM ROLLING AT 50% FASTER SPEED.

THEY LIVE THE LIFE OF PRIVATE RILEY

RAILROADS WORK TOGETHER

TROOP MOVEMENTS ARE SECRET. BUT THIS WE CAN TELL YOU — TROOPS FOR EMBARKATION MAY ARRIVE IN DOZENS OF TRAINS, FROM DIFFERENT PARTS OF THE COUNTRY. YET THESE TRAINS PULL INTO PORTS IN A PRECISELY-TIMED STREAM. NO CONFUSION. NO DELAY. JUST MILITARY EFFICIENCY IN TERMS OF RAILROADING.

TODAY'S SOLDIER TRAVELS TWICE AS MUCH

IN 1918, A SOLDIER IN TRAINING MOVED AN AVERAGE OF 3 TIMES. TODAY, WITH MORE INTENSIVE TRAINING, SOLDIERS ARE MOVED FROM CAMP TO CAMP AN AVERAGE OF 6 TIMES.

ON OVERNIGHT JOURNEYS, TROOPS USUALLY TRAVEL IN PULLMANS. WITH THE SOLDIERS GOES THEIR FULL EQUIPMENT—SMALL ARMS, TRUCKS, FIELD GUNS, TANKS, KITCHENS.

CHESAPEAKE and OHIO LINES
One of America's Railroads...ALL MOBILIZED FOR WAR!

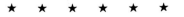

Advertisements . COURTESY C&O
HISTORICAL SOCIETY

-261-

Today this is a "MILITARY OPERATION"

Today, most railroad operations are military in ultimate purpose and effect. It may be just throwing a switch to start a carload of bomb cases on their way to Australia . . . or a whole division of troops and equipment across the Atlantic. Every railroad is a vital arm of the forces that fight for world freedom. Like all other railroads, Chesapeake and Ohio Lines hail as their most important customer a certain Old Gentleman with gray chin-whiskers. Uncle Sam knows he can count on his boys in uniform to give a first-rate account of themselves. And he knows that he also can count

on the steel-railed supply lines at home to back him . . . and them . . . to the limit.

So far, commercial shippers have had little to worry about while Chesapeake and Ohio was handling their goods. We hope it will always be that way. But any time a big military operation comes along — it comes first. We know you understand. In asking your co-operation, we also offer our co-operation. Just call our nearest representative, or communicate with Geo. W. Wood, Freight Traffic Manager Solicitation, Chesapeake and Ohio Lines, Cincinnati, Ohio.

CHESAPEAKE AND OHIO LINES
Geared to the war GO of America!

The long freight climbing the Divide
is in a race against the Axis!

DAY and night, long Milwaukee Road freight trains are climbing up and over the giant hump of the Rockies. Rolling westward loaded with guns, planes, tanks and munitions . . . returning with livestock, grain, fruit and lumber.

These heavy duty trains are in a race against time, charged with a basic part of the war program. And they're winning the race, partly because types of power best fitted for the hauling job are used: big electric "motors" over the mountains — a giant diesel bridging the inter-mountain

gap — mighty steam locomotives east of the Rockies.

The Milwaukee Road's skilled, experienced personnel keeps the 11,000 miles of line clear for these titans of the rails and their vital cargoes.

* * *

The railroads are a powerful weapon in the arsenal of democracy because they have adequately maintained — and improved — their facilities even in times of adversity. The Milwaukee Road is efficiently handling immense quantities of war materials. To this essential service we will continue to dedicate our best efforts.

The MILWAUKEE ROAD   BUY WAR BONDS AND STAMPS

Straight as a bomber to its target . . .

freight trains cross Lake Michigan!

WHAT!—*on tracks?* Yes, on tracks built into the broad, capacious decks of Pere Marquette Carferries. In an average year, over 100,000 cars travel this time-saving route . . . avoiding delays in congested areas . . . cutting out many roundabout miles between the Northwest and the East.

Now, as war needs place an extra premium on speedy delivery, this "water bridge across Lake Michigan" is doing yeoman ser-

vice for America. Daily, between Ludington, Michigan, and Milwaukee, Manitowoc and Kewaunee, Wisconsin, Pere Marquette Carferries move whole freight trains back and forth across the lake. There's no breaking bulk, for the loaded cars are switched onto the ships, carried to the other shore and switched back onto mainline tracks to continue their journey. Route your shipments this way and save precious time!

PERE MARQUETTE Railway
THE RAILROAD THAT CROSSES LAKE MICHIGAN

Railroads were born fighting . . .

First, it was wilderness . . . savage Indians. Later, the desert . . . blazing heat, dust and thirst! But the railroads fought through and won. They united a nation with bands of steel . . . Then fought to preserve it!

Today, our fight is bigger than ever before. The enemy more ruthless than wilderness or Indians. The issue greater than a stretch of track . . . greater than any one nation!

No longer must we drop our tools to grab a rifle. Our tools and equipment themselves are weapons . . . Modernized weapons kept always in fighting trim . . . Weapons used to transport the countless essentials of this *Fight for Freedom!*

And the railroads wield these tools with a vengeance! Every second of every hour, Long trainloads of troops and materials speed forward To take their parts in the conflict. Every second of every hour, The railroads are on the job . . . fighting . . . Helping to forge Victory for Democracy!

CHESAPEAKE AND OHIO LINES
ONE OF AMERICA'S RAILROADS—
All Mobilized for War

AVOID UNNECESSARY TRAVEL   BUY WAR BONDS INSTEAD!

-262-

Information booth in the Pennsylvania Railroad
Station, New York City, August 1942. LC-USW3-6960-E

A trainload of tanks on the Atchison, Topeka and
Santa Fe Railroad between Seligman, Ariz., and
Needles, Calif., March 1943. LC-USW3-21355-E

Tanks being transported by the New York Central Railroad, 1942. LC-USZ62-99541

Interior view of Union Station, Washington, D.C., in March 1943. This was one of the busiest stations in America during the war, but fell into disrepair as train travel diminished. Today it has been restored to its prewar elegance and still serves as a railroad station but also as a center for retail shops. LC-USW3-18393-C

"All abo-o-o-ard" sounds in a clear, high voice on this as on many other Pennsylvania Railroad commuter trains in the Philadelphia area. As men left for service, they were replaced by women. FDR

In a scene played out again and again in towns large and small, families and friends crowd the railway station to see the boys off. These young men are leaving on a troop train from Marlinton, W.Va., on April 29, 1942. POCAHONTAS COUNTY HISTORICAL SOCIETY

A troop train rounds a curve near Peach Springs, Az., on the Atchison, Topeka and Santa Fe Railroad, March 1943. Millions of troops were moved around the country and to ports of embarkation by troop trains in a major undertaking unprecedented in the history of the country.
LC-USW3-21356-E

CALIFORNIA STATE RAILROAD MUSEUM

The government seized American railroads in December 1943 to prevent a work stoppage and disruption of this critical part of war production. The railroads were returned to private ownership on Jan. 8, 1944, after the government agreed to a nine cent hourly raise and vacation and overtime concessions to 1,450,000 railroad workers.

THE WESTERN PACIFIC RAILROAD COMPANY

N O T I C E

BY EXECUTIVE ORDER DATED THE 27TH DAY OF DECEMBER, 1943, THE PRESIDENT OF THE UNITED STATES, ACTING THROUGH THE SECRETARY OF WAR, HAS TAKEN POSSESSION AND CONTROL OF THE TRANSPORTATION FACILITIES OF THIS COMPANY EFFECTIVE AS OF SEVEN P.M., DECEMBER 27, 1943.   THIS ACTION WAS TAKEN TO AVOID A THREATENED INTERRUPTION OF VITAL TRANSPORTATION SERVICE.   THE CONTINUED OPERATION OF THE FACILITIES THEREBY TAKEN IS ESSENTIAL TO THE SUCCESSFUL PROSECUTION OF THE WAR.

HENRY L. STIMSON,

SECRETARY OF WAR.

The elaborate Union Terminal at Cincinnati, Ohio, was a busy place during the war. C&O HISTORICAL SOCIETY

A crowd of passengers waiting to board The George Washington is checked in by a conductor at the St. Louis, Mo., station, 1943. C&O HISTORICAL SOCIETY

Airlines at War

Airlines had unprecedented growth during the 1930s with new all-metal passenger planes flying passengers from coast to coast. Even before the war, the nation's airlines were already devoting many of their seats to military passengers.

Once the war started several of the major airlines were virtually turned into an arm of the military machine.

Pan American Airways, which pioneered overwater routes to Europe and the Orient with their flying boats, was put into immediate service on routes to Australia and across the Atlantic to Africa, the Near East and India.

American, United and Northwest airlines were pressed into service, flying around the world and to the distant outposts of Alaska. Many of the airline pilots donned military uniforms and began to train other military men as pilots.

Domestically the airlines were much in the same position as the railroads with the military taking most of the seats and transporting critical war materials both at home and abroad.

Timetables. COURTESY DON THOMAS, DUNEDIN, FLA.

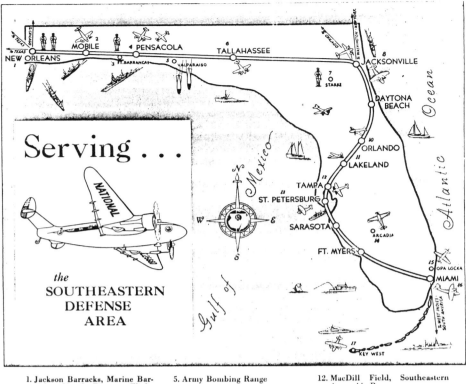

Serving...

the SOUTHEASTERN DEFENSE AREA

1. Jackson Barracks, Marine Barracks, Naval Reserve Flight Training Base, Army Air Corps Training Detachment, Army Supply Base, Coast Guard Training Station
2. Brookley Field, Southeast Army Air Depot
3. Ft. Barrancas, Army Training
4. Naval Air Training Station
5. Army Bombing Range
6. Army Flying Field
7. Camp Blanding, Army Training
8. Naval Training Station Coast Guard Division Headquarters
10. Army Flying Field
11. Civilian Air Corps Training School
12. MacDill Field, Southeastern Army Air Base
13. Coast Guard Air Station
14. Army Air Training School
15. Naval Reserve Air Station
16. Coast Guard Station
17. Navy Station Submarine and Air Training Station

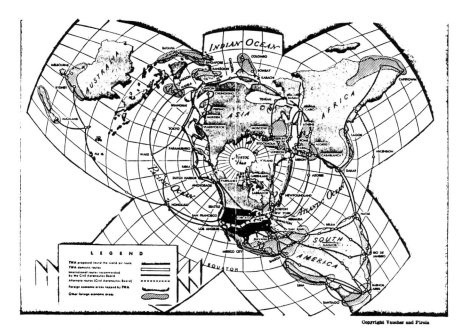

Copyright Vaucher and Piroia

The curtain rises on "Trans-World" Aviation

From TWA's 17,000,000 miles of international flying, touching 44 foreign countries and 5 continents, we offer a workable pattern for the sound development of United States international aviation:

It recognizes that competition between individual companies will foster international amity to a far greater extent than competition between nations and their chosen instruments.

It recognizes that, as a matter of history, new forms of transportation generate their own traffic. In other words, that airlines will create a new volume of traffic—not merely divide up the traffic that existed in the past.

It recognizes 26 areas of the world that are important enough to the economy, diplomacy and security of the United States to support trunk line air transportation.

TWA seeks to serve 10 of these economic areas through a single globe-circling route that will bring the farthermost point within 38 hours flying time of our borders.

TWA POINTS THE WAY

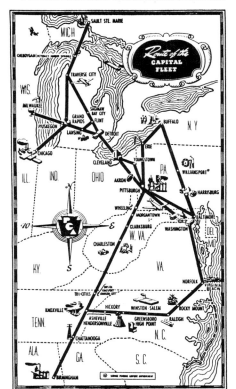

WESTERN AIR LINES

SAN DIEGO - LOS ANGELES - SALT LAKE CITY - GREAT FALLS - LETHBRIDGE, CANADA

Read Down—Northbound   AM—Light Face   JUNE 25, 1942   PM—Dark Face   Read Up—Southbound

12		2	10		Miles		Daily	War Time	Miles	9			3	
		11:25	4:36		0	Lv SAN DIEGO		(PT) Ar	1402	11:00			4:05	
		12:05	5:15		97	Ar LONG BEACH		Lv	1306	10:20			3:25	
		12:15	5:25		97	Lv LONG BEACH		Ar	1306	10:10			3:15	
		12:30	5:45		127	Ar LOS ANGELES		Lv	1275	9:55			3:00	
12		2	10							9	5			11
*5:00		*1:00	*6:15		127	Lv LOS ANGELES		Ar	1275	9:50	4:20			9:50
9:35		2:35	7:50		383	Ar LAS VEGAS		Lv	1019	9:15	2:45			8:15
9:45		2:45	8:00		383	Lv LAS VEGAS		(PT) Ar	1019	9:05	2:35			8:05
12:50		5:50	11:05		743	Ar SALT LAKE		(MT) Lv	659	*7:00	*1:30			*7:00
		6(1)										1(1)		
		*8:00			743	Lv SALT LAKE		Ar	659			8:36		
		8:55			893	Ar POCATELLO		Lv	509			7:40		
		9:10			893	Lv POCATELLO		Ar	509			7:30		
		—			941	Ar IDAHO FALLS		Lv	461					
		—			941	Lv IDAHO FALLS		Ar	461			*6:10		
		10:30			1116	Ar BUTTE		Lv	286			5:50		
		10:50			1116	Lv BUTTE		Ar	286					
		—			1158	Ar HELENA		Lv	244					
		—			1158	Lv HELENA		Ar	244			*9		
		11:40			1237	Ar GREAT FALLS		Lv	165			5:00		
		12:00			1237	Lv GREAT FALLS		Ar	165			4:40		
		12:35			1329	Ar CUT BANK		Lv	73			4:05		
		12:56			1329	Lv CUT BANK		Ar	73			3:45		
		1:25			1400	Ar LETHBRIDGE		(MT) Lv	0			3:15		

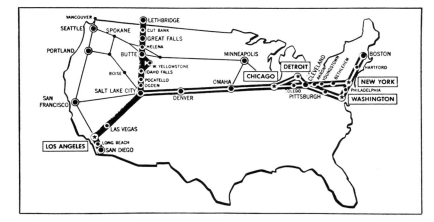

Wartime License Plates

During the war some of the most delicate and contro-versial alternative substances used were those that were substituted in license plate manufacture for the steel, aluminum, and other metals that had already been used. Many states created fiberboard of various compositions to take the place of metal. While the material was inex-pensive and allowed the plates to be printed rather than embossed, there were several problems not anticipated by the states that issued them. Illinois introduced the first of the infamous 'fiberboards,' as they were commonly known, although the actual material in use varied from masonite to sugarcane to soybeans. The 1943 Illinois plate was a combination of soybean and paper pulp, chemically treated to strengthen it for use in both winter and summer. These plates attracted nationwide atten-tion when an Illinois newspaper published a photograph of a goat nibbling the corner of one. The news service ran the photo and caption nationwide, and soon it was com-mon knowledge that goats, cows, horses, mules, pigs and even dogs were merrily chomping away on 1943 Illinois license plates while registration offices across the state were kept in a frenzy supplying duplicates. Nevertheless, Illinois continued annual issues through 1948. Louisiana developed a similar substance for their 1944 plates, pre-pared from a crushed sugarcane compound known as "bagasse." Many states also issued stickers for wind-shields and small aluminum tabs for older license plates.

Stickers

Alabama - 1943
Arizona - 1943-44
Arkansas - 1943
California - 1944
Hawaii - 1943-45
Idaho - 1943-44
Iowa - 1943-45
Kentucky - 1943, 1945
Louisiana - 1943
Maine - 1943
Massachusetts - 1943-44
New Mexico - 1943
North Dakota - 1943
Ohio - 1943
Oklahoma - 1943
Oregon - 1943-45
Rhode Island - 1943
South Dakota - 1944
Utah - 1943
Washington - 1943-44
West Virginia - 1944

Fiberboard Plates

Alaska - 1945
Arizona - 1944
Arkansas - 1944
Illinois - 1943-45
Louisiana - 1944
Missouri - 1942-43
Montana - 1944
Utah - 1944
Virginia - 1942-44

Information. COURTESY MICHAEL C. WIENER, ALBUQUER-QUE, N.M.

PASSENGER
METAL PLATE NO.

38511

19 NEW MEXICO 43

MFG. LICENSED UNDER U.S. PAT. 1955569 PAT. 1898993 OTHER PAT'S PEND.

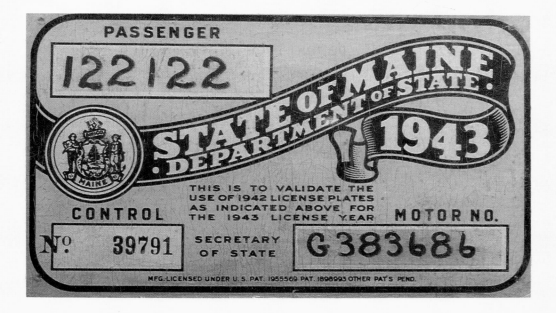

PASSENGER

122122

STATE OF MAINE
DEPARTMENT OF STATE
1943

THIS IS TO VALIDATE THE
USE OF 1942 LICENSE PLATES
AS INDICATED ABOVE FOR
THE 1943 LICENSE YEAR

CONTROL
Nº 39791

SECRETARY
OF STATE

MOTOR NO.
G 383686

MFG. LICENSED UNDER U.S. PAT. 1955569 PAT. 1898993 OTHER PAT'S PEND.

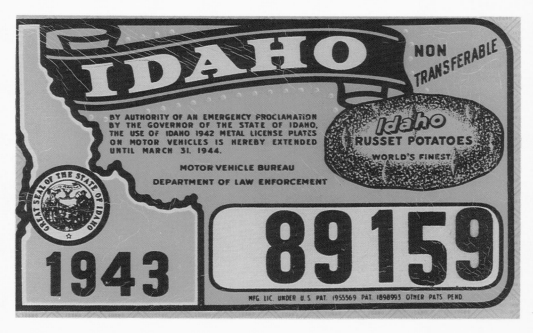

IDAHO
NON TRANSFERABLE

BY AUTHORITY OF AN EMERGENCY PROCLAMATION
BY THE GOVERNOR OF THE STATE OF IDAHO,
THE USE OF IDAHO 1942 METAL LICENSE PLATES
ON MOTOR VEHICLES IS HEREBY EXTENDED
UNTIL MARCH 31, 1944.

MOTOR VEHICLE BUREAU
DEPARTMENT OF LAW ENFORCEMENT

Idaho
RUSSET POTATOES
WORLD'S FINEST

GREAT SEAL OF THE STATE OF IDAHO

1943

89159

MFG. LIC. UNDER U.S. PAT. 1955569 PAT. 1898993 OTHER PATS. PEND.

License stickers. COURTESY WELFRED A. STAHL, LARGO, FLA.

Faced with a ban on buses for sightseeing purposes in the nation's capitol, Jimmy Grace puts ingenuity to work and conducts daily tours of points of interest in a horse-drawn wagon. FDR

Sharing taxis outside Union Station in Washington, D.C. *TIME/LIFE* PICTURE SERVICE

Joseph B. Eastman, director of the Office of Defense Transportation, in 1942 inspects a new 15-passenger "war workers' coach" made from a standard five-passenger sedan and only 300 additional pounds of steel. Left to right: Francis W. Feeney, president of the Fitz John Coach Company, which made the vehicle; Mr. Eastman; Frank H. Shepard, special assistant in the ODT's Local Transportation Division, and Guy A. Richardson, director of the Local Transport Division. FDR

Government workers leave their autos at a car park and crowd into buses going the last leg of their trip to Washington, D.C. FDR

Car pooling bulletin board at the Glenn Martin aircraft plant in Baltimore, Md., 1942. FDR

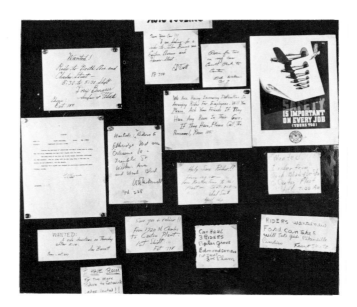

Car pooling poster at the Lockheed Vega aircraft factory in California, 1942, encouraging another very important way of conserving precious gas and rubber. FDR

In Denver, Clarence Werthan, chairman of transportation, discusses his committee's plans for coordinating transportation schedules and informing the public. Offices and industries agreed to stagger hours so as not to tax public transportation during peak periods. Housewives were urged to shop at times when people would not be going to their jobs in defense plants. The committee made surveys of the needs for transportation at factories, and passed out information on rubber conservation, car and truck care and share-the-ride programs. The committee's efficient work paid off, because while the transportation system was often crowded, there was no break-down in it. COLORADO HISTORICAL SOCIETY

This wartime-issue road map is unusual in that points of military interest in the state have been removed. One wonders how many enemy agents would have been interested in Montana, a state almost 500 miles from the Pacific Coast.

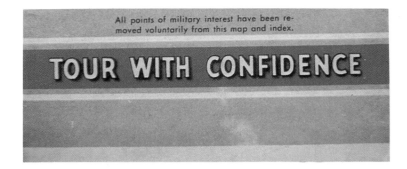

Civilians and military passengers waiting for a bus at the Chicago Greyhound terminal. Military travel took priority in all forms of transportation. LC-USW3-37790-E

Waiting room at the Greyhound bus terminal in Pittsburgh, Pa., in September 1943. Every mode of transportation in the country was taxed to the limit during the war. LC-USW3-37346-E

Workers arrive to start a shift at Ford's Willow Run bomber plant, 1943. With gas rationing in effect, buses became very important in transporting the millions of workers to their daily jobs. HENRY FORD MUSEUM and GREENFIELD VILLAGE

This bus, built about 1933, is being boarded in the Indianapolis, Ind., terminal in September 1943. Old buses such as this were brought out of retirement because of the increased amount of bus travel around the country. LC-USW3-37757-E

THE
ARSENAL
OF
DEMOCRACY

An Armco security guard proudly raises, along with the American flag, the coveted Army-Navy "E" pennant, which was awarded for excellence in meeting high production quotas for defense. FRANK B. ELAM PHOTO

There's work to be done and a war to be won... **NOW!**

SEE YOUR U. S. EMPLOYMENT SERVICE
WAR MANPOWER COMMISSION

MILES OF HELL *to Tokyo!*

WORK WHERE YOU'RE NEEDED

CONSULT YOUR U.S. EMPLOYMENT SERVICE OFFICE
WAR MANPOWER COMMISSION

Look to the Sky....

Western
WORLD CHAMPION AMMUNITION

SHOT SHELLS ... CARTRIDGES ... TRAPS AND TARGETS

Oct. 6-'44

FOR skill, industry, and devotion on the production front of the greatest war in history, this Army-Navy Production Award emblem is hereby presented

TO *George H. Holden*

SUNFLOWER ORDNANCE WORKS

OF _____

Under Secretary of War   *Under Secretary of the Navy*

An Invitation to Employees and their Families

THE employees of Sunflower Ordnance Works, Hercules Powder Company, have been honored with the Army-Navy Production Award for high achievement in the production of war materials. Because this is the highest award that can be won by industrial soldiers, special ceremonies commemorating the occasion will be held at the plant, 3:45 P. M. Friday, October 6, 1944. At this time, the "E" flag will be raised and employees will be presented with "E" pins. All employees and members of their families are cordially invited to attend.

SUNFLOWER ORDNANCE WORKS, LAWRENCE, KANSAS

Living Conditions

Defense housing in Erie, Pa. A central utility building (right) with toilets, showers and laundry facilities was maintained for every 60 trailers at this site. Each trailer, which could accommodate up to four people, was set on a plot of ground measuring 25 by 50 feet, and each was equipped with a gas stove, an icebox and davenport beds. FDR

A trailer camp for Consolidated-Vultee aircraft workers on Murfreesboro Road, Nashville, Tenn., June 1941. TENNESSEE STATE ARCHIVES

Thousands of war workers would spend all or part of their wartime years living in small trailers such as this. With the defense industries expanding greatly in 1941, thousands of these trailers were set up in trailer parks near defense plants. This one, in San Diego, Calif., was occupied by a family from Minnesota. The husband worked for Consolidated Aircraft. LC-USF34-39331D

Aerial view of the Kaiser shipyards in Portland, Ore., one of many producing liberty ships on the west coast. OHS

War plant housing at Vanport, Portland, Ore. OHS

Donald Nelson, head of the War Production Board (WPB), was formerly an executive with Sears, Roebuck & Company.

Because of the housing shortage, an Erie, Pa., defense worker and his family of three lived in this attic room. The expansion of defense industries, even before America entered the war, made it difficult to house the workers. Eventually trailers and pre-fab homes were provided, but the shortage of adequate housing persisted throughout the country during the war years. FDR

A "Westcraft Home," a pre-fabricated house, built by the Western Trailer Company of Los Angeles to help alleviate the great nationwide shortage of housing for war workers. FDR

COCA-COLA

Perhaps no other product made in America reminded the GI of home as much as Coca-Cola. The company, headquartered in Atlanta, Ga., went to war in a big way. Their ads throughout the war reflected their patriotic ideals both at home and for the servicemen and women overseas. One important ingredient of Coca-Cola was sugar which soon became scarce and was rationed early in the war. The company reprinted a 1917 ad from WWI stating that: "Again, Sugar enlists for Victory. Whatever any of us may have, or may not have, Victory we must have above all else!" At times Coca-Cola for domestic consumption was in short supply because of the sugar situation, but Coke followed the troops overseas and 64 bottling plants were built for the troops, 59 transported at government expense as a military priority. Robert Woodruff, president of the Coca-Cola Company stated: "We will see that every man in uniform gets a bottle of Coca-Cola for five cents, wherever he is and whatever it costs." The company lived up to Mr. Woodruff's statement throughout the war.

Coke bottle dated 1943.

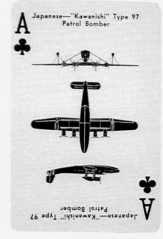

The Coca-Cola Company published these sets of playing cards as a patriotic gesture and as a learning tool for spotting Allied and Axis airplanes.

WAR-TIME WORKER'S HAND BOOK

You're Helping!

Every time you charge a retort or pull a sleeve, you're driving another nail in Hitler's and Hirohito's coffin!

Did you know that every sleeve of magnesium will make 24 incendiary bomb casings?

Magnesium Wins Wars!

The magnesium you make at Permanente is helping win the war of the skies!

Just one of the sleeves you pull out of the retorts will make 29 control wheels for a Flying Fortress!

ENLISTED IN FREEDOM'S FIGHT ★

OFF the assembly line they roll—sleek, streamlined Harley-Davidson motorcycles for Uncle Sam's forces and the armies of our Allies. Day and night, whirring wheels, clicking automatics, pounding presses roar ceaselessly as raw materials are fashioned into still more Harley-Davidsons. ★ Today's Harley-Davidson motorcycles are duplicating the splendid record made by their predecessors in World War I. The hard-riding scouts who lead the advance of the armored divisions know that the staunch and sturdy construction of their mounts will not let them down. ★ All the exacting care and skill of determined loyal workers—all the resources and experience of the Harley-Davidson organization are enlisted to give freedom's fighters the best in motorcycles. That we pledge till victory is won.

Harley-Davidson Motor Company, Milwaukee, Wisconsin

HARLEY-DAVIDSON

Indian MOTORCYCLE NEWS

ARMY E NAVY

ARMY-NAVY PRODUCTION AWARD

"FOR YOUR FINE RECORD IN THE PRODUCTION OF MATERIALS NEEDED IN THE WAR EFFORT"

★ AUGUST-SEPTEMBER 1943 ★ VOL. X · NO. IV ★

Published By The Indian Motocycle Co., Springfield, Mass., U.S.A.

MEN TRENTWOOD *has* AN AXIS SMASHING, HISTORY MAKING *JOB* FOR YOU

GET STARTED TODAY!

APPLY: S.101 HOWARD STREET PLANTSITE TRENTWOOD OR U.S. EMPLOYMENT SERVICE

TRENTWOOD ALUMINUM ROLLING MILL

B-24 *Liberator* bombers on the assembly line at Ford's giant Willow Run plant in Michigan. America's ability to produce on this scale spelled doom to the Axis powers. FDR

5000TH
Ford Built
Liberator

The 5,000th B-24 *Liberator* built at the Willow Run plant in Detroit, Mich. HENRY FORD MUSEUM and GREENFIELD VILLAGE

Women workers at the Long Beach, Calif., plant of Douglas Aircraft Company groom lines on the transparent noses of A-20 attack planes. FDR

Airplane Production

In 1944 the United States produced over 96,000 aircraft.

P-39 *Airacobra* aircraft on the final assembly line at the Bell Aircraft Corporation's Elmwood Avenue plant in Buffalo, N.Y. This view, looking toward the beginning of the line, shows the airplane taking form. Yet to be attached are the rear fuselage, engine, fuselage armament, wings and armor plate. A large number of these planes were shipped through Alaska for Lend-Lease to Russia. FDR

Camouflage netting covers a parts stockyard at the Consolidated-Vultee aircraft plant, July 1943. In the foreground are assemblies for waist-gun turrets for PBY Catalina patrol bombers. NA

PB2Y patrol bombers and aircraft parts parked under camouflage netting at the Consolidated-Vultee aircraft plant in San Diego, Calif., July 1943. NA

This remarkable photo shows the Boeing Aircraft plant in south Seattle covered by camouflage to resemble a residential area. Boeing Field is in the background. This vital war industry would have made an inviting target for Japanese bombers had they ever appeared. AL LLOYD, SEATTLE

Wing sections, each containing two Wright engines, await mating with fuselage sections of B-17F models in Boeing's Seattle plant. OWI VIA VMI

Maximum B-17 production at Boeing's Seattle, Wash., plant was reached in April 1944, when 16 B-17Gs per day were rolled out. AL LLOYD, SEATTLE

C-47s on the assembly line at the Douglas Aircraft plant in California. The C-47 was the workhorse of the U.S. Army Air Corps during the war and flew in every major theater. OWI VIA VMI

Two midgets atop a wing assembly exhibit. Because of their small size, little people were employed in the B-24 bomber factory at Willow Run, Mich., to work on the inside of the giant plane's wings. USN

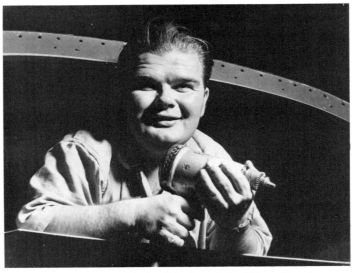

Joe Cobb, former "fat boy" in the original "Our Gang" comedies, helped build B-25 bombers at the Inglewood, Calif., plant of North American Aviation. FDR

Aircraft designer, Donald Douglas witnessed the first airplane flight at Kitty Hawk and in the 1930s designed the DC series airplane. The most famous was the DC-3 (C-47 in military use). Over 10,000 were built during the war.

Rows of nose sections of the B-29 *Superfortress* on Boeing's Wichita, Kan., assembly line. In the background are huge double bomb bay sections. The Bell plant in Georgia and the Martin plant in Nebraska also produced B-29s. KANSAS STATE HISTORICAL SOCIETY

Propellers ready for assembly. OWI VIA VMI

Lockheed aircraft employees arriving at work. Those who lived within four miles of the plant could purchase bicycles with company help and sell them back when they left the job. With gas rationing, bicycles were a natural alternative to the automobiles. NA 171-G-10C-11

An aircraft engine assembly line at the Douglas Aircraft plant in California. NA 80-G-412712

With men from every profession going into the military, it was up to women to fill the thousands of job vacancies, even in traditional fields such as railroading. UTAH STATE HISTORICAL SOCIETY, *SALT LAKE TRIBUNE* PHOTO

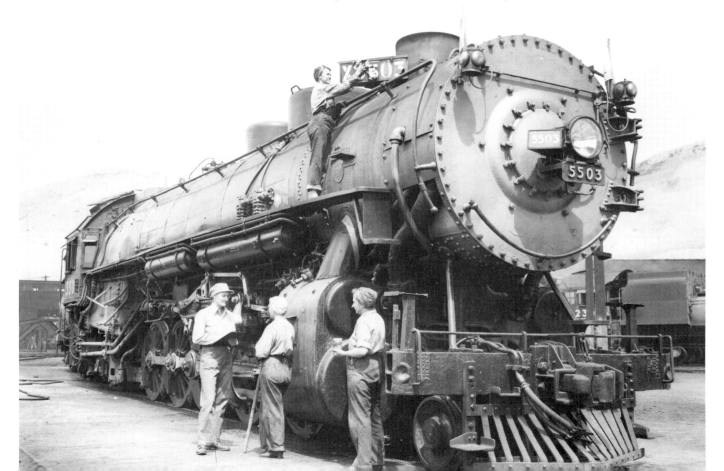

Women Wartime Workers

Six National Youth Administration girls model work clothes created by the design department of the Illinois NYA. Left to right, the clothes are intended for: two woodshop workers, a welder, a radio assembly worker, an aviation ground mechanic and a machine operator. FDR

Men and women shared the burden of building the war machine needed to fight a global war. FDR

Another woman war worker puts the finishing touches on the bombardier's nose cone of a B-17F bomber in the Douglas plant. FDR

Women learning welding in Deland, Fla. Women, as well as men, went to school to learn the skills needed for work in an aircraft plant established in the Deland area in 1942. FDR

Experienced men helped train women in all phases of airplane construction in this Douglas Aircraft Company plant in Long Beach, Calif. FDR

Workers in a Midwest aluminum factory assembling 37mm armor-piercing shells prior to a heat-treating operation. FDR

Fern Evans, whose husband was one of the sailors killed on the *USS West Virginia* during the Pearl Harbor attack, at work in an aircraft factory, supporting herself and her 20-month-old son and helping to avenge her husband's death in a small way. FDR

Mrs. Eloise J. Ellis, left, at work at the Naval Air Base in Corpus Christi, Texas. Formerly a sociology major at the University of Southern California, she took a Civil Service job in the assembly and repair department, providing assistance in solving housing and other personal problems in order to help maintain morale among women workers. FDR

Madelon O'Leary operates a punch press in a well-cut, one piece coverall. The visor-front cap completely covers her hair for safety and neatness. FDR

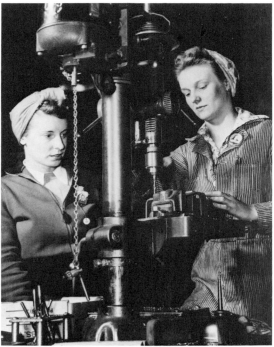

Drill press workers at the Commercial Iron Works plant in Portland, Ore., 1943. OHS, *OREGON JOURNAL* PHOTO

Women welders on their way to work at the Todd Erie Basin dry dock in Pennsylvania, 1943. LC-LCW33-25834-Z0

SIGN UP for VICTORY!

ON this VICTORY FLEET DAY, September 27, 1943, I solemnly pledge that I will pour into the production of SHIPS FOR VICTORY so full a measure of my muscle, mind and money that the fighters of our UNITED NATIONS will never lack war materials to blast into oblivion the enemies of free labor, wherever they may be found.

"Rosie the Riveter" was named after Rosina Bonavita, and this nickname became the catch-phrase for all American women working in defense industries.

Mr. Kaiser and His Liberty Ships

by Jean Sherrell
from *The Californians*, The Magazine of California
Sept./Oct. 1988 issue

"Westerners," a New Yorker once said, "are so damned dumb, they didn't know they couldn't accomplish the impossible but then, damn it, they go ahead and do the impossible." In this respect, note historians Warren Beck and Susanne Gaskins, Henry J. Kaiser was a true son of the American West. His genius and determination eventually brought him on the scene at the moment his country needed someone who "never knows what he can't do" (as a rival once described Kaiser). The year was 1940, Britain was fighting the enemy alone and U-boats were sinking ships faster than British yards could build them: German submarines had sent 150 ships to the bottom of the Atlantic in the first nine months of the conflict.

Earlier, the Merchant Marine Act of 1936 had sought to revive the lost art of shipbuilding in America by establishing a maritime commission and a radical policy frankly authorizing construction and operating differential subsidies so American shipbuilders and operators could compete with foreign-flag ships. (The cost of constructing a cargo vessel in a U.S. shipyard was twice that of foreign competitors, and operating costs 50 percent higher.) Taking into account the various trade routes, U.S. Maritime Commission design teams produced three standard type ships - the early C1, C2 and C3, which proved to be excellent turbine vessels with no equal. According to maritime historians L.A. Sawyer and W.H. Mitchell, this far-sighted and original concept of standardization for individual purposes was immensely important to the speed with which the U.S. was able to turn to prefabrication at a critical time, but even so by 1940 American shipyards were still not geared to a wartime program.

Meanwhile, Kaiser's success in cement and contracting had assured him (and others) that his peculiar brand of brash creativity could overcome a challenge to which experienced shipbuilders had not yet risen. To learn the basics of shipbuilding, in 1939 Kaiser's Six Companies joined Todd Shipbuilding. In December of 1940, after the British said that they needed 60 freighters, and quickly, the Kaiser-Todd combine began laying out new yards at Portland, Oregon, and Richmond, California, for two 30-ship contracts. Though the Americans wanted to build their own lighter, faster, more sophisticated vessels, time was the deciding factor: the British wanted "ships built by the mile and chopped off by the yard," and the only way to achieve this was to use the existing British designs and rush into mass production.

Fortunately for the war effort, Kaiser was willing "to have a go" at the impossible task of "quickly" constructing 60 ships. As soon as the Grand Coulee Dam project was finished, Kaiser brought in his construction managers and many of his construction workers - practically none of whom had ever even seen a shipyard before. Kaiser's team regarded a ship as just another large structure to be built as well and efficiently as possible, and so approached the task with open minds. Ships were traditionally built by skilled craftsmen, but there was no time to train such people so Kaiser simplified ship construction so that it could be done by less experienced workers on an assembly line. E.g., whereas it took years to train a person in vertical or overhead welding, a worker could learn horizontal welding in just a few days. Therefore, "jigs and cranes were built so that sections could be turned on their side and joined by horizontal welds."

Traditional shipbuilders laughed at Kaiser and assembly-plant shipyards that welded together the 30,000+ components produced en masse in thousands of factories in more than 32 states. They were also amused when Kaiser spoke of "front" and "back" ends of a "product." Kaiser, of course, not only had the last laugh but also kept all his promises - including the one that California would have its own steel plant to avoid delays and frustration of waiting for steel supplies from back East. Asked about what he intended to use for iron ore, he replied "We'll prospect for it out here." (They did, and found it in Utah.)

By 1941 German submarines were sinking twice as many ships as America and Britain combined could produce. Nine new emergency shipyards (five under the Todd/Kaiser group) were expected to produce 260 ships that year. Though welding was controversial, it was a calculated risk that Kaiser was willing to take, for welding was the only alternative to the slower approach of using four-man rivet crews to punch holes in the steel plates and rivet them to the frame.

In February, newspapers across the nation dubbed the emergency ships "ugly ducklings" after President Franklin D. Roosevelt contemptuously described them as "dreadful-looking objects." Maritime Commission chairman Admiral Emory Scott Land, attempting to change the new ship type's image, began referring to them as the "Liberty Fleet." He also nominated September 27, 1941, as Liberty Fleet Day. That same day, as 15 Liberty ships were launched throughout the nation, President Roosevelt made no mention of "dreadful-looking objects" as he praised each new ship as a blow struck "at the menace to the nation and for the liberty of the free peoples of the world." In this same speech the President announced his determination to set aside the laws that prevented American merchant ships from being armed and entering combat zones, although war was still more than two months away for the United States.

The Liberty shipbuilding program

swung into full-scale production, setting and then breaking incredible records again and again. Kaiser delivered his first 10,400-ton ship in 197 days, but constantly improving techniques quickly cut production time. In April of 1942 one Liberty ship was built in 86 days, in May 74 days, and the *Joseph N. Teal*, delivered in October 1942, was built in 14 days. The industry's speed record was set by Kaiser when the *Robert E. Peary* was delivered in four days, 15 hours and 30 minutes.

Though Kaiser's innovative style of ship production accounted in large part for his yards' speed and efficiency, historian Newell Bringhurst believes that the good employer-employee relations the company fostered contributed significantly. Workers who came up with good new ideas not only saw them "adopted forthwith" but also the mark that went on their company record stood them in good stead with Kaiser as long as they lived and wanted a job. Besides paying top wages, the Kaisers also provided for their workers outside of the shipyard. If adequate housing was scarce, they built more; and in return for a nominal payroll deduction Kaiser employees received unlimited medical treatment in Kaiser-run hospitals. Company-run daycare, after-school care and nursery schools were established near the Kaiser yards, and these 24-hour centers also sold inexpensive pre-cooked food for the family's supper which parents could buy when they called for their children at the end of the work shift.

Kaiser's visibility, flamboyance and success despite his lack of shipbuilding experience made him powerful enemies, including William Randolph Hearst, the disgruntled newspaper magnate who'd dubbed Kaiser "a coddled new deal pet" (even though the entrepreneur was a registered Republican). A widely publicized series of charges ranging from inadequate welding to stockpiling and profiteering were all eventually proven groundless. Perhaps the most serious was the allegation of inadequate welding: many lives were lost when two welded ships broke in Arctic waters. Between 1942 and 1944, more Kaiser-built vessels were affected by this cracking, leading to the charges. But it was found that the plating fractures were aggravated by severe Arctic cold, which turned ordinary steel brittle, and that because the Kaiser yards were near the North Pacific, a disproportionate number of his ships were assigned to those cold waters. As soon as the cause was discovered, crack-arresting procedures were introduced.

Despite early structural problems, the welded hulls were impressively sound. Many Liberty ships performed tremendous wartime service, surviving terrific punishment under extreme conditions. The *Cornelia P. Spencer*, for example, stayed afloat until a *third* torpedo sank her. In all, more than 200 Liberty ships were lost during the war.

Many others were salvaged and refit for further service until the mid-to-late '60s, when the relatively high fuel consumption of the Liberty ships compelled most private owners and governments to scrap the slow, worn-out vessels in favor of faster, more modern and more economic tonnage.

Kaiser's extraordinary wartime ship production, for which one observer dubbed him "Sir Launchalot," account for 27 percent of total ship tonnage turned out under the wartime emergency program - a record of production efficiency that deserves closer examination now that American industry must find ways to increase its overall efficiency in the face of stiff foreign competition.

Launching the liberty ship, *Booker T. Washington*, on Sept. 29, 1942, at the California Shipbuilding Corp. It was named for a famous black educator, christened by black singer, Marian Anderson and commanded by Hugh Mulzac, a black. FDR

The first liberty ship launched was the *S.S. Patrick Henry* and the last was the *S.S. Benjamin Warner*.

The launching of the *USS Albany* (CA-123) at the Bethlehem Steel Company's shipyard in Quincy, Mass., June 30, 1943. NA 80-G-345486

Cake-cutting ceremonies to celebrate the commissioning of the *USS Barbel* in 1944 in Oakland, Calif. The submarine and all hands were lost to enemy action in February 1945. FRED MAE COLLECTION

The launching of the *USS Missouri* (BB-63), which is still in active service, at the New York Navy Yard, Jan. 29, 1944. Left to right: Rear Adm. Monroe Kelly, commandant of the yard; Rear Adm. S.S. Kennedy; Sen. Harry S. Truman of Missouri, and Miss Margaret Truman, sponsor of the ship. NA 80-G-44891

Assault boats are lined up at the Higgins Industries plant, New Orleans, La., in September 1942. These boats were vital for the seaborne invasions in both the European and Pacific Theaters of war. FDR

Wooden boats under construction at Higgins Industries, New Orleans. As the boats were finished, they were pushed out the far door onto the water. FDR

Views of Henry J. Kaiser's Richmond, Calif., massive Liberty ship shipyards. Kaiser didn't win the war by himself, but he had a lot to do with the country's ability to overpower the Axis with industrial might. COURTESY ARUE SZURA, CASTRO VALLEY, CALIF.

Launching LST 492 at Evansville, Ind. Thousands of smaller naval ships were built on the inland waterways of the United States in small and large boat factories on the Ohio and Mississippi rivers and their tributaries. FDR

Assault boats for the U.S. Marine Corps stored in a gymnasium formerly used as a recreation center by plant employees. FDR

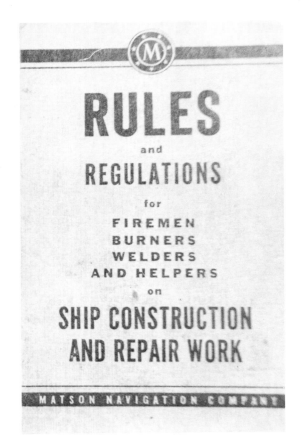

RULES
and
REGULATIONS
for
FIREMEN
BURNERS
WELDERS
AND HELPERS
on
SHIP CONSTRUCTION
AND REPAIR WORK

MATSON NAVIGATION COMPANY

President Roosevelt on a visit to the Higgins Industries boat yard, New Orleans, La., in 1942. USN

The Electric Boat Company in New London, Conn., was the largest builder of submarines (74) and PT boats (398) during the war.

Ford's River Rouge plant in May 1941. Since coal, limestone and iron ore are all used to make steel in automobile manufacture, and since this plant was basically self-contained, it would become a vital link in America's war production. FDR

A view of the end of three main assembly lines of a giant tank factory which built 28-ton M-3 tanks. Mass production methods developed in the automobile industry were used in the manufacture of war material. FDR

Chrysler had the largest tank factory in the country and built 25,000 during the war.

A truck assembly plant where workmen are stenciling on U.S. Army serial numbers. FDR

The last civilian automobile leaves the Ford factory on Feb. 10, 1942. Its serial number was 30-337509. Ford converted entirely to war production after this.
FDR

JOHN DEERE COMPANY

M-2 Military Tracto
Cleveland Tractor Co
(Ordnance Dept.)
War Assembly Plant

The John Deere Company built this armored tractor equipped with trailer in early 1941. It was tested by the U.S. Army at the Aberdeen Proving Grounds, but like hundreds of wartime designs, did not prove practical. JOHN DEERE COMPANY

43105   1-9-41   ABERDEEN PROVING GROUND   Ordnance Dep't.
Three-quarter right front view of John Deere Model A armored tractor equipped with trailer.

John L. Lewis, president of the United States Mine Workers of America. NA

Labor Relations

Total Union membership rose from 10.5 million at the start of the war to 14.75 million at the end. Unions bargained to obtain higher wages in the war-fueled economy and for safer working conditions.

One of the most important union leaders during the war was the United Mine Workers chief, John L. Lewis. His career was marked by bitter strikes and sharp conflicts with union opponents.

In 1935 he formed the Committee for Industrial Organization (CIO), changing its name in 1938 to the Congress of Industrial Organizations. Under Lewis' leadership, the CIO organized strong indus- trial unions in the mass-production industries.

There was much strife and many strikes in the coal fields during the war and for a time the govern- ment had to seize and run the coal industry to keep America's war industries running.

Lewis took his UMW union out of the CIO in 1942, rejoining in 1946.

NOTICE

In accordance with the proclamation of the President of the United States, Government possession of the coal mines of this mining company has been taken by Order of the Secretary of the Interior.

Harold L. Ickes

SECRETARY OF THE INTERIOR

Miners leaving a coal mine near Bishop, W.Va., at the end of their shift. Bituminous coal was one of the most important natural resources produced for the war effort. It powered the electrical generating plants, most of the nation's rail-roads, heated millions of homes and was used to produce many industrial chemicals. Despite union confrontations with management and government during the war years, coal production was at an all-time high and contributed greatly to the war effort. No color barriers were evident in the underground mines.

A major chromite mining complex at Mouat, Mont., in 1942. The only known chromium deposit in North America was located in the Stillwater Complex of south-central Montana and was established to produce the metal for America's steel industry. Supplies of this vital metal, used in the production of high-grade steel, had been reduced considerably by war activity and by increased demand. LC-USW3-9000-E

Loading oil, vital to war production, at the Mid-Continent Refinery in Tulsa, Okla., in October 1942. Oil played a major part in the great industrial victory of the United States, while the Axis powers had a constant problem keeping their war machine fueled. LC-USW3-10047-D

A section of the war emergency oil pipeline built from Longview, Texas, to Norris City, Ill., to insure a steady flow of oil, a vital natural resource for the war industries of the midwest and east. German submarines were sinking oil tankers along the Atlantic coast in the early days of the war, and an overland pipeline was a natural alternative. LC-USW3-9341-D

The Guayule Project

When Japanese occupation of the Pacific cut off natural rubber production, another source had to be found. Guayule, a plant that grew well from central California to Texas and produced a latex material, proved to be the answer. The U.S. Forest Service set up a pilot program in Salinas, Calif., to grow seeds and research rubber extraction from the plant. By the spring of 1944 over 200,000 acres of guayule had been planted and 1,500 tons of rubber were produced by the end of the program in 1945.

Dr. William B. McCallum of Intercontinental Rubber Producers, considered to be the world's leading expert on guayule culture. LC-USF34-70977-D

Planting guayule seed in the nursery at Salinas, Calif., in May 1942. The fine seed was planted with a mixture of sawdust and sand. LC-USF34-72532-D

Bales of guayule stored in a barn at the Salinas, Calif., facility, November 1942. LC-USW3-35374-D

Slab of Rubber From Kok Sagyz

A smooth, round slab of black rubber, first evidence of the product of the Russian dandelion or Kok Sagyz grown in this country, has been received at Forest Service headquarters from H. Basil Wales, field director for the Department of Agriculture in the North Atlantic states.

The rubber was produced from the roots grown in this country last year, appearing to be of satisfactory composition.

Sixty acres of Russian dandelion are being planted in the state this spring by the Forest Service in further continuing the experiment initiated by the Department of Agriculture.

One of many small shops making defense-related items located across the nation. This one, the Dante Electric Company, of Durham, Conn., made electrical parts for submarines. FDR

A corner of an assembly room where workmen are putting together the parts of the M-1 Garand rifle, the main infantry weapon used by American soldiers during the war. FDR

Two men guard stacks of vital magnesium produced at Basic Magnesium's giant plant in Nevada. Magnesium is the lightest of all metals and was used to make incendiary bombs, tracer bullets and aircraft parts. FDR

The only two-man labor-management War Production Drive Committee in the country. Jake Sparling, left, 60-year-old head of Sparling Pulley Manufacturing Company, Bay City, Mich., and Percy Fogelsonger, 79-year-old ex-lumberjack, who worked 15 hours a day seven days a week for 18 months. With no other help, they produced 18,000 steel flanges for war equipment and earned a citation which put them at the top of the list of plants formally enrolled in the War Production Drive, August 1942. FDR

Plant #8 of the Reynolds Metals Co., in Louisville, Ky., where airplane parts, as well as rod and sheet aluminum stock was manufactured 24 hours a day. FDR

As part of the War Production Drive, a ceremony takes place at a corner of the Westinghouse plant complex in Bloomfield, N.J. The streets were renamed "MacArthur Avenue" and "MacArthur Plaza" in honor of Gen. Douglas MacArthur, leader of troops in the Southwest Pacific. FDR

Sign in a plant that produced drills for war production. FDR

A meeting of automobile manufacturers executives and union leaders, held in Washington in January 1941, a year before Pearl Harbor, to discuss the conversion of the industry to war work. Left to right: Walter Reuther, R.J. Thomas, Sidney Hellman, W.S. Knudsen and C.E. Wilson. FDR

A soldier guards a sand-bagged oil well pump in a southern California oil field. After the attack on Pearl Harbor, major industrial complexes along America's coastline were guarded by Army troops.
BETTMANN ARCHIVE

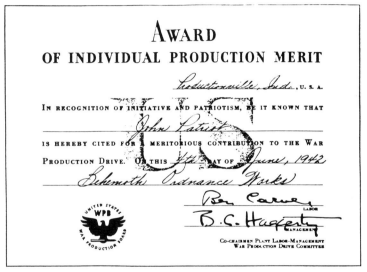

AWARD
OF INDIVIDUAL PRODUCTION MERIT

Productionville, Ind., U.S.A.

IN RECOGNITION OF INITIATIVE AND PATRIOTISM, BE IT KNOWN THAT

John Patriot

IS HEREBY CITED FOR A MERITORIOUS CONTRIBUTION TO THE WAR PRODUCTION DRIVE. ON THIS 4th DAY OF June, 1942

Behemoth Ordnance Works

Ben Carver
LABOR

B.C. Hafferty
MANAGEMENT

CO-CHAIRMEN PLANT LABOR-MANAGEMENT
WAR PRODUCTION DRIVE COMMITTEE

Seven crew members of the B-26 bomber "Old Hellcat," visited Ashland Oil employees and construction workers in 1943 to relay the urgent need for completion of the new 100 octane aviation fuel plant.
COURTESY FRANK B. ELAM

A guard at the Anaconda Copper Mining Company's smelter at Anaconda, Mont. MONTANA HISTORICAL SOCIETY

A defense plant worker makes adjustments to the warhead section of a Navy torpedo at a Pontiac Motor Division, General Motors factory, circa 1944. NA

A form filled out by H.B. Alexander of Port Republic, Va., as part of a census undertaken in the Shenandoah Valley of Virginia to identify skilled machine workers. FDR

A ceremony at the Briggs Manufacturing Company in Detroit, Mich., in September 1942. The "E" flag was awarded to manufacturers for increased war production. LC-USW3-9154-C

Government workers in Washington, D.C., step from the War Wagon trailer, which was sponsored by the Office of Defense Transportation. Built on a steel frame, the coach was made principally of wood and masonite. It was 12 feet long and seven feet wide and held 24 people. OWI VIA VMI

The government ordered all distilleries in the country to stop production of liquor and to convert to war production. KENTUCKY HISTORICAL SOCIETY

A sign outside the Commercial Iron Works plant in Portland, Ore. Absenteeism was a problem in many American plants, and much effort was made to reduce it. OHS

A sign outside the Anaconda Copper Mining Company in Butte, Mont., September 1942. Another attempt to curb absenteeism. LC-USW3-8231-D

This sign appeared at a power plant in Yakima, Wash., in late 1941, months before the Pearl Harbor attack. LC-USW3-9431-D

POSTAL HISTORY

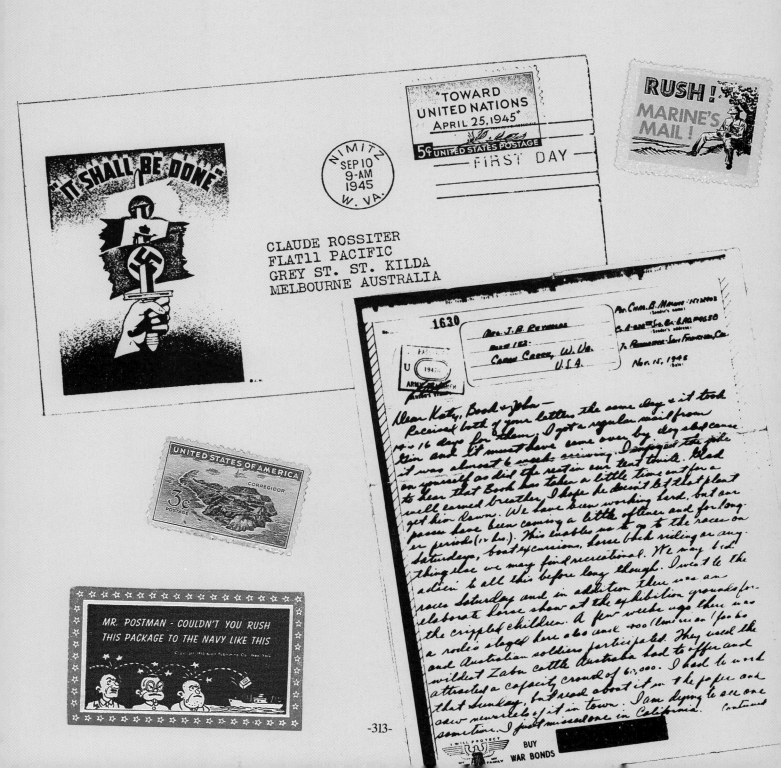

Remember
Pearl Harbor

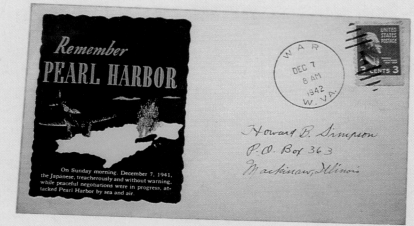

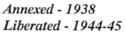

Annexed - 1938
Liberated - 1944-45

Stamp series issued in 1943 to commemorate countries of the world overrun by Axis forces.

Annexed - 1910
Liberated - 1945

Occupied - 1940
Liberated - 1944

Occupied - 1941
Liberated - 1944

Occupied - 1940
Liberated - 1944

Occupied - 1940
Liberated - 1944

ALBANIA

WASHINGTON
NOV 9
9-AM
1943
D.C.

FIRST DAY OF ISSUE

UNITED STATES POSTAGE

**Annexed - 1938
Liberated - 1945**

H. Beard
260 11 Ave
New York City 1 N Y

Zi
V
ALBANIA

**Occupied - 1941
Liberated - 1944**

WASHINGTON
NOV 23
9-AM
1943
D.C.

FIRST DAY OF ISSUE

UNITED STATES POSTAGE

THE DAY OF LIBERATION
SHALL NOT BE SO FAR OFF

AUSTRIA

designer

H.D.MULLON.
P.O.STAFF-MILITARY CAMP
WAIOURU. NEW ZEALAND.
NEW ZEALAND.

WASHINGTON.
SEP.
14
9:00 AM
1943
D.C.

FIRST DAY OF ISSUE

UNITED STATES POSTAGE
BELGIUM

BELGIUM

**Occupied - 1940
Liberated - 1944**

**Occupied - 1940
Liberated - 1945**

WE FIGHT ON-WE WILL WIN

THE "SLEIPNER"

NORWAY

designer

WASHINGTON
JUL 27
9-AM
1943
D.C.

FIRST DAY OF ISSUE

UNITED STATES POSTAGE

U.S. CENSOR
EXAMINED
9807

H.D.MULLON.
P.O.STAFF MILITARY
CAMP.
WAIOURU. NEW ZEALAND.
NEW ZEALAND.

**Occupied - 1940
Liberated - 1945**

CX

DENMARK

**Occupied - 1941
Liberated - 1944**

WASHINGTON
DEC 7
9-AM
1943
D.C.

FIRST DAY OF ISSUE

UNITED STATES POSTAGE

PII
1931

WE WILL NOT GIVE UP!
E GEN DRAJA MIHAILOVICH

YUGOSLAVIA

WASHINGTON
OCT 26
9-AM
1943
D.C.

FIRST DAY OF ISSUE

UNITED STATES POSTAGE

V-Mail Service provides the most expeditious dispatch and reduces the weight of mail to and from personnel of our Armed Forces outside the continental United States. When addressed to points where micro-film equipment is operated a miniature photographic negative of the message will be made and sent by the most expeditious transportation available for reproduction and delivery. The original message will be destroyed after the reproduction has been delivered. Messages addressed to or from points where micro-film equipment is not operated will be transmitted in their original form by the most expeditious means available.

INSTRUCTIONS

(1) Write the entire message plainly on the other side within marginal lines.

(2) PRINT the name and address in the two panels provided. Addresses to members of the Armed Forces should include rank or rating of the addressee unit to which attached, and APO or Naval address.

(3) Fold, seal, and deposit in any post office letter drop or street letter box.

(4) Enclosures must not be placed in this envelope and a separate V-Mail letter must be sent if you desire to write more than one sheet.

(5) V-Mail letters may be sent free of postage by members of the Armed Forces. When sent by others, postage must be prepaid at domestic rates (3¢ ordinary mail, 6¢ if air mail is desired).

Post Office Department Permit No. 17

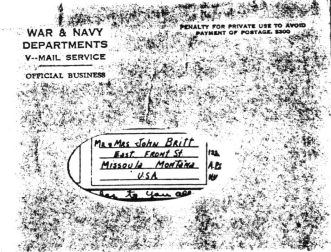

WARTIME STAMP ISSUES

THE END OF THE WAR

P. O. Box 693
Evanston, Ill.

The "Sultan of Swat," Babe Ruth, with war bonds. Ruth, the most famous player in baseball history, played for the New York Yankees through most of his career, which ended in 1935. NATIONAL BASEBALL HALL OF FAME

Sporting events, whether individual, amateur or professional, have always been an institution in the United States. The idea of canceling these activities during the war was never seriously considered by government authorities.

Only one sport, auto racing, was canceled for the duration - understandably - because of gas rationing and the rubber shortage. Horse racing at most of the nation's tracks flourished; gambling let off some steam from the stress of war work. But in 1945, horse racing also was banned due to severe travel restrictions.

High school sports continued even though travel was curtailed and supplies were limited (balls made of rubber disappeared). Intercollegiate sports managed to function in spite of the number of players going into the service. This was somewhat offset by the military men who were sent to the nation's colleges for training, although they were supposed to be there for studies in their specific field, not to participate in fun and games. Professional sports took the worst beating as players were at the prime age for military service.

All in all, sports activity was a valve for letting off pressure, and provided a sanctuary from the day-to-day stresses.

College football took something of a back seat to all-service teams made up of former college and professional players. The two service academies dominated college standings. This was especially true of West Point in 1944-45 with standout players such as Felix "Doc" Blanchard and Glenn "Junior" Davis.

College basketball continued on a somewhat limited scale. Stanford was the 1942 national champion, with Wyoming winning the championship and a special tourney against the NIT winner, St. John's, in 1943. Utah took it all in 1944, and Oklahoma A&M, with seven-foot Bob Kurland, beat a DePaul team with a soon-to-be superstar, George Mikan, in 1945.

The National Basketball Association (NBA) was not established until 1946 but two leagues did function during the war: the National Basketball League (NBL) and the American Basketball League (ABL).

Professional boxing continued, but with a noticeably inferior crop of fighters. The "Brown Bomber," Joe Louis, much-admired heavyweight champion of the world in the 1930s, was drafted in 1942. He served throughout the war in special services and helped promote the black cause for equal rights in the military.

Baseball

All professional and college sports experienced a drastic decrease in the number of players during the war. Baseball was the hardest hit. More than 5,700 men played in the major and minor leagues in 1941, and more than 4,000 of them eventually served in the military. Forty-one minor leagues were in existence at the start of the war, but only nine continued throughout the war years. Night baseball was suspended in many cities until 1944, which resulted in many twilight games.

President Roosevelt advocated the continuance of professional baseball and in a letter to baseball commissioner, Judge Kennesaw Mountain Landis in January 1942 stated:

"Baseball provides a recreation which does not last over two hours or two hours and a half, and which can be got for very little cost... 300 teams use 5,000 or 6,000 players, these players are a definite recreational asset to at least 20,000,000 of their fellow citizens - and that in my judgment is thoroughly worthwhile."

The 1941 season was over before the Pearl Harbor attack, but the raging war in Europe was already exacting a toll on the players. Hank Greenberg, the American League's most valuable player in 1940, was the first major leaguer to enter the service, after playing in only 19 games in 1941.

The attention-grabber for the 1941 season was, of course, New York Yankees player Joe DiMaggio and his 56 consecutive game hitting streak that started on May 15 and ended on July 17, a feat that has yet to be broken. The World Series, playing to record-breaking crowds in Yankee Stadium, saw the New York Yankees beat their cross-town rivals, the Brooklyn Dodgers, four games to two.

In the first wartime season, 1942, many players were drafted or enlisted. The St. Louis Cardinals brought up Stan Musial, a 21-year-old outfielder from the minors who would be immortalized in the game, although his career would be interrupted by military service in 1945. The Red Sox's great player, Ted Williams, would also have his career interrupted.

The New York Yankees won the pennant again with Joe McCarthy at the helm but lost in the series to the St. Louis Cardinals. The biggest news of the season happened not on the field but in the front office when Branch Rickey, who had built up the Cardinals with a strong farm team system, jumped to the rival Brooklyn Dodgers, as their new general manager.

During the last two-and-a-half-years of the war, the major league teams scrambled for players, mainly very young or older players, some of whom were called out of retirement. Travel restrictions were imposed, and a government order limited spring training to the northern cities, further hindering the orderly development of the game.

Baseball did serve a very useful purpose, in helping people to forget, even for a few hours, the violent headlines of war news. Many famous stars, however, including Joe DiMaggio, Phil Rizzuto and Ted Williams, were gone in 1943.

New York once again became the American League champs and they clobbered the Cardinals in the World Series five games to one.

Further depletion in the ranks of major league stars occurred in 1944, and more players from the 1930s came out of retirement to fill up the ball teams to keep the league functioning.

The year would be noted for a down-to-the-wire finish in the American League pennant race with the St. Louis Browns edging out New York, Boston and Detroit. Their cross-town rivals won the National League pennant in the most lopsided race since the early 1900s.

St. Louis was assured of a world

championship, but it would not go to the Browns, who lost four games to two. It would be their only World Series appearance.

Baseball would play its final season of the war almost through world series time. Travel restrictions canceled the All-Star game, the only year this occurred during the war. The game also got a new commissioner when Kentucky's U.S. Senator, Albert B. (Happy) Chandler was selected to replace Judge Kennesaw Mountain Landis, who died in November 1944.

Some players started returning to civilian life in 1945, including the Tigers' Hank Greenberg, who donned his old uniform in mid-season. His return helped his team win the pennant and beat the Chicago Cubs four games to three in the World Series.

The national pastime had weathered the storm, as had other American institutions. In all, the National League sent 31 players to the service in 1942, 100 in 1943, 174 in 1944 and 204 in 1945. The American League sent 40 in 1942, 119 in 1943, 168 in 1944 and 180 in 1945.

Branch Rickey, president of the Brooklyn Dodgers, had promised his mother that he would not go to the ballpark on Sundays. He broke his promise only once - when a war bond sale was dedicated to his Dodgers, and he was honored before the game. He left before the game started. Here Rickey is speaking into a mike held by well-known sports announcer, Red Barber. NATIONAL BASEBALL HALL OF FAME

Hank Greenberg, left, famous baseball player for the Detroit Tigers, and Harry Gowdy, right, coach of the Cincinnati Reds. Greenberg was the first major league player to join the military, just a few days after the Pearl Harbor attack. He joined the U.S. Army Air Force and became an administrative officer for a B-29 unit in China. He attained the rank of captain and was discharged in June 1945. Gowdy had been the first major league player to join the military during the First World War. NATIONAL BASEBALL HALL OF FAME

Brooklyn Dodgers contributed 10 percent of their salaries to war bonds during the war years and then voted to buy an extra $50 bond each to be given away by the Treasury Department during the month of April. It was veteran outfielder, John Cooney, who conceived the idea of the players buying bonds to be given away as a sales stimulant. Cooney first presented the plan to club manager, Leo Durocher, and then to players, who gave it an immediate favorable response. Left to right: Kirby Higbe, Bucky Newson, Valerie Harding, chairman of the Canteen Corps, A.W.V.S. of Brooklyn, Leo Durocher, John Cooney, Betty Leggatt, co-chairman, and Mickey Owen. Photo taken at Ebbetts Field, Brooklyn, New York. NATIONAL BASEBALL HALL OF FAME

The 1944 World Series pitted cross-town rivals, the St. Louis Cardinals and the St. Louis Browns. This scene in the fourth inning of the final game on Oct. 9 shows the Card's Ray Sanders starting his slide into home plate. The Cards scored three runs, won the game three to one and the series, four games to two. It was the only World Series appearance by the St. Louis Browns. NATIONAL BASEBALL HALL OF FAME

Football

The National Football League (NFL) had been in existence for some two decades when America entered the war. The Western Division consisted of five teams: the Chicago Bears, Chicago Cardinals, Green Bay Packers, Detroit Lions and Cleveland Rams. The Eastern Division also had five teams: the New York Giants, Brooklyn Tigers, Washington Redskins, Pittsburgh Steelers and Philadelphia Eagles.

The league sent 638 men to the service during the war; two players, Young Bussey of the Chicago Bears and Jack Lummies of New York, would die in action.

The 1941 title game, played two weeks after the Pearl Harbor attack, had an understandably low attendance. The Chicago Bears beat the New York Giants, 37 to 9.

The 1942 title game, played before a much bigger audience in the wartime capital, was won by Washington over the Bears, 14 to 6.

Montana State College (now University) located in Bozeman, Mont., lost its entire 1940-41 football season team during the war. It was the only college to experience this disaster. The roster included: end Dana Bradford; tackle John Burke; tackle Newell Burke; guard Bernard Cluzen; end John Hall Jr.; guard Joseph McGreener; backfield John Phelan; backfield Rick Roman; backfield Wendell Scabad; quarterback Alton Zempel and center Albert Zupin.

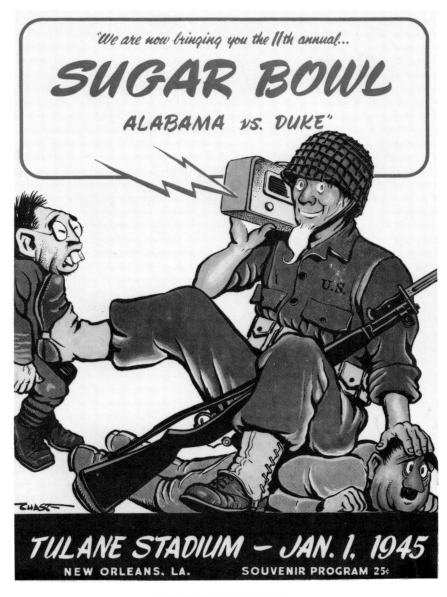

DUKE UNIVERSITY ARCHIVES

Because of the depleted ranks of players, Philadelphia and Pittsburgh merged for the 1943 season. Sid Luckman of the Chicago Bears and Sammy Baugh of the Washington Redskins, two of the league's greatest players, played in the 1943 title game with Baugh's team coming out on top, 41 to 21.

During the 1944 season teams again combined because of the shortage of players. The Chicago Cardinals and Pittsburgh Steelers merged into the Western Division with a new franchise at Boston, called the Yanks, and the Cleveland Rams returned to the Western Division after suspending the 1943 season. The Green Bay Packers beat the New York Giants in the title game, 14 to 7.

In the last year of the war, the Brooklyn Tigers merged with the Boston Yanks in the Eastern Division and Cleveland squeaked by Washington 15 to 14 in a bitterly cold title game.

Washington Redskins pose in front of the U.S. Capitol. PRO FOOTBALL HALL OF FAME, CANTON, OHIO

A halftime ceremony at Memorial Stadium, University of California in Berkeley, 1942. ROBERT STINNETT, OAKLAND, CALIF.

ROSE BOWL

55,000 football fans jammed the stadium at Durham, N.C., for the 1942 Rose Bowl game. DUKE UNIVERSITY ARCHIVES

The annual Rose Bowl game on New Year's Day is one of America's greatest sports spectaculars. Duke University from North Carolina and Oregon State were the opposing teams for the 1942 game to be played in Pasadena, Calif. The game was to be played just three weeks after the Pearl Harbor attack and the West Coast was still in a state of panic, with the possibility of a Japanese attack still on the minds of the citizens. Duke had been to the Rose Bowl in 1939, and this time expected to travel west in its own train called the "Blue Devil Special." But because of wartime scares in California, it was decided to move the game away from the coast. It was thought that thousands of fans jammed into the Rose Bowl would offer a tempting target for Japanese planes. There was talk of moving the game to Soldiers Field in Chicago, but Duke's coach, Wallace Wade, was concerned about bad weather at that time of year. The Rose Bowl directors ultimately accepted an offer to move the game to Durham, N.C., where the weather was better and the threat of an enemy air raid was remote. (Did anyone think of a possible German air attack?) The Oregon State team came across country by train and won the game before 55,000 spectators jammed into a 35,000-person stadium. (Bleachers had to be placed in the end zone.) As it turned out, the weather was awful that day in Durham, which was not unusual for that time of year. Coach Wade spent more of his time hosting Oregon State than coaching his own team.

DUKE UNIVERSITY ARCHIVES

Personalities

Many sports personalities from college and pro teams as well as individual sports stars served in the military.

Several famous boxers served their country. Heavyweight boxing champ Jack Dempsey was rejected by the army as being overage but was accepted by the Coast Guard and became a physical fitness director and morale officer at a base in New York. He also participated in the Okinawa campaign.

Famous 1930s heavyweight Joe Louis was drafted into the army in 1942 and gave boxing demonstrations for the troops. On Jan. 12, 1942, he fought Buddy Baer for a Navy Relief Society benefit. By a special waiver Louis was buried in Arlington National Cemetery although he was not in combat during the war. Rocky Marciano and Barney Ross, famous boxers before and after the war, also served.

Baseball contributed many men to the military. Hank Greenberg, of the Detroit Tigers, was the first major league player to enlist, a few days after the Pearl Harbor attack. Hank Gowdy was the only pro baseball player who served in both world wars. Lou Brissie, a pitcher, lost part of his leg in combat but, after many operations, was fitted with an aluminum plate and continued to play ball until 1953.

Other well-known baseball players who served in the military included: Stan Musial, Warren Spahn, Joe DiMaggio and his brother Dominick, Bob Feller, "Yogi" Berra, Gil Hodges, Hoyt Wilhelm, Ted Williams, Jackie Jensen, "Pee Wee" Reese, Jackie Robinson and Phil Rizzuto.

Several baseball managers or future managers and executives also served including Bill Veeck, Danny Murtaugh, Ralph Houk and Hank Bauer.

The sport of football also contributed its share of servicemen. "Woody" Hayes, longtime coach at Ohio State University, ran exercise programs for navy recruits. Tom Landry, former Dallas Cowboys coach, flew B-17s in Europe. Jack Lummus, All-American player at Baylor University, was killed on Iwo Jima. Pro players Johnny Lu-Jack, Ernest Pannell and Ken Kavanaugh also served.

Olympic track star, Charles Paddock, once known as the fastest man in the world, joined the Marines and was killed in a plane crash in Alaska. Tennis stars Gardner Mulloy and Bobby Riggs were both in the navy, and famous race car driver, Barney Oldfield, who was already in his 60s, became an army public relations officer.

Songwriter Frank Loesser read about Navy Chaplain Howell Forgy, who was stationed on board the *USS New Orleans* during the Pearl Harbor attack. Forgy called out to a sailor during the attack and stated his now famous phrase, "Praise the Lord and pass the ammunition." This became one of the most famous expressions to come out of the war.

AMERICA'S SONGSTRESS

Of all the performers on radio during the war years, none could match the versatile, robust, Kate Smith. Her untrained voice was familiar to most Americans, especially in her rendition of Irving Berlin's "God Bless America," which was an unofficial national anthem during the war. Along with her theme song, "When the Moon Comes Over the Mountain," she rivaled and ultimately displaced Rudy Vallee as the number one radio show attraction of the 1930s. Perhaps her greatest contribution to the war effort was her vast radio appeal which produced the largest war bond sales by an entertainer. In her career she introduced more than 700 songs, 19 of which sold more than a million copies each. After the war she starred in her own television show and made numerous guest appearances. She died in Raleigh, N.C., in June 1986.

The music that you hear in malls, supermarkets, etc., *Muzak*, originated in Cleveland in 1934, transmitting music over telephone lines to hotels and restaurants. New vistas opened for *Muzak* with studies showing that it reduced fatigue among war plant workers.

Glenn Miller
written by Edward F. Polic

Alton Glen Miller, better known as Glenn Miller, was born in Clarinda, Iowa, on 1 March 1904. In his early years the Miller family moved several times. In Grant City, Missouri, at the age of 12, Glenn Miller acquired his first trombone. In 1918 the family moved to Fort Morgan, Colorado, where Glenn Miller honed and polished his skills on that instrument. From an early age his first love was music. He missed his high school graduation to take his first professional job on the road as trombonist with the Boyd Senter band.

When the Senter job ended he returned to Colorado to attend the University of Colorado in Boulder, while at the same time playing in local bands. Music took precedence over studies and before long Miller was playing in territory bands. In 1925 in Los Angeles, he joined Ben Pollack and His Californians as trombonist and arranger. The Pollack band took him to Chicago for two years and then to New York City in early 1928. In New York his playing and arranging talents were much in demand. Not only was he a member of the bands of Paul Ash and Red Nichols, but he was also on hundreds of recordings by many bands.

In 1932 Glenn Miller put together and managed a band, in addition to arranging and playing in it, for Smith Ballew. That was his first taste of running a musical organization. In 1934 he put together, played in, and arranged for, the Dorsey Brothers' Orchestra. In 1935 he organized the Ray Noble Orchestra. While with Ray Noble, Glenn Miller put together a pick up group and made the first recordings under his own name. In mid-1936 he worked with Vincent Lopez, and later that year did free-lance recordings. He was now ready to head out on his own.

At the beginning of 1937 he used his savings to organize his first band. The band was good, and made several recordings, but had no identifiable style, and had some personnel problems. The next year he started with a new band and during that year developed his very distinctive five reed sound (clarinet and tenor saxophone playing the melody an octave apart, with the other three reeds providing the harmony in between). Very quickly that band rose

Capt. Glenn Miller and the 418th Army Air Force Band at the Shangri-La War Bond and Stamp Rally, July 28, 1943 at the Yale Bowl, Yale University, New Haven, Conn. This was a rally to raise money for a new aircraft carrier named Shangri-La. COURTESY EDWARD POLIC, MILPITAS, CALIF.

to the top in popularity polls and record sales. In 1942 they completed their second (and very successful) motion picture, "Orchestra Wives," and the United States was at war.

Glenn Miller did much to promote the sales of War Bonds and Stamps, and to play tribute to and entertain the U.S. troops. That was not enough for him. In the summer of 1942, at the peak of his popularity, he attempted to enlist his entire band in the U.S. Navy, as an entertainment unit, but the Navy was not interested. He then went to the Army and offered his services to organize modern musical units to entertain the troops. The Army accepted. At the end of September 1942, amid the tears of his fans and band members, Glenn Miller broke up his band and a few days later became Capt. Alton Glenn Miller.

Within six months Miller put together what was to become the most famous band that had ever existed or will ever exist. The band started its life on 20 March 1943 as the 418th AAF Band, located at Yale University in

New Haven, Connecticut, playing for base functions. Two months later the band began a local radio program called "I Sustain the Wings," the motto of the U.S. Army Air Forces. In July 1943 the band began broadcasting "I Sustain the Wings" coast-to-coast. At the same time the band was continually playing and entertaining at War Bond and Stamp Rallies, recruiting drives and hospitals. The band was one of the largest fund raisers and morale boosters in existence.

That was not enough for Glenn Miller. He wanted to entertain the fighting troops in person and made every effort to get his band transferred to England. With D-Day came a telegram from Gen. Dwight D. Eisenhower transferring the band to England, where it became designated "Glenn Miller Band Special." For six months in England the band did hundreds of broadcasts and hundreds of concerts at theaters and bases all over England, bringing a touch of home to the troops.

At the end of 1944, with France liberated, Glenn Miller wanted to take his band closer to the troops, in France. With a supreme effort in an 18-day period the band pre-recorded 83 broadcasts, while maintaining their normal schedule of broadcasts and concerts, in order to cover their broadcasting schedule while they would entertain the troops in the Paris area. On 15 December 1944 Glenn Miller took off, with a pilot and another officer, in a small single-engine aircraft, for Paris, to make preparations for his band. Three days later the band flew to Paris, only to find that Miller had never arrived. No trace of the aircraft has ever been found. The official missing aircraft inquiry concluded that the aircraft went down in the English Channel.

It is a tribute to Glenn Miller's organizational talents that his band continued very successfully under the musical leadership of Ray McKinley (drummer in the band) and Jerry Gray (arranger in the band). The band entertained the troops in France, and after V-E Day, all over Europe. They returned to the U.S. in August 1945 and resumed their "I Sustain the Wings" broadcasts. At the end of 1945 the band members were discharged.

In January 1946 most of the band members of Glenn Miller Army Air Force Band became members of the Glenn Miller Orchestra under the direction of Tex Beneke, which continued the distinctive Glenn Miller music. The Glenn Miller Orchestra remains fully booked even as you read this. Original Glenn Miller recordings are still being issued. Radio stations still feature his music, and several television specials on Glenn Miller have aired.

For more information on Glenn Miller, join the Glenn Miller Birthplace Society, P.O. Box 61, Clarinda, Iowa 51632, or The Glenn Miller Society, 3 Pine View Close, Verwood, Wimborne, Dorset BH21 6NN England. For a detailed account of Glenn Miller's last band read, *The Glenn Miller Army Air Force Band* by Edward F. Polic, Scarecrow Press, P.O. Box 4167, Metuchen, NJ 08840, 1-800-537-7107.

Famous songwriter Irving Berlin made a rare screen appearance in a film adapted from his 1942 stage tribute to the army. He sang one of his most popular songs from the show, the World War I song, *Oh, How I Hate to Get Up in the Morning,* in a quavering voice. The film was released by Warners in 1943.

WARTIME HIT PARADE

No other war had so many memorable songs, many that are still in vogue today.

• *I LEFT MY HEART AT THE STAGE DOOR CANTEEN* Sammy Kaye/Don Cornell • *DADDY* Sammy Kaye • *CHICKERY CHICK* Sammy Kaye • *DER FUEHRER'S FACE* Spike Jones • *MY DREAMS ARE GETTING BETTER ALL THE TIME* Les Brown/Doris Day • *SATURDAY NIGHT (IS THE LONELIEST NIGHT OF THE WEEK)* Frank Sinatra • *SOMEBODY ELSE IS TAKING MY PLACE* Benny Goodman/Peggy Lee • *I DON'T WANT TO SET THE WORLD ON FIRE* Horace Heidt/Larry Cotton/Donna Wood & Don Juans • *YOU'LL NEVER KNOW* Dick Haymes • *CHATTANOOGA CHOO CHOO* Glenn Miller/Tex Beneke/ The Modernaires w/Paula Kelly • *I'VE HEARD THAT SONG BEFORE* Harry James/Helen Forrest • *I'LL BE SEEING YOU* Bing Crosby • *MAIRZY DOATS* Merry Macs • *RUM AND COCA COLA* Andrews Sisters • *DANCE WITH A DOLLY (WITH A HOLE IN HER STOCKING)* Russ Morgan/Al Jennings • *I'LL WALK ALONE* Dinah Shore • *PIANO CONCERTO IN B FLAT* Freddy Martin/Jack Fina, piano • *THERE! I'VE SAID IT AGAIN* Vaughn Monroe • *IT'S BEEN A LONG, LONG TIME* Harry James/Kitty Kallen • *OH! WHAT IT SEEMED TO BE* Frankie Carle/Marjorie Hughes • *DON'T FENCE ME IN* Bing Crosby & Andrews Sisters • *SENTIMENTAL JOURNEY* Les Brown/Doris Day • *GREEN EYES* Jimmy Dorsey w/Bob Eberly & Helen O'Connell • *I'LL NEVER SMILE AGAIN* Tommy Dorsey w/Frank Sinatra & Pied Pipers • *BOOGIE WOOGIE BUGLE BOY* Andrews Sisters • *PISTOL PACKIN' MAMA* Al Dexter • *JINGLE, JANGLE, JINGLE* Kay Kyser/Julie Conway/Harry Babbit • *TILL THE END OF TIME* Perry Como • *WHEN THE LIGHTS GO ON AGAIN (ALL OVER THE WORLD)* Vaughn Monroe • *TO EACH HIS OWN* Ink Spots • *PRAISE THE LORD AND PASS THE AMMUNITION* Kay Kyser • *DON'T GET AROUND MUCH ANYMORE* Ink Spots • *SWINGING ON A STAR* Bing Crosby • *I'LL GET BY (AS LONG AS I HAVE YOU)* Harry James/Dick Haymes • *AS TIME GOES BY* Rudy Vallee • *IN THE MOOD* Glenn Miller • *COMIN' IN ON A WING AND A PRAYER* Song Spinners • *SHOO SHOO BABY* Andrews Sisters • *DON'T SIT UNDER THE APPLE TREE (WITH ANYONE ELSE BUT ME)* Glenn Miller/Marion Hutton, Tex Beneke, The Modernaires • *YOU ALWAYS HURT THE ONE YOU LOVE* Mills Brothers • *THERE ARE SUCH THINGS* Tommy Dorsey/Frank Sinatra & Pied Pipers • *AC-CENT-TCHU-ATE THE POSITIVE* Bing Crosby/Andrews Sisters • *DEEP IN THE HEART OF TEXAS* Bing Crosby • *(THERE'LL BE BLUEBIRDS OVER) THE WHITE CLIFFS OF DOVER* Kay Kyser

In the four months after Pearl Harbor, wedding ring sales jumped 300 percent. Then across the nation, the war wrenched sweethearts apart, and Tin Pan Alley set to music every possible twist in the story of "*A Boy in Khaki - A Girl in Lace*." While the women back home tearfully mused, "*If He Can Fight Like He Can Love*," in boot camp men hummed "*I've Got a Gal in Kalamazoo*" while "*Cleaning My Rifle (And Dreaming of You)*." Though he'd left promising "*I'll Be Home for Christmas*," as the war dragged on, he soon changed his tune to "*I Won't Be Back in a Year, Little Darlin'*." But when her soldier sang "*Wait for Me, Mary*," she chorused "*I'll Keep the Love Light Burning*." Then finally he was able to croon, "*I'll Be Walking with My Honey Soon, Soon, Soon*." At long last she could sing "*Welcome Home*." After she trilled "*I'm Glad I Waited for You*," they sang in perfect harmony "*It's Been a Long, Long Time*."

Well-known music personalities who served in the military included Woodrow Wilson, "Woody" Guthrie, Lyle "Skitch" Henderson, Al Hirt and Henry Mancini.

Irving Berlin, America's greatest songwriter, wrote many patriotic songs during the war including, *Any Bonds Today* in 1941 and *Angels of Mercy* in 1942.

Eddy Duchin, famous pianist, enlisted in the Navy in 1942 and trained with anti-submarine detection equipment because of his perfect pitch and excellent hearing. He took part in the D-Day, Iwo Jima and Okinawa invasions.

HOLLYWOOD GOES TO WAR

This 1944 film was adapted from Ted Lawson's popular wartime narrative of the daring April 18, 1942, air raid on Tokyo.

Spencer Tracy, as General James Doolittle, approves a romantic twosome, Phyllis Thaxter and Van Johnson

MGM's "THIRTY SECONDS OVER TOKYO"

Hollywood's first wartime propaganda film concerned the heroic fight for Wake Island in December 1941.

BRIAN DONLEVY
MACDONALD CAREY
ROBERT PRESTON
WAKE ISLAND
ALBERT DEKKER
WILLIAM BENDIX
WALTER ABEL
DIRECTED BY JOHN FARROW
A PARAMOUNT PICTURE

A prewar film released by MGM in 1939, *Babes in Arms*, starred Mickey Rooney as President Roosevelt and Judy Garland as Mrs. Roosevelt, a highly unusual team to impersonate the first family. This scene is from the patriotic finale, "God's Country."

Those War Films - Fact, Fiction, Impact

by Jack W. Jaunal

The war films that "Hollywood was eager and willing" to produce during World War II were made for two basic reasons, profit and propaganda. Between 1942 and 1945, propaganda was of prime importance. It was only during the last six months of the conflict that films appeared which depicted war in more realistic terms. As might be expected, some of these pictures were of high quality while others rated poorly. *The Story of G.I. Joe*, based on the Pulitzer Prize awarded stories of war correspondent Ernie Pyle, received praise from critics as well as from combat-wise soldiers themselves. Of the films rated less enthusiastically, *A Yank on the Burma Road*, was one of the first, and worst. Released only seven weeks after the Japanese attack on Pearl Harbor it was, according to one film critic, "glib humbug." Lacking realism and plausibility, films of the latter quality were justly criticized, particularly by those individuals who knew about war from their own experiences.

A war film can be defined as one in which individuals are portrayed in battle in a recognized military action or in which they are directly or indirectly influenced by actual combat. The war films of that time had two special stimuli peculiar to them alone: (1) there was a great public want for information about the war, even in recreated, edited, artificial from; and (2) war films bolstered home front morale by showing audiences "the American fighting man" and "our boys" in combat. They also motivated war industry workers with the importance of their jobs in manufacturing arms and equipment, "the tools of war."

Stories for war films usually originated in the studio story department, which searched all possible sources of material in magazines, books, stage plays, news reports and old pictures. Even one of President Franklin D. Roosevelt's "fireside chats" provided the source for a film, *The Story of Dr. Wassell* (1944). Roosevelt told about the exploits of a navy doctor, Commander Corydon M. Wassell, who stayed with

This idyllic film was released in 1940. Just a year later this part of the world would erupt in savage warfare and movies such as *Wake Island* and *Bataan* would immortalize the American soldier even in defeat.

eight wounded sailors, all stretcher cases, during the Japanese invasion of Java, and managed to get all of them to Australia alive. Unfortunately, Wassell's "saga of simple heroism" became submerged amid "a typical Hollywood entertainment feature." Roosevelt told the story more briefly and cogently.

Books relating to the war, especially firsthand accounts by individuals like war correspondent Richard Tregaskis, *Guadalcanal Diary* (1943); Captain Ted W. Lawson, *Thirty Seconds Over Tokyo* (1943); and Colonel Robert L. Scott, *God Is My Co-Pilot* (1943); were eagerly sought. Screen rights for Scott's book had been purchased before the book was published.

Guadalcanal Diary was "a resourceful adaptation of correspondent Richard Tregaskis' best selling war book, and a straightforward, exciting picture" about the U.S. Marines in America's first counter offensive in World War II. While the film is true to the spirit of the book, it was primarily a film version of history which involved some altering of fact for dramatic effect. One example is the ill-fated Goettge patrol from which there were only three survivors. In the film there is only one survivor of the slaughtered patrol. The film has a documentary quality about it, especially the first half, and follows the Marines from their pre-landing shipboard briefings through two months of hardship and fighting until they are relieved by fresh army troops. However, "the picture never makes clear how desperately expendable the Marines felt on Guadalcanal."

Thirty Seconds Over Tokyo was a "re-created picture" of one of America's "boldest blows" in the Pacific war, the famous "Doolittle raid" over Tokyo (April 18, 1942). Although intended to be factual, for security reasons the film did not tell the entire story of the raid. The actual bombing did little damage to the targets at the cost of every one of Doolittle's planes. By the use of true names of many of the raiders, well-staged battle sequences and aerial photography, the feel of a war documentary was provided. Even with its flaws the film was "a very sincere effort to...remain true to a true story."

God Is My Co-Pilot, after 16 months of preparation, 12 weeks of filming, cooperation of the army air corps, "and the expenditure of thousands of dollars," was released to the public (1945). "Colonel Scott's popular, vivid story of his career as a fighter pilot in the Far East" became just "another rather cheaply theatrical war film."

By combining fact and fiction, the studios produced many dramatic films to bring to life the conflict for audiences. However, the wartime populace preferred fiction to fact as evidenced by the poor response to the many feature length documentaries about the war. Documentaries were fact, real names and real people dying. Audiences preferred to see *Edge of Darkness* in which Errol Flynn killed hundreds of Germans or *Objective Burma* in which he killed the same number of Japanese; fiction was "more interesting." A film review of *Edge of Darkness* (1943) reported that "The final, climactic battle between the Nazis and the villagers is a pip; so many have not fallen so graphically since the United States Cavalry and Mr. Flynn died very gallantly with their boots on back there at the Little Big Horn." "At the rate Errol Flynn and company knock off the Japanese" in *Objective Burma* (1945), reported one film review, "it makes you wonder why there is any good reason for the war to outlast next weekend...."

Most films of this genre always said the right thing about the enemy. The Nazis were portrayed as cultured swine; they could be brutal, but were intellectual about it all. This view is brought forth by the German garrison commander in the film, *The Moon is Down* (1943). Because all Germans were not Nazis, a distinction was sometimes made between them and the callous Nazi that became the most common stereotype. The captured German flyer in the film *Sahara* (1943) is one example

of the Nazi who remained dedicated to Hitler's philosophy of the master race. The Italians were stereotyped as being "unlike the Germans." They were portrayed, for the most part, like an Italian prisoner in the film *Sahara*, who makes a statement that the Fascist uniform covered only the body, not the soul. The Japanese were presented as savages, very fanatical, and sneaky, dirty fighters. Because the Chinese were our allies, racial slurs implicit in such terms as "yellow cowards," eventually were eliminated and the Japanese just became dirty cowards, rats and savages. The Japanese enemy always seemed to be more brutal, indulging in torture and rape to excess, and doing these things with obvious pleasure. In this way war films sought to impress the public with some of the realities of war, and in so doing stimulate patriotism, the war effort and ultimate victory of America.

Ultimate victory as a theme was stated in many of the initial films that dramatized the American armed forces in combat. The first was a fictionalized version of the Marines defending Wake Island in December of 1941. The film *Wake Island*, released in September 1942, succeeded both as wartime propaganda and engrossing entertainment. The story of the Marines at Wake was intended to be nothing less than a clarion call for the defense of freedom and a rallying point for all Americans. As history it was flawed, but so were many of the contemporary news reports about the battle, such as one account which wrongly reported that one of the last messages from Wake Island was, "Send us more Japs." After the war and his release from a Japanese prisoner of war camp, the commanding officer of the Marines defense battalion, Major James P.S. Devereux, claimed the message never originated from Wake because "More Japs was one thing we didn't need." The message, which the media tried to immortalize, had originated merely as padding to protect the cryptographic integrity of a message sent from Wake Island to Pearl Harbor. Immediately

after the message became public, three film companies registered "Send Us More Japs" as a film title.

Bataan (1943), another film based on news reports, told the story of a rear guard action by a squad of doomed American soldiers and one sailor in the final days of defending the Philippines. Like many war films, the idea for the film came from a screenwriter, who suggested a story set in the Philippines similar to *The Lost Patrol* (1934), a film about a British patrol lost in the desert and wiped out by Arabs. *Bataan* had stereotyped characters with individual identities and traits with which many people in the audience could identify. Among the characters portrayed is "one Negro soldier from the engineers...whose placement in the picture is one of the outstanding merits" of the film. *Bataan* was the first of the very few war films (*Sahara* was another) that had a realistic black character. Although the army was not then integrated, the portrayal of the black soldier is plausible considering combat conditions on Bataan at that time. Regardless of the film's fictional story and technical errors, as propaganda it prepared American audiences for a long struggle in the war and at the same time provided a feeling of pride in the gallantry of American soldiers as they faced certain death.

Another film of the "Lost Patrol" genre was *Sahara*, a story about an American tank and its crew in the Battle of El Alamein. The film not only had the stereotyped Nazi and Italian characters, but also a small group of other soldiers of various nationalities as well: three American tank crewmen, four British soldiers, a South African medical officer, a Free French soldier and a black Sudanese corporal. It is the black corporal who captures the Italian soldier and kills the Nazi prisoner in hand-to-hand combat. The film provides action, drama, and several propaganda messages. However, it was not World War II as it was being fought, since American tanks did not fight at El Alamein with the British Army. The film was "first rate entertainment" with an "unusual amount of honesty about war." For that reason "the whole unlikely affair seems believable."

"The most popular films with military heroines, *So Proudly We Hail*, depicted the struggles and bravery of army nurses on Bataan." The story was adapted from firsthand accounts of the fighting at Bataan and Corregidor during the Japanese invasion of the Philippines. The film, released in 1943, was an honest tribute to the spirit of American women, and it made a clear statement on the value of their part in the war. One noticeable fault in the film is the disheveled glamour of the film's nurses compared to the contemporary news photographs of the real army nurses at Bataan and Corregidor. One Army nurse survivor of Corregidor, Second Lieutenant Leona Gastinger, remarked that when she "saw the movie" after the war, she "knew it wasn't true." The nurses were not "zonked out from being in love" and no one "blew herself up with a hand grenade. Those things just didn't happen." The film does, however, present "a heartfelt, but highly fictional, tribute to the army nurses on Bataan."

In the *Air Force* (1943), the "heroine is a Flying Fortress named Mary Ann." Beginning with the historical fact that a squadron of Flying Fortresses arrived in Hawaii during the attack on Pearl Harbor, the film follows the "Mary Ann" across the Pacific to Wake Island, to the Philippines, to the Battle of the Coral Sea and a crash landing on the coast of Australia. The film is an effective blending of historical facts with a fictionalized story which creates an illusion of reality. One of the historically false statements in the picture is the Japanese sabotage of American aircraft on the ground at Hickam Field during the attack on Pearl Harbor. Regardless of the propaganda messages it offered,

most audiences seemed to enjoy *Air Force* as escapist entertainment.

Early war films, such as *Wake Island, Bataan, So Proudly We Hail*, fiction based on factual events, aroused audience emotions and brought forth a surge of national pride. The message was always there: America will win the war, we lost the first battles against a sneak attack and overwhelming enemy forces, but in the end victory will be ours. Not only did the early war movies provide a message of hope for ultimate victory, but acted as a catharsis for Pearl Harbor and early battles lost. The climactic scenes of *Air Force*

Not all movies made during the war portrayed death and destruction. *Meet Me in St. Louis*, released by MGM in 1944, starred Judy Garland and Tom Drake, and centered around a romantic theme at the 1904 St. Louis World's Fair.

Yankee Doodle Dandy, released by Warners in 1942, had a patriotic theme but was good solid entertainment and was one of the most popular films of the period. James Cagney played famous songwriter, George M. Cohan. Cohan would accept only Cagney in the role, and Cagney, himself a song-and-dance man in the early days of his career, leaped at the opportunity.

in which hundreds of Japanese are killed in the Battle of the Coral Sea brought forth not only applause, but shouts of joy from audiences. Films of this type which prophesied victory, repeated enough times, inevitably provided a positive influence on home front morale and the war effort.

As American forces shifted from the defense to offensive action in 1942, the Guadalcanal and North Africa landings, war pictures began to reflect those events. American successes on the battlefield provided a source with greater historical fact, either depicting actual events or a synthesis of several combat actions that were combined for dramatic effect. Although the majority of war movies, especially the early ones, emphasized the Pacific war, it was the war in Europe that provided some of the most authentic contemporary products.

War films, regardless of authenticity, were not the favorites of the military overseas. According to the Army Overseas Motion Picture Service surveys, soldiers overseas preferred "musicals, comedies, mysteries, romantic dramas, documentaries, and newsreels showing authentic war action." A similar survey conducted by *Newsweek* in 1943 follows the same pattern. Only two war films and two with military themes were among the favorite films listed. *Wake Island* and *Sergeant York* were the war films. *To the Shores of Tripoli* and *Captains of the Clouds* had military themes. One year later, 1944, a Time survey reported that, "Almost without exception, G.I.s liked musical comedies best, comedies next best, and then adventure films and melodramas." Without exception, "they disliked tinhorn war and home-front heroics." "But *Destination Tokyo*, a war film about submarine warfare, earned a certain respect."

Destination Tokyo, released in December 1943, depicted a submarine crew that was united in their effort to win the war and return home as quickly as possible, a wartime goal still in the future when the film was released. Although not a true story, many of the fictionalized incidents in the film reflected what did happen during the war. Submarines did enter Tokyo Bay, a submarine did radio weather information for Doolittle's raiders, and an American submarine did sink a Japanese aircraft carrier. *Destination Tokyo* was the second of only two war films of World War II to receive The New York Times "Best Film of the Year" award. *Air Force* received the award for 1943, *Destination Tokyo* for 1944. Both films were factual if fictionalized, and considered first rate entertainment for wartime showing.

Some of the most authentic war films were released in the last few months of the war, and two *They Were Expendable* (1945) and *A Walk in the Sun* (1946) were still in production when the war ended. Films like *Bataan* only hinted at the true nature of the war because much of the story came from a screenwriter's imagination. In contrast, *The Story of G.I. Joe*, released in April 1945 showed the reality of World War II ground combat. It did so because the film was based on the reporting of Ernie Pyle, who had experienced combat and was able to put what he had seen into words. *G.I. Joe* had no plot or story that built up to a climax. It simply followed a group of infantrymen in Italy as they fought the enemy. Documentary in style, the film succeeded in visualizing Pyle's newspaper columns. Soldiers' names may have been changed but their combat experiences were real. Although the film version of Captain Henry T. Waskow's death is faithful to Pyle's description in one of his stories, the character in the film is named Walker. Some critics of the film have remarked that the name was changed because Waskow was not an American name. Regardless of any name changes, Pyle and nine fellow correspondents supervised and vouched for the film's authenticity. Some of that was provided by 150 soldiers, all combat veterans of the Italian campaign, who were used in the film. The result is an illusion of reality that few war films achieve. *The Story of G.I. Joe* "deliberately sets out to show that war is hell," succeeding "so well that it may be Ernie Pyle's most enduring memorial." The film was released the same month that Pyle was killed on Ie Shima.

They Were Expendable is a version of William L. White's best selling book with the same title. Based on fact, the story is an account of Navy Motor Torpedo Squadron Three during the Japanese invasion of the Philippines. "In trying to steer between war melodrama and straight documentary reporting," the film is a reminder that in war anything can be expendable - money or gasoline or equipment or, most usually, men. "The MTB's were like the rest" of the American forces in the Philippines, "the expendable to fight without hope to the end." Because the film was released after the war ended, it was not successful with an audience that was tired of war films. By that time the defense of the Philippines had become history.

The last of the World War II war films in production when the war ended, *A Walk in the Sun*, was a fictionalized account of one small combat action, a platoon-sized attack on a German fortified farmhouse a few miles inland from an Italian beachhead. By focusing on one small battle, the film provided a "feeling of reality" and demonstrated what actually happened on many battlefields of a global war. Some veterans of the U.S. Army's 36th (Texas) Infantry Division may have memories of a farmhouse attack, similar to the film's "Texas Division" soldiers. The film, released five months after the end of the war, was not popular with audiences. The realities of war had been replaced by musicals and escapist entertainment films.

Among the many war films produced there were several feature length documentaries about the war. Despite their overall excellence and favorable reviews, none of the war documentaries were very successful with the audiences. Like the better war films, by the time the best and least-censored of all documentaries were released, the public was tired of the war.

Because of the bravery of combat cameramen and the increasing skill of military film makers, the documentaries provided a panorama of the war in a manner which indicated that film was to be a history book of the future. Among the best of the documentaries was *The True Glory* (1945). It provides a history of the war in Europe from the Normandy invasion to the final days of Berlin, with the emphasis on the cooperative nature of the Allied war effort. Every nationality that took part in the battles to Berlin is represented in the film, which describes history through the eyes of the individuals who helped make it. Another very good documentary was *To The Shore of Iwo Jima* (1945), a motion picture that demonstrated "more clearly than any previous film, that war in its critical essence is neither dramatic nor even particularly human, but paroxysmic: that it is simply hell on earth." *Marines at Tarawa* (1944) was the first war documentary to show the American public an entire military operation in the Pacific war: the pre-landing bombardment, the tremendous enemy fire as the Marines waded ashore, the inch-by-inch advance against enemy positions, the "Stars and Stripes finally fluttering over the blood-soaked atoll." Although the film did not show any "Americans being wounded or killed," it was "war in the least expurgated form" for audiences at that time. *The Fighting Lady* (1945) was a "thrilling color record of an aircraft carrier," in scenes of violent action and visual magnificence. *The Battle of San Pietro* (1945) is among the best and the last of the war documentaries. San Pietro, set on the lower slopes of Mount Sammucro in Italy, had observation across a mile wide valley which American troops called "Death Valley." The Americans could only capture the town by outflanking it, and dominating the heights above it. This they did and the combat cameramen at San Pietro recorded the cost in American lives. "These lives were valuable," states the narrator (John Huston), "valuable to their loved ones, to their country, and to the men themselves."

Documentaries such as these comprise an excellent pictorial history of the war and the ultimate hard won victory.

The movies of World War II presented a united America facing its enemies who were very real and very determined to win. The enemy was clearly perceived and the battle lines drawn; it was "us or them" and there was no question about it. "Us" were the "good guys" fighting for a noble cause. The brutal truths of World War II have been softened by time for a war whose issues and dangers are historical fact. Many of the films of that era, although fictionalized, are based on historical happenings. For that reason motion pictures in the genre of *Wake Island* to *The Story of G.I. Joe* provide a history of the war from Wake Island in the Pacific to the battlefield of the Italian campaign. They may not show later generations very much about the actual war. They will, however, show them many things about the American people of the time and consequently are in themselves recorded history.

Bette Davis sings "They're Either Too Young or Too Old," lamenting that the only available males in wartime are either "too gray" or "too grassy-green," from Warners 1943 movie, *Thank Your Lucky Stars*.

The *March of Time*, produced by *Time* magazine, was a very popular movie featurette which was issued every four weeks and depicted news both at home and overseas.

Famous songwriter, Irving Berlin, made a rare screen appearance in a film adapted from his 1942 stage tribute to the army. He sang one of his most popular songs from the show, the World War I song, *Oh, How I Hate to Get Up in the Morning*, in a quavering voice. The film was released by Warners in 1943.

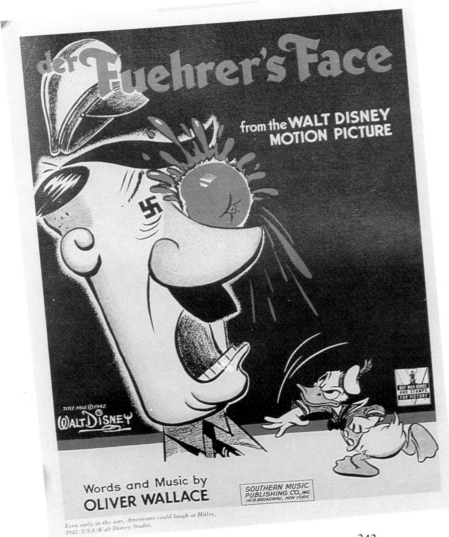

The entire business of the Walt Disney Studios was devoted to the war effort from 1942 on. Many military symbols such as those of the Seabees and the Flying Tigers came from the studio. This 1942 film, *Der Fuehrer's Face*, poked fun at the Führer using one of Disney's most popular cartoon characters, Donald Duck. The music score was written by Oliver Wallace and recorded by Spike Jones and his City Slickers.

This 1943 movie portrayed one of America's greatest military defeats in the Philippines in the spring of 1942.

Joe E. Brown, Hollywood comedian, traveled over 200,000 miles during the war to entertain troops. He and correspondent Ernie Pyle were the only civilians during the war to be awarded the Bronze Star. Brown traveled at his own expense. His son was killed in a military plane crash.

A rather fictionalized version of the trial of flyers who crashed in China and were captured by the Japanese following the famous Doolittle Raid on Tokyo on April 18, 1942.

Rationing was the theme of this 1944 movie starring two old-time actors, Wallace Beery and Marjorie Main.

Movies were a prime vehicle for propaganda against the Nazi menace. Hitler was a villain in most of these movies.

ONLY the Nazis don't think it's so funny

The amazing adventures of a cockney scrubwoman who set out from London to get that 'orrid 'itler man—and almost succeeded! ... Laugh and thrill as you see the Nazis go nuts over the "super-spy in soapsuds!"

PASSPORT TO DESTINY

with
LANCHESTER · OLIVER · AUBERT

Produced by HERMAN SCHLOM · Directed by RAY McCAREY
Original Screen Play by Val Burton and Muriel Roy Bolton

Copyright 1944 RKO Radio Pictures Inc.   Country of Origin U.S.A. 44/78

THEY LIVE IN FEAR
A COLUMBIA PICTURE

America's youthful rug-cutters meet a young ex-Hitler cut-throat in America.

PRINTED IN U.S.A.

One of Hollywood's most well-known directors, John Ford, joined the navy before the Pearl Harbor attack to command a photographic unit. He filmed many historical events during the war including the departure of Jimmy Doolittle's B-25s from the *USS Hornet* to bomb Tokyo in April 1942, and the Battle of Midway in June 1942, where he was wounded. His two wartime documentaries, *December 7th* and *The Battle of Midway*, both won Oscars.

The Oscar is Hollywood's major yearly award for outstanding pictures and performances. It is made of a mixture of tin, copper, antimony and electroplated nickel, gold and copper. During the war it was made of plaster, to be exchanged for the real thing at the end of hostilities.

WARD BOND
DOROTHY TREE
"HITLER—
DEAD OR ALIVE"

WARREN HYMER · PAUL FIX · RUSSELL HICKS · FELIX BASCH
BOB WATSON · BRUCE EDWARDS · FREDERICK GIERMANN

Prewar and Post-war movie and TV personalities who served in the military sometime between 1940-45.

ARMY

Desi Arnaz
James Arness
Joey Bishop
Neville Brand
Mel Brooks
Art Carney
John Derek
Hugh Downs
Allen Funt
Lorne Greene (Canadian Army)
Van Heflin
Hal Holbrook
William Holden
John Huston
George Kennedy
Stanley Kramer
Burt Lancaster
Karl Malden
Tim McCoy
Robert Mitchum
George Montgomery
Arthur O'Connell
Bert Parks
Sidney Poitier
Tony Randall
Ronald Reagan
Carl Reiner
Will Rogers Jr.
Mickey Rooney
Telly Savalas
Rod Serling
Red Skelton
Eli Wallach
Jack Warden
Efrem Zimbalist Jr.

NAVY & COAST GUARD

Eddie Albert
Richard Boone
Raymond Burr
Sid Caesar
Tony Curtis
Richard Denning
Billy De Wolfe
Buddy Ebsen
Tom Ewell
Henry Fonda
Rock Hudson
Gene Kelly
Jack Lemmon
Victor Mature
Robert Montgomery
Don Rickles
Jason Robards Jr.
Soupy Sales
Robert Stack
Rod Steiger
Robert Taylor

MARINES

Sterling Hayden
Bob Keesham
Ed McMahon
Hugh O'Brien
Tyrone Power
George C. Scott
James Whitmore
Jonathan Winters

AIR FORCE

Gene Autry
Charles Bronson
Bruce Cabot
Jackie Coogan
Robert Cummings
Sabu Dastagir
Clark Gable
George Gobel
Charlton Heston
Don Herbert
Alan Ladd
Norman Lear
Walter Matthau
Burgess Meredith
Cameron Mitchell
Tom Poston
Robert Preston
Dan Rowan
Mort Sahl
Jimmy Stewart
Dick Van Dyke
Jack Webb

MERCHANT MARINE

Carroll O'Connor
Cliff Robertson

Between 1942 and 1945 Hollywood produced some 1,700 feature films; of these, more than 500 dealt with the war in one form or another.

By March 1943 more than 27,000 members of the motion picture industry were in uniform including 132 members of the Screen Directors Guild.

Carole Lombard's press photo from her last movie, *To Be or Not To Be*, 1942. LARRY EDMUNDS BOOKSHOP, HOLLYWOOD, CALIF.

Hollywood's highest paid star in 1937 and one of its most popular, Carole Lombard appeared in dozens of movies beginning in 1921. In 1941 she, along with Jack Benny, starred in the movie *To Be or Not To Be*, set in Poland at the onset of the German invasion. They played two temperamental Shakespearian thespians who led their troupe in outwitting the Germans. Lombard was killed in an air crash on Jan. 16, 1942, when the TWA Lockheed Skyclub plane in which she was a passenger crashed into Mt. Potosi near Las Vegas, Nev. She was returning from a war bond drive in which she had sold more than $2 million worth of war bonds in Indianapolis, near her hometown of Fort Wayne, Ind. The plane also carried Lombard's mother, her press agent and 19 other passengers and crew. She left a heartbroken widower, Clark Gable, whom she had married in 1939 after a much-publicized courtship. President Roosevelt cabled the following message to Gable: "She brought joy to all who knew her, and to millions who knew her only as a great artist....She is and always will be a star, one we shall never forget, nor cease to be grateful to." Carole Lombard was 33 years old at the time of her death.

The "Oscar" Operation

Famous movie actor, Douglas Fairbanks Jr., was involved in a secret operation during WWII which did not become public until after the war. He served as a uniformed advisor to the U.S. Navy on camouflage projects.

In early 1943 Fairbanks devised a concept for the creation of a dummy paratrooper that could be used to deceive the enemy before and during paratroop invasions. His first design was for an 18-inch lead figure resembling Hollywood's Oscar, which accounts for the code name, "Oscar." Eventually the dummies evolved into four-feet high creatures made of a black rubberized material inflated by a CO_2 bottle.

They were used twice during the war: dropped once in the invasion of southern France in August 1944 and again in the operation to liberate Manila in the Philippines in January 1945. Gunfire simulations were also used in both drops to further confuse the enemy.

All 22 on Airliner Dead, Including Miss Lombard, 15 Flyers

Las Vegas, Nev., Jan. 17.—(AP)—Bodies of 22 persons, including breezy, outspoken Carole Lombard, Hollywood movie star, were found scattered for hundreds of yards today on the slopes of Table mountain 35 miles southwest of here where a TWA passenger plane crashed last night, killing everybody aboard.

Horseback searchers found the bodies and wreckage of the Los Angeles-bound plane. It plunged mysteriously against the 8,500-foot mountain soon after take-off here at 7:07 p. m. under clear skies.

Killed with Actress Lombard were her mother, Mrs. Elizabeth K. Peters, Otto Winkler, M-G-M studio publicity man, Mrs. Louis Hamilton of Detroit, three plane crew members and 15 officers and men of the air corps' Long Beach, Cal., ferrying command.

The bodies will have to be brought out by horseback and this may require a day or so. A party with extra horses, being rounded up tonight, expected to leave for the crash scene at daylight tomorrow.

11-Mile Trip.

It is an 11-mile trip up from Good Springs at the mountain's base, with few trails.

The 32-year-old Miss Lombard, formerly Jane Peters of Fort Wayne, Ind., was returning to Hollywood from Indianapolis where on Thursday she sponsored sales of defense bonds totaling nearly $2,500,000. The trip was an assignment by Gable, chairman of an actors' committee handling personal appearances to boost bond sales.

Hollywood friends heard the return trip by plane resulted from a coin toss-up between her and Winkler, she wanting to come back by air and he by train. Their eastward journey was by train.

Mrs. Hamilton was en route to join her husband, Lieutenant Linton D. Hamilton, aviator stationed on the west coast.

Crew victims on the ill-fated plane were Pilot Wayne Williams, 41, of Reseda, Cal., near Los An-

PIN UPS

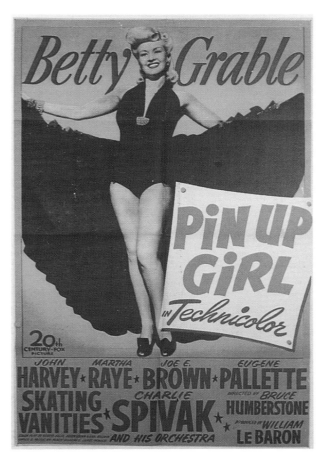

America's most popular box office actress during the war was the curvaceous queen of the pinups, Betty Grable. She was born in St. Louis in 1916 and arrived with her mother in Hollywood in 1930. Although only in her teens (she lied about her age), she worked as a song-and-dance girl in films and campus comedies. Her marriage to film star Jackie Coogan lasted from 1937 to 1940.

Her big break came when she replaced Alice Faye in the movie, *Down Argentine Way*, and she was put under contract to 20th Century-Fox. Many of her musicals during the 1940s were mediocre, but she continually ranked in the top 10 film stars.

This top ranking made her a favorite pinup of the millions of GIs around the world, especially after her famous over-the-shoulder photo was released. Her personal statistics were memorized by GIs: 34-23-35, and it was said that thoughts of her encouraged the men to win the war and return home to their loved ones.

Not only was her figure well-proportioned, but she was declared the winner of the "best legs" in Hollywood, and her shapely limbs were insured by Lloyds of London for $1 million.

In 1943 she married bandleader Harry James who appeared with her in the 1942 movie, *Springtime in the Rockies*. Their marriage lasted for 22 years and produced two daughters.

After the war her popularity began to wane as Marilyn Monroe came on the scene. Betty Grable starred in her last two movies in 1955 and then retired. She died in 1973 of cancer.

Her wartime contributions cannot be calculated in dollars, but her friendly, folksy manner and beautiful figure made millions of GIs around the world think of home.

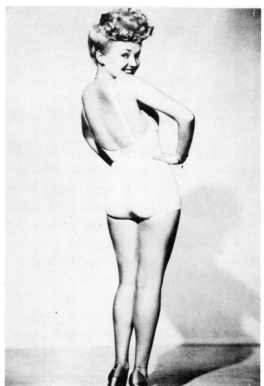

Rita Hayworth, another very popular Hollywood actress, and GI pin up.

Destination Unknown

Lt. and Mrs. Ronald Reagan (Jane Wyman) Say, "Live for Today—Tomorrow Takes Care of Itself!"

HE'S IN THE ARMY NOW, and ex-actor Ronald Reagan has already adopted the philosophy of Uncle Sam's fighting men. Not long after any soldier puts on his uniform and plans his days around the Army routine, he learns that the best way to waste his energy is to make plans beyond the present day. For who knows—tomorrow he might be of better service thousands of miles away!

At this writing Lieutenant Reagan is assigned to the motion picture unit of the Army Air Corps at Culver City, Calif. But he and his pretty wife Jane Wyman, are fully prepared for the possibility of his being transferred elsewhere tomorrow. Ronald and Jane have learned to make each day complete in itself, with no strings left over to be tied together the next. Nor do they ever put off until tomorrow what they can do today. For as far as they know there may not be any tomorrow—until Messrs. Hitler, Tojo and Company have been put out of business.

One break for Jane is that her man is at the moment living at home. His present post at Culver City does not provide living quarters for officers. The fact that he has to report for duty every morning at the very crack of dawn is no trial for the Reagans. When a star is at work on a picture, the day begins long before the first note of reveille has sounded, and early rising in the Army is practically late sleeping to him!

Even before the war started, the Reagans preferred evenings at home to pub-crawling. Now they still enjoy little dinner parties at home with a group of intimate friends. A recent visit to a popular night spot confirmed their preference for the domestic life. Ron, Jane and two of their friends went to the club for cocktails, and stayed for one round. When the bill came to $21, meaning $5.25 for each drink, the Reagans voted that home was easier on a first lieutenant's budget!

Having finished work on *Princess O'Rourke* in September, Jane now spends her days taking care of Maureen Elizabeth, her two-year-old daughter. If the Lieutenant is transferred, there will be regrets, but the Reagans know that the exigencies of war are of primary importance in their own future and their daughter's

Former movie actor, Ronald Reagan, President of the United States, 1981–1989.

Picture of a happy couple, Ron and Jane have learned the secret of security in wartime

Proof ... that she was recently voted ... Modern life ...

22

"Footlight Serenade" proved she could rate beside veterans like Betty Grable. In *Princess O'Rourke* she is with Olivia de Havilland and Bob Cummings.

This 1944 film was adapted from Ted Lawson's popular wartime narrative of the daring April 18, 1942, air raid on Tokyo.

The USAAF's First Motion Picture Unit (FMPU), established in July 1942, was commanded briefly by Col. Jack Warner, but saw its greatest growth under Lt. Col. Paul Mantz. The FMPU was based at the old Hal Roach Studios in Culver City, Calif. The aging sound stages of "Fort Roach," where Laurel and Hardy, Harold Lloyd, and the Our Gang Comedy kids had once cavorted, echoed for the duration of the war with the narrative voices of the Culver City Commandos. Its ranks comprised such minor Air Force personages as Capt. Clark Gable, Alan Ladd, Ronald Reagan, George Montgomery, Lt. Van Heflin, Joseph Cotten, Arthur Kennedy, and Craig Stevens.

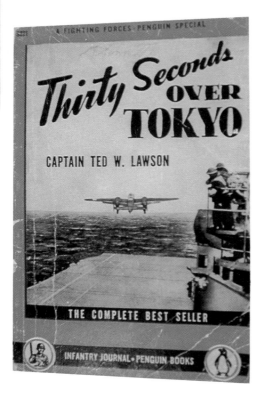

A FIGHTING FORCES—PENGUIN SPECIAL

Thirty Seconds OVER TOKYO

CAPTAIN TED W. LAWSON

THE COMPLETE BEST SELLER

INFANTRY JOURNAL · PENGUIN BOOKS

Two of the many propaganda movies produced during the war. At right, Walter Huston appeared in *Mission to Moscow*, and left, Robert Watson appeared as Hitler in *The Hitler Gang*.

Lew Ayres was a well-known Hollywood actor and husband of Ginger Rogers from 1934 to 1941. He declared himself a conscientious objector during the war and served in the Army Medical Corps under fire. His declaration almost cost him his acting career: his films were banned in 100 Chicago theaters. FDR

Hollywood actor Robert Montgomery had a varied military career during the war. He was a volunteer in France for the American Field Services as an ambulance driver. In August 1941 he joined the U.S. Navy Reserve and served as a naval attaché in London. He also served as a PT-boat commander and on a destroyer during the D-Day landings. He starred as PT commander John Bulkeley in the 1945 movie, *They Were Expendable*. FDR

GIVE

The Greatest Mother in the World

AMERICAN RED CROSS
1943
WAR FUND

The first USO Club, located at 1182 West Pioneer Way,
Oak Harbor, Wash. USO WASHINGTON, D.C.

Servicemen stream into the Newark, N.J., YMCA, which became a beehive of activity during the war. YMCA OF THE USA ARCHIVES, UNIVERSITY OF MINNESOTA

The Elks, like many fraternal and service organizations throughout the country committed their people and resources to the war effort. BOB STEPHENS, KALISPELL, MONT.

American Legion members from Chicago serving food to servicemen and women. AMERICAN LEGION

New York American Legion members visit a wounded serviceman, Staff Sgt. Jerome Martin, of Texas, who was wounded at St. Lô, France. AMERICAN LEGION

The annual American Legion Poppy Day sale to support war veterans got an assist from the Boy Scouts in Detroit in May 1941. AMERICAN LEGION, *DETROIT FREE PRESS*

A USO Club at the
Pocatello, Idaho, railroad
station, Jan. 31, 1945. UTAH
STATE HISTORICAL SOCIETY

USO Club in Pensacola,
Fla., in 1944. FDR

The "Victory Book
Campaign," conducted
cooperatively by the
USO and the American
Library Association,
distributed over 13
million books to service-
men along with over
three million magazines
and 280,000 newspapers.

The canteen at the Milwau-
kee Railroad Depot in
Aberdeen, S.D. SOUTH
DAKOTA STATE HISTORICAL
SOCIETY

USO

The organization was born a year before this country entered World War II. With the prospect of millions of Americans being called to the Colors, 18 organizations - including the YMCA, YWCA, Salvation Army, National Jewish Welfare Board, National Catholic Community Service and Travelers Aid-International - met with other private organizations. They wanted to explore the possibility of providing wholesome recreation and other morale supporting services to the young Americans who would soon be serving in the nation's defense.

With their combined resources, they created a single organization to raise funds, develop a program of services and serve as a liaison with the Federal government. The new organization, called the United Service Organizations for the National Defense (USOND), was established Feb. 4, 1941.

USOND got the full support of the War and Navy Departments. The Federal government donated $15 million for furnishing USOND clubs. The organization had raised $14,345,000 in public contributions before the United States entered the war. Soon the name was shortened to USO.

USO clubs, located near military installations and in major cities, were designed as "homes away from home." It was a place where lonely servicemen could drop in for a cup of coffee and doughnuts, play a game of cards, or perhaps meet a "nice young girl." When war was officially declared USO activities rapidly expanded.

Wherever soldiers served - they could count on two things: being preceded by a mysterious character named "Kilroy," and being entertained by USO-sponsored show troupes. At the peak of World War II there were a total of 3,035 USO operations, and USO Camp Shows gave more than 438,000 performances to military audiences totaling 213 million.

During and immediately following the war, USO raised more than $236 million through public donations. The government provided funds to equip 332 USO clubs at a cost of $20 million.

President Roosevelt's silhouette presides over a plug for the USO. FDR

The site of the North Platte Canteen, commemorated by the Union Pacific Railroad when it demolished the North Platte station. The park was dedicated on July 23, 1975. JIM REESDORFF, DAVID CITY, NEB.

Interior view of the Lincoln County Historical Society Museum, North Platte, Neb., showing memorabilia of the North Platte Canteen. JIM REESDORFF, DAVID CITY, NEB.

Hungry servicemen descend on the canteen from an eastbound train. UNION PACIFIC RAILROAD

Red Cross

1945

MOISTEN GUMMED EDGES AT TOP AND BOTTOM AND APPLY TO WINDOW

provided service to disaster victims and military personnel throughout the world. The *Motor Service* provided transportation for both Red Cross and military personnel and civilians in need. The *Gray Lady Service* served in hospitals, giving aid and comfort to war casualties and civilians alike. The *Volunteer Nurse Aide Service* assisted nurses in the military and civilian hospitals. The Red Cross also instituted a new service during World War II: the prisoner of war packaging project. Five national centers were set up to provide more than 27 million packages for American and Allied prisoners in Europe and the Far East.

In war, as in peace, the Red Cross assumed a vital role as an instrument of the American people. It extended vital services to the able-bodied, the sick and the injured who served their country both at home and abroad, as well as to millions of American civilians.

The demands of World War II brought the American Red Cross the greatest challenge in the organization's history. Drawing upon its experiences from World War I and its large-scale disaster relief operations, the Red Cross immediately swung into action. When the armies began to move, the Red Cross moved with them.

The American people responded magnificently both with volunteer manpower and financial commitments. Over 7,500,000 volunteers served and $785 million was donated during the war years. At the same time, 39,100 paid workers - both at home and abroad - administered the various functions of the Red Cross. Eighty-six paid and volunteer workers died while serving overseas. Over 16 million Americans were in uniform during the war, and over one million became combat casualties (killed, wounded, missing or prisoners of war). These numbers created incredible demands on the organization and its tireless workers.

In addition to the expansion of traditional Red Cross services given to members of the armed forces, the organization also developed a blood donor service, provided an extensive overseas club program, established prisoner of war documentation and aid, stepped-up recruitment of medical personnel for the military, and itensified a communications program and extended home care between servicemen and women and their families. Disaster relief was another important function of the Red Cross within the United States. Whether in wartime or peacetime, natural disasters occur. The organization gave millions of dollars of aid and donated thousands of man-hours to the victims of fires, floods, tornadoes and other natural disasters.

Branches of the Red Cross performed a myriad of functions during the war. The *Production Service* provided surgical dressings, hospital garments and clothing for the military and war victims. The *Canteen Service*

PRISONERS OF WAR BULLETIN

Published by the American National Red Cross for the Relatives of American Prisoners of War and Civilian Internees

VOL. 3, NO. 5   WASHINGTON, D.C.   MAY 1945

Reports on German Camps

-357-

American Red Cross
War Fund Campaign—March, 1944

$200,000,000—to Help Him—Win for Us and to Guard the Home Front

HOW IT WILL BE SPENT

Red Cross Service in Army and Navy Hospitals	$ 26,200,000
Service in Camps and Combat Zones	36,000,000
Blood Donor Service	4,000,000
Emergency Financial Assistance to Service Men and Their Families	3,500,000
Chapter Production of Surgical and Clothing Items	2,100,000
Servicemen's Clubs Overseas	27,000,000
Service to U. S. Prisoners of War	1,500,000
Other War Services	79,700,000
Total, War Service of Red Cross	$180,000,000
Normal Civilian Red Cross Activities	20,000,000
Total 1944 Budget	$200,000,000

The Missoula-Mineral County Share
$37,500.00

This will provide about $12.50 for each of our 3,000 men and women in the service.

THIS IS WHERE WE COME IN

OF OUR DONATIONS:—

$22,500.00 goes to the National Red Cross

$15,000.00 for Red Cross Services in Missoula and Mineral Counties.

Missoula and Mineral Counties Need
This $15,000.00 for

Home Service for Servicemen and their families	$ 5,800
Nursing Service	200
Volunteer Special Services (surgical dressings and clothing production, nurse's aides and canteen corps)	3,000
Administrative, Educational and other activities	6,000
Total 1944 budget	$15,000

90 Cents of Each Dollar

Goes to Help HIM

In Missoula and Mineral Counties in 1943

Local Red Cross volunteers spent 24,726 hours preparing 282,000 dressings for your wounded boys.

Home Service sent and received 1,200 wires and cables and made loans and grants of $3,200 to servicemen and their families.

Local Red Cross workers gave 29,800 hours in making 4,582 hospital and comfort items for men in the armed services.

A total of 458 people were trained in first aid work and 42 instructors trained for teaching first aid.

In addition a total of 196 people were trained and given certificates in water safety, accident prevention, home nursing, and nurses aides while 43 instructors were trained for these same lines of work.

★ ★ ★ ★ ★ ★ ★ ★ ★ ★ ★ ★ ★ ★

Missoulian

IBM

MATSON NAVIGATION CO.
CONSTRUCTION & REPAIR DEPT. - MAINTAINANCE DIV.
WAR CHEST, RED CROSS CAMPAIGN

In recognition of the needs of my country, our men in the Armed Forces and our Allies and in consideration of the gifts of others I hereby pledge to my HOME WAR CHEST AND RED CROSS CHAPTER 75c per week for 12 weeks . . . A TOTAL OF NINE DOLLARS.

As a convenience to me in carrying out my above pledge, my employer is hereby authorized to deduct 75c a week (adopted as the standard contribution for this campaign by the Bay Cities Metal Trades Council) over a period of 12 consecutive weekly deductions, beginning not later than November 14, 1943.

Signature .... Badge No. .... Home City ....
Place of Present Residence.

KINDLY SIGN and TURN THIS CARD IN TO YOUR LEADERMAN TODAY at end of shift.

An Album of Red Cross Activities

Red Cross volunteers wrapping bandages in the Masonic Hall, Gallipolis, Ohio. MAJ. GEN. and MRS. GEORGE E. BUSH, GALLIPOLIS, OHIO

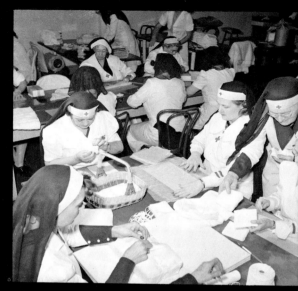

On Dec. 8, 1941, Red Cross personnel began wrapping bandages at their San Francisco, Calif., headquarters. LC-USF34-81870-E

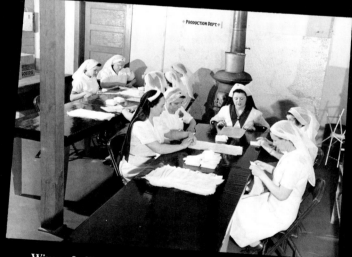

Wives of officers at Fort Dix, N.J., make up surgical dressings in May 1942. ARC

The wife of Montana's Governor Sam Ford packs Red Cross kits for GIs. MONTANA HISTORICAL SOCIETY

Red Cross personnel receiving the 29,000,000th produced Ford car at the Ford factory in Detroit, April 29, 1941. HENRY FORD MUSEUM & GREENFIELD VILLAGE

A Milwaukee, Wis., Red Cross group uses a production-line system to pack "comfort kits" for the troops. The ARC production corps turned out more than four million surgical dressings in 1943. ARC

Volunteer canteen workers pack food kits for shipment to American prisoners of war. The Red Cross was given the job of providing necessities to POWs throughout the world when the Germans, Italians and Japanese would let the packages through. ARC

Red Cross canteen workers feed the Massachusetts State Guard in the Blue Hills near Milton, Mass. ARC

Members of the Nassau County, N.Y., Red Cross chapter use an old electric car and a bicycle because of gas rationing. ARC

Jane Briggs, daughter of Detroit industrialist and Detroit Tigers baseball club owner, Walter O. Briggs, waits to pick up a pair of pilots who have just landed at a Ferry Command base in Detroit. To become a member of the Volunteer Motor Corps of the Red Cross, she had to pass tests in mechanics and first aid. ARC

Famous radio commentator Gabriel Heatter, whose voice carried war news throughout the nation on broadcast hook-ups, is shown on July 8, 1942, inspecting an ambulance which Mrs. Heatter, extreme right, presented to the Nassau County, N.Y., Red Cross chapter for use in its Freeport, N.Y., branch. ARC

A volunteer of the Red Cross Motor Corps, at the loading of the exchange ship *Gripsholm*, paints the destination of boxes of clothing, food, etc., being sent to American prisoners of war in Japan and the Far East. LC-USW33-42498-ZC

Volunteers provide food and drink to wounded soldiers on an ambulance plane that stopped in Toledo, Ohio, on Thanksgiving Day in 1944. The Red Cross provided aid to wounded servicemen throughout the country during the war years. ARC

Members of the San Francisco Volunteer Motor Corps-Mounted, of the Red Cross, practice transferring a "victim" from a canvas litter to a stokes stretcher atop a horse. ARC

BLOOD DRIVE

Arthur Godfrey founded an organization to recruit blood donors for the Red Cross and called it GAPSALS - "Give A Pint, Save A Life Society."

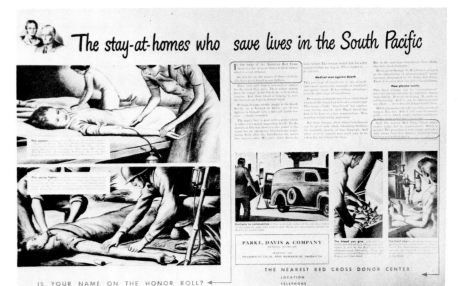

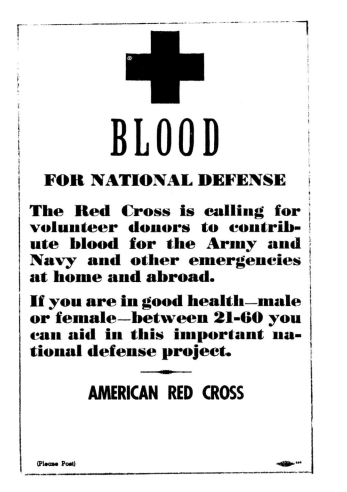

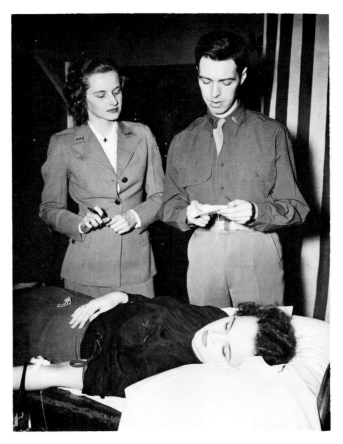

Military personnel were on hand at the Ashland, Ky., Red Cross Center when several women donated their blood for the troops. FRANK B. ELAM PHOTO

While Dwight D. Eisenhower served as Commanding General of Allied Forces in Europe, he sent this message back home: "If I could reach all America, there is one thing I would like to do - thank them for blood plasma and for whole blood. It has been a tremendous thing." A Red Cross chapter in Birmingham, Ala., first suggested a blood transfusion service in 1929. An initial experimental service began in Augusta, Ga., in 1937. The 1940 "Plasma for Britain" project was a pilot program that shipped plasma to beleaguered Britain. In January 1941, at the request of the Surgeon Generals of the U.S. Army and Navy, the Red Cross established the Army-Navy Blood Donor Services. Between February 1941 and September 1945, over six and one-half million individuals donated more than 13 million pints of blood.

A poster advertising a blood drive set up at an air raid station. Blood collecting was one of the primary functions of the Red Cross during the war. More than five million pints were collected for use overseas and on the home front. LC-USW3-39988

Nuns prepare to donate blood at the Red Cross blood plasma center in Milwaukee, Wis., during their Christmas vacation in 1942. They were among the 100 nuns to donate a pint of blood in the center, which collected 50,000 pints during the year. ARC

"Whitey" Kurowski, third baseman for the St. Louis Cardinals, gives a pint of blood during a St. Louis Red Cross blood drive, 1942. ARC

Red Cross volunteers deliver blood plasma to the gangplank of a U.S. Navy ship. The Red Cross collected thousands of units of dry blood plasma as part of the national defense effort in 1941. The plasma underwent an intricate series of processes, and was ready for delivery after being frozen, dehydrated and hermetically sealed in glass flasks. It was restored to liquid form when distilled water was added. ARC

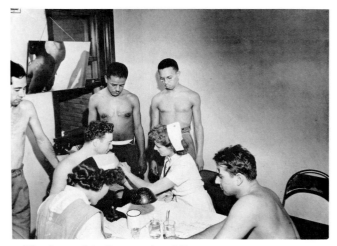

Members of the International Fur and Leather Workers Union, CIO, donate blood at a Red Cross blood station in 1944. ARC

HOSPITALS FROM HOTELS AND RESORTS

There were many naval hospitals located throughout the country to serve the thousands of casualties coming in from the world's battlefields. There were also convalescent hospitals established for patients who required little treatment other than rest, diet, psychotherapy or physiotherapy, before being discharged or returned to duty.

By June 1945 the range of functions was so wide that the title was changed to that of special hospitals. By the end of the war these hospitals had a total of more than 18,000 beds.

The Bureau of Yards and Docks leased and converted for use many hotels and schools around the country, thus holding down costs (instead of building from scratch) and opening units quickly.

The first such hospital was the Harriman estate in New York's Catskill Mountains donated by Averell Harriman. A hotel was leased in Santa Cruz, Calif., in early 1943 followed by facilities in Asheville, N.C., Glenwood Springs, Colo., Sun Valley, Idaho, and Yosemite National Park.

By 1945 facilities had opened at Arrowhead Springs, Banning and Beaumont, Calif., Brooklyn, N.Y., Springfield, Mass., Asberry Park, N.J., Palm Beach, Fla., Camp White near Medford, Ore. and Camp Wallace at Galveston, Texas.

In Klamath Falls, Ore., a large Marine Corps hospital was constructed. The U.S. Army also established many convalescent hospitals and like the navy had taken over various hotels, resorts and schools.

Perhaps the most famous hospital site in the country was the famous historic Greenbrier Resort nestled in the hills of eastern West Virginia. This resort, which had been in existence for over 150 years, was the summer White House of presidents and was frequented by the rich and famous from around the world.

Right after the Pearl Harbor attack it was taken over by the government for use as an internment center for enemy diplomats. In 1942 it was bought by the U.S. Army and converted to the Ashford General Hospital. It was not to open again until three years after the war ended.

America's first and premier ski resort at Sun Valley, Idaho, closed for the duration on Dec. 20, 1942. Since it was fairly isolated, travel was mainly by railroad which was converted to war work, and most of the able-bodied men were off to war, Sun Valley had no choice but to shut down. It would not open again for four years.

On July 1, 1943, Sun Valley was formally commissioned as United States Naval Special Hospital, Sun Valley, Idaho. The Navy obtained the resort through a trade-off - they got the whole resort for free but paid the taxes and carried the insurance.

The ski slopes were again opened for recreation along with other activities and summer facilities. In the nearby town of Ketchum gambling, which was legal at the time, appeared to be one of the main attractions for the recovering sailors.

The nation's large and small hotels and resorts contributed much to the war effort.

Sailors pose near the magnificent Ahwahnee Hotel in Yosemite National Park, which was converted to a naval hospital during the war. YOSEMITE NATIONAL PARK

Sailors look out over world-famous Yosemite Valley from the Wawona Tunnel in Yosemite National Park. YOSEMITE NATIONAL PARK

The 604th Ordnance Co., from Fort Ord, Calif., poses on the Fallen Monarch, Mariposa Grove of Big Trees, at Yosemite National Park, Calif., July 1943. YOSEMITE NATIONAL PARK

The beach at Waikiki, Honolulu, during the war. The large building in the background is the famous Royal Hawaiian Hotel, The Pink Palace, which was taken over by the U.S. Navy for use as an R and R Center for submarine personnel. HAWAII ARCHIVES

ROYAL HAWAIIAN REST & RECREATION CENTER

MEALS

Date Aug, 27/1942

Register No. 29147   Room No. 446

Name Azbell, W. B.

Cashier J. Johnson

SERVICE

Nº 19988

HAWN. PTG. CO. 40050

A dance at the Huntington Women's Club for servicemen, Huntington, W.Va. MARSHALL UNIVERSITY ARCHIVES, CATHERINE ONSLOW PAPERS

The milk bar at the Grove Park Inn in Asheville, N.C., in 1944. The Inn served as an Army Redistribution Station for soldiers on Rest and Recreation from July 1944 to August 1945. THE GROVE PARK INN

Six hundred officers and men of the 260th Coast Artillery from the District of Columbia visit Carlsbad Caverns National Park in New Mexico, May 1941 (top). Some of the 2,255 servicemen that toured the caverns in January 1943 (left). The park was a popular attraction for the thousands of men stationed in the El Paso, Texas, and eastern New Mexico area. CARLSBAD CAVERNS NATIONAL PARK

The American Legion Bath House at Nashville, Tenn., 1944. TENNESSEE STATE ARCHIVES

When the hotel at Mt. McKinley National Park, now called Denali National Park, was taken over by the Alaskan Defense Command as a Rest and Recreation Center for troops stationed in Alaska, different recreational activities were offered, depending on the time of year. ARC and U.S. ARMY MILITARY HISTORY INSTITUTE

U.S. ARMY MT. McKINLEY RECREATION CAMP

Miss Connie Norden of San Francisco, a Red Cross representative, teaches downhill skiing to army troops on leave, probably in Mt. McKinley National Park area, January 1943. ARC

Somewhere in Alaska a Red Cross worker entertains soldiers and an Army stenographer in this remote, isolated theater of war. ARC

This sailor presents an unusual sight as he skis in his uniform and hat near Donner Summit, Calif., where the ski facilities were used as a rest area. DR. FRANK HOWARD, SAN RAFAEL, CALIF.

FACTS and FIGURES

The mother of three soldiers in Placquemines Parish, La., June 1943. LC-USW3-33909-D

In a scene repeated by thousands of couples, Lt. and Mrs. Harry F. Keene, USNR, leave Mission San Buena Ventura, Ventura, Calif., after their marriage in March 1944. War caused romance to flourish, and speeded up the dating-to-marriage timetable. *OAKLAND POST ENQUIRER*, FRED MAE PHOTO

a.ug 21, 1943

Wedding Joins Navy Couple

First Wave to be married to a United States navy man in Oregon is Yeoman Dorothy Mae Nash, daughter of Mr. and Mrs. John H. Nash, 2943 N. E. 27th avenue, who became the bride of William A. Tunstall, aviation machinist's mate, first class, Saturday at the Fremont Community Methodist church.

They met over an ice cream soda at ship's service at the naval air station at Sand Point, near Seattle, where they are both on duty. Machinist's Mate Tunstall, of Springfield, Mass., has just returned from service on the aircraft carriers Saratoga and Hornet in major battles in the Pacific area, including the Tokyo raid and the battle of Midway. Yeoman Nash had just reported to the station following completion of her yeoman's training at Georgia State Teachers college.

She enlisted in the Waves December 9, 1942, and reported to the Waves indoctrination school at Hunter college of Columbia university, New York city, on February 17, 1943.

Maid of honor at the first navy wedding of its kind in Oregon was Yeoman Betty Jean Nash, cousin of the bride, also on duty at the Sand Point station; best man was William Knight, aviation machinist's mate, second class.

School children and grown-ups in Salt Lake City read about D-Day - the Allied invasion of France - in the *Salt Lake Telegram* on June 6, 1944. UTAH STATE HISTORICAL SOCIETY

Times Square in New York City on D-Day, June 6, 1944. LC-USW3-54022-C and LC-USW3-54016-C

Times Square in New York City on D-Day, June 6, 1944. LC-USW3-54022-C

Washington, D.C. in Wartime

Washington, D.C., shoppers jam the Milstone's Acme liquor store in late December 1941 in anticipation of a shortage of alcohol. All forms of alcoholic beverages were in short supply throughout the war. FDR

Christmas shopping at Hecht's Department Store in Washington, D.C. The American people continued to be well fed and clothed compared to the populations of other Allied countries. FDR

A massive building boom to house the expanded government occurred in the nation's capital during the war. These are temporary buildins going up for the Navy near the Lincoln Memorial. FDR

Hotel space in Washington, D.C., was at a premium during the war with many people having to share a room or even spend the night in the lobby. FDR

The scene of the disastrous fire at the Cocoanut Grove nightclub in Boston, Mass., on Nov. 29, 1942. More than 250 people were killed here in one of the worst fires in the country during the war years. NA 171-G-13-D-3

Race riots broke out in several major American cities during the war. This one occurred in New York's Harlem in August 1943. The worst riots happened in Detroit in June 1943. NA 171-G-38-3

Civilian Conservation Corps

The Civilian Conservation Corps (CCC) was one of President Roosevelt's first New Deal agencies, established in 1933. Its purpose was to provide employment for thousands of the nation's unemployed youth in conservation work. The agency lasted for nine years (1933-1942) and eventually employed over three million young men. Billions of trees were planted, forest fires fought, parks established, dams built, historical sites restored, soils and grazing areas were rehabilitated and the nation's youth were given a chance for employment and learning a trade. The thousands of camps were run by the U.S. Army thus giving some minimal military training to the enrollees, training which would prove valuable to both the army and men in the 1940s. By 1940 the nation was shifting to a national defense posture and the emphasis of work and training was shifted from conservation to skills needed for defense purposes. The agency went out of existence in July 1942 as the nation's youth was called to duty with the military. Many of the camps were turned over to the military or used to house Japanese-American internees or Axis prisoners of war. Some of the buildings were even shipped to Canada and Alaska for use in the construction of the Alaska Highway.

CCC boys line up for roll call at a camp in the Chippewa National Forest, Minnesota, in August 1940. The U.S. Army ran the camps, the U.S. Forest Service provided the work projects and overhead personnel. NA

National defense training at Camp Lake Fork Co. #2939 in McCall, Idaho, July 1941. This was a school for radio repair, a skill that would be very useful for these boys who would soon be entering the military. NA

National defense training at Camp Sun Valley, Sunburg, Pa., April 1941. The CCC boys are taking an aircraft mechanics course, another skill that would be useful in the military. NA

Soldiers attending Officer Candidate School hear a lecture on East Cemetery Hill at the Gettysburg National Battlefield in 1943. NATIONAL PARK SERVICE

The movie, *War Nurse*, at the Palace Theater in Juneau, Alaska, 1943. ALASKA STATE LIBRARY

Movie actress Maureen O'Hara poses with typewriters donated by the RKO studio to the war effort. A shortage of typewriters resulted from the tremendous increase in paper work and numbers of government employees. Some of these machines came from the Script Department, where each played a role in creating countless scenes for the screen. Miss O'Hara helped collect more than 70 typewriters and added her own before posing. FDR

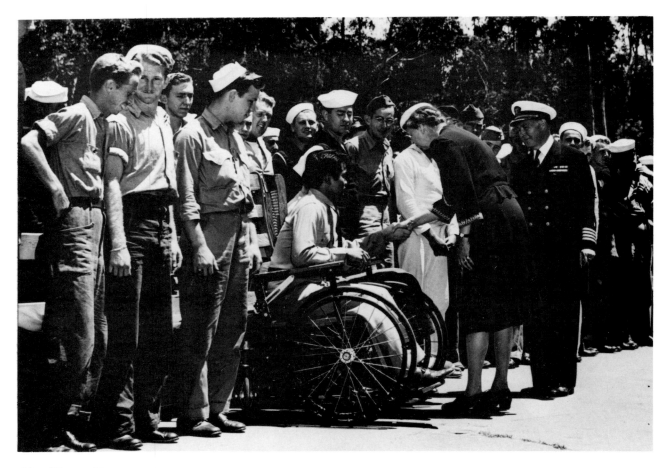

Mrs. Eleanor Roosevelt visits San Diego Naval Hospital in July 1944. She visited the wounded whenever possible and made a maximum effort to work on defense-related projects. FDR

PROTECT YOURSELF AGAINST VENEREAL DISEASES

ARMY — NAVY — CIVILIANS
FREE PROPHYLAXIS
AT

CENTRAL EMERGENCY HOSPITAL
135 POLK STREET

HARBOR EMERGENCY HOSPITAL
88 SACRAMENTO STREET

ARMY MEDICAL STATION
143 EDDY STREET

OPEN DAY AND NIGHT

PROPHYLAXIS MUST BE TAKEN PROMPTLY

DON'T DELAY

OPERATED BY THE CITY AND COUNTY OF SAN FRANCISCO
DEPARTMENT OF PUBLIC HEALTH
IN COOPERATION WITH THE U. S. ARMY AND U. S. NAVY

15769 8-42 10M   STATE PRINTING OFFICE

Window display in a general store in Emmitsburg, Md., February 1943. LC-LCW3-17681-D

The entire Hurlbut family gathers at home in Southington, Conn., in May 1942, for a Sunday dinner honoring Cpl. Robert Hurlbut, 21, home on his first furlough from the Army. The corporal is not the only member of the family serving his country. His father works in a defense plant and his mother, and the children who are old enough, are enrolled in volunteer services. LC-USW3-41991-D

Sign in a Klamath Falls, Ore., telephone company office, July 1942. LC-USF34-73318-E

The Fulton Fish Market in New York City, June 1943. LC-USW3-31327-E

The Victory Task Force patch. The force was created in mid-1942 and consisted of 1,200 soldiers assigned to the Army War Show. The mission of the force was to perform live shows in 14 large American cities to raise funds for the Army Emergency Relief Fund. The show, using infantry and artillery weapons and tanks, was also meant to impress the audience with the Army's capabilities. The show ran from June 12 to September 21, and then the soldiers were returned to their units. The "V" on the patch was a major symbol for victory during the war and the bright red color was used to attract attention.

Wives of California state legislators sell cookbooks in the Senator Hotel, Sacramento, to raise money for the "boys overseas," 1945. *OAKLAND POST ENQUIRER*, FRED MAE PHOTO

Lucky Strike cigarettes substituted a white and red bull's-eye logo for its green and red one since the green ink contained a metal needed for war production.

A "silver nickel" made with 35 percent silver. To save nickel, a strategic metal, for the war effort, it was removed from five-cent coins from October 1942 through the end of 1945. On the reverse, above Monticello, the "silver nickels" had large mint-marks which included the first "P," for Philadelphia, mint-mark in history. LITTLETON COIN COMPANY

A 1943 steel cent. The traditional U.S. penny was temporarily replaced in order to conserve copper, which was essential for the manufacture of war materials. The replacement was made of steel covered with zinc, and 1943 was the only year of issue. LITTLE-TON COIN COMPANY

The "Iron Duke," a mobile kitchen that saw service in London during the blitz, on the campus of Duke University, Durham, N.C., in April 1941. Donning a tin hat, Robert L. Flowers, president of the university, accepted, on behalf of the university, a package of ashes from a London fire caused by a German plane. DUKE UNIVERSITY ARCHIVES

An important food conference was held at Virginia's Homestead Hotel in May 1943. BETTMANN ARCHIVE

Government Agencies

Some of the most important government boards, commissions and administrations established for the management of the war.

WPB - War Production Board
WLB - War Labor Board
WMC - War Manpower Commission
WRA - War Relocation Authority
OPA - Office of Price Administration
OWI - Office of War Information
WSA - War Shipping Administration
OWM - Office of War Mobilization
OSRD - Office of Scientific Research and Development
ODT - Office of Defense Transportation
ANMB - Army and Navy Munitions Board
RFC - Reconstruction Finance Commission
OCD - Office of Civilian Defense
RRC - Rubber Reserve Corporation
SSS - Selective Service System

The present day riverboat *Delta Queen* that plies the Ohio and Mississippi rivers as a tourist boat served the war effort as the *U.S.S. Delta Queen* (YHB-7). Along with her counterpart, the *Delta King*, she was stationed at Yerba Buena and Treasure Island in San Francisco Bay from 1940 to 1946. The ships were painted a dull battleship gray and put to work shuttling troops around the bay and serving as a barracks and training boat for naval reservists. In the bay's high winds and tricky currents, the flat bottom boats became, according to the boat's skipper, "an immense box kite, which knocked down some of the best piers ever built in San Francisco Bay." After the war, the *Delta Queen*, which was built in 1926, was put up for auction and acquired by Capt. Tom Greene. He took her on the open sea, through the Panama Canal, to New Orleans and up the Mississippi to Cincinnati. She was refurbished and relaunched in 1948 and is still in operation, listed now on the National Register of Historic Places. USN

American Women in World War II

1. 350,000 women served in the military during the war.
2. 280,000 women were on active duty when the war ended.
3. 17,000 WACs served in every combat area overseas.
4. 8,000 women were on active duty in the European Theater of Operation at war's end.
5. 4,400 women were on active duty in the Pacific Theater of Operation when the war ended.
6. 565 WACs in the Pacific won combat decorations.
7. More than 200 Army Nurses died in combat situations. 17 are buried in U.S. cemetaries overseas.
8. 1,600 Army Nurses won combat and non-combat decorations, including Distinguished Service Medals (the highest non-combat award), Silver Stars, Bronze Stars, Air Medals, Legions of Merit, Commendation Medals, and Purple Hearts.
9. Six Army Nurses were killed at Anzio when the Germans bombed and strafed the beachhead hospital tents. Four Army Nurses among the survivors won Silver Stars for bravery.
10. 66 Army Nurses and 11 Navy Nurses were captured when Bataan and Corregidor fell. They remained prisoners of the Japanese for 37 months.

Women's Air Force Service Pilots

1. 25,000 applied for the Women's Air Force Service Pilots program, 1,830 women were selected and 1,074 completed the program.
2. WASPs flew 60 million miles and ferried 12,650 aircraft to U.S. bases and overseas bases. They flew every type of plane the Army Air Corps had, including the superfortresses: B-17s and B-29s. They flew trainers, Mustangs, Thunderbolts, B-25s, B-26s, C-54s, P-38s (nicknamed Lightning), P-39s, P-47s and P-51s. They towed gunnery targets and trained hundreds of male Army Air Corps pilots how to fly.
3. 38 WASPs lost their lives in air crashes while ferrying planes to military bases.
4. The WASP was deactivated on December 20, 1944.
5. On May 21, 1979, the Assistant Secretary of the Air Force presented the first official WASP discharge. Veterans benefits were at last awarded to these women who had served their country more than 35 years earlier.

KNIT A SWEATER FOR A SOLDIER

A sweater for a soldier—
We have the finest khaki service yarns

The boys in our fighting forces will appreciate one of these hand knitted sweaters.

It can be sent direct to your own soldier

or to

THE CITIZENS COMMITTEE FOR THE
ARMY AND NAVY, Inc.
8 West 40th Street, New York City

See knitting instructions on other side

ARC 400-2
Rev. Jan. 1942
Code K-1

MAN'S SOCK
(Medium Size)

Equipment Needed: 4 ozs. 4/14 sock yarn of suitable color.

Needles: Four needles to fit the Red Cross Needle Gauge for socks. Gauges available from Area Offices.

Scale: 7 stitches to the inch, 9 rows to the inch. Make a sample to find out how many stitches are required for you to knit an inch. If your scale is not that given here, try a smaller or larger needle until you obtain this scale. If you have to use a different size needle from that called for above, it will not in any way alter the garment provided you knit 7 stitches to the inch and 9 rows to the inch.

When knitting the second sock of a pair, always count the rows of the first sock to insure uniform size when finished. These knitting directions are given as a guide. Other simple sock directions may be used so long as the garment is the proper size and of correct proportions.

INSTRUCTIONS FOR MAKING

The sock when finished should measure: Foot, 11½ inches; leg, 14 inches.

On 3 needles and with a double thread cast on loosely 60 sts., having 20 on each of 3 needles. Join, being careful not to twist sts. Work with double thread for first row only. This helps to prevent fraying.

Work in ribbing of knit 2, purl 2 for 3 inches.
Work in plain knitting for the next 8 inches.

Heel: Divide sts. as follows: 30 on 1st needle (for heel) and 15 sts. each on 2nd and 3rd needles. On heel needle always slip first

The zoot suit clothing fad originated among teenagers in Harlem and other urban slums. This garb, worn mostly by minority street gangs, consisted of a long jacket with overstuffed shoulders, baggy trousers and a key chain, and was considered a 1940s show of independence. These outfits were favored by the pachucos, teenage Mexican-Americans, and after several clashes occurred between them and servicemen, the Los Angeles City Council declared the wearing of the suits a misdemeanor.

Sample of a food sack for Russian war relief. KANSAS STATE HISTORICAL SOCIETY

Home front display at the Kansas State Historical Museum in Topeka. KANSAS STATE HISTORICAL SOCIETY

Perhaps the most popular form of graffiti during the war was a mischievious character called Kilroy, whose wide-eyed, bald-headed face peering over a fence, turned up all over the world - on buildings, sidewalks and bathroom walls. The term "Kilroy Was Here," became a fad expression meaning "A U.S. serviceman was here," or "A stranger was here."

United States Forest Service in WWII

Wood was of very strategic importance during the war, and the U.S. Forest Service was called upon to supply a great quantity of it and to do so without sufficient manpower or critical machinery.

The military needed wood for pontoon bridges, railroad ties, gunstocks, ships and docks, buildings of all kinds and aircraft manufacture. Wood cellulose provided a main component of explosives from dynamite to nitroglycerin. The single biggest demand for wood was for the manufacture of packing crates for everything from complete airplanes to food products. The Forest Service calculated that in 1942 alone, military and civilian use would consume eight billion board feet of timber.

The Forest Service also had to protect its vast, nationwide acreage from natural and man-caused fires and had to prepare for the possibility of enemy sabotage. The Japanese did send over incendiary balloons late in the war to try to set the forests of the Pacific Northwest ablaze but, fortunately, the experiment did not work.

Loggers and sawmill workers were exempted from the draft, and even German prisoners of war were used to keep lumber production in pace with demand.

Like many other government agencies, the Forest Service fulfilled its task under very difficult circumstances.

Spam
by Steve McCartney, *World War II Times*

It came to be known as a joke, if not a running gag. Spam (from Spiced Ham) went to war during World War II and was a major contribution to America's war effort.

Invented, or rather, developed and introduced just before the war (its 50th anniversary a couple of years ago was heralded by its parent company), Spam was joked about, eaten and complained about.

What was so special about this ham in a can? It was compact, allowing shipping space to be kept to a minimum. That alone was important when ships were being built almost as fast as they were being sunk, and at a time when shipping space in the available surviving ships was limited.

It could also be mass produced and prepared in a multitude of ways, although, after a while, the multitudes weren't too happy about any form of Spam.

Housewives could find an equal number of uses, if and when they could find it on the ration system. The British, who were shipped Spam by the ton, fell for it, and 30 years later Monty Python comedy troupe was still able to parody the British affinity for it in a now famous skit.

Sad Sack, that loveable yet down at heart eternal GI comic strip character, even got into the "I-hate-Spam" routine when his creator depicted Sad Sack being fed Spam morning, noon and night until he was obviously sick of it. When a care package from home arrived - you guessed it - Spam.

Today, Spam is still a million dollar seller, although many an ex-GI will not touch it much as AAF vets won't touch scrambled eggs due to the horrible powdered eggs they endured during the war.

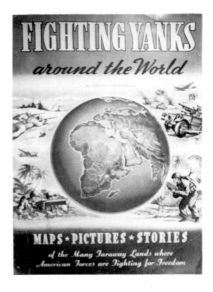

END OF THE WAR

UNDER PRIVATE ENTERPRISE WE AMERICANS HAVE ENJOYED— AND WILL ENJOY AGAIN — AFTER VICTORY—MORE CONVENIENCES THAN ANY OTHER PEOPLE ON EARTH

Ella's **LUNCH**

V-J Day Closed

Besides we are too God-damned tired

Ella and the crew

— We Need —
~~Females~~
~~Fry Cook~~
~~Waitress~~
~~Dishwasher~~
Good Shifts-Top Wages

God Bless America and All the Boys

WAITRESS WANTED

A GALLANT LEADER FRANKLIN D. ROOSEVELT

The Last Journey

On March 29, 1945, the President left for a rest at Warm Springs. He had prepared a speech for broadcast on April 13. Roosevelt had written: "The only limit to our realization of tomorrow will be our doubts of today. Let us move forward with strong and active faith." April 12 began as usual. The President read newspapers and mail that had been flown from Washington. He planned to attend a barbecue in the afternoon. Before the barbecue, Roosevelt was working at his desk while an artist, Mrs. Elizabeth Schoumatoff, painted his portrait. Suddenly he fell over in his chair. "I have a terrific headache," he whispered. these were Roosevelt's last words. He died a few hours later of a cerebral hemorrhage. As news of his death spread, a crowd gathered in front of the White House, silent with grief. Millions of people in all parts of the world mourned the dead President. Roosevelt was buried at Hyde Park. His home and library there have been set aside as the Franklin D. Roosevelt National Historic Site.

The hearse bearing the President's body arrives at the Warm Springs, Ga., station where the body was transferred to the train for the journey north to Washington, D.C., and Hyde Park, N.Y. FDR

Awaiting FDR's funeral train at Washington's Union Station, left to right: James F. Byrnes, secretary of state; President Harry S. Truman; and Henry A. Wallace, secretary of commerce. FDR

Railroad stations and rights-of-way all the way from Warm Springs to Washington, D.C., were lined with people paying their last respects to Roosevelt. This aerial scene was taken at Greenville, S.C. NA 208-PU-170C-6

The Casualty List of April 13, 1945, was headed by President Roosevelt. Thousands of mourners lined the streets of Washington, D.C., to honor the nation's wartime commander in chief.

Today's Army-Navy Casualty List

Washington, Apr. 13.—Follow ing are the latest casualties the military services, includin next-of-kin.

ARMY-NAVY DEAD

ROOSEVELT, Franklin. D., Commande in-Chief, wife, Mrs. Anna Eleanor Roo velt, the White House.

Navy Dead

DECKER, Carlos Anthony, Fireman 1 Sister, Mrs. Elizabeth Decker Metz, Concord Pl., Concord, S. I.

SEILER, Edwin Norton, Lt. Mother M

The funeral procession heads down Pennsylvania Avenue towards the White House on April 14, 1945. NA 208-PU-170C-72

Grief-stricken crowds watch Roosevelt's cortege arrive for funeral services at the White House. NA 208-PU-170C-65

The flag-draped coffin containing the body of the late President was guarded by enlisted men of the four branches of the armed forces, prior to the funeral services which were held in the Executive Mansion in Washington, on April 14, 1945. NA 208-PU-170C-65

New York State Trooper Honor Guard at the grave of President Franklin D. Roosevelt. FDR

V-E Day, May 8, 1945, two down and one to go.

V-E Day in Portland, Ore. OHS

V-E Day in Wilmington, Del. DSA

Street scene in New York City on V-E Day. BETTMANN ARCHIVE

Bernice Tierney (left) and Rose Greco (right), workers at the Casco Company of Bridgeport, Conn., take time out from their jobs to carry a sign around the plant reminding fellow workers of the importance of continuing the job to defeat the Japanese. The company made fuses for mortars and napalm bombs. BETTMANN ARCHIVE

On May 14, 1945, a German U-boat, the U-858, surrenders to the Americans at Fort Miles, Lewes, Del. DSA

After 1943, with the Allies on the offensive throughout the world, post-war planning began for the civilian population. EASTERN WASHINGTON STATE HISTORICAL SOCIETY, SPOKANE, WASH.

Albert Einstein
Old Grove Rd.
Nassau Point
Peconic, Long Island

August 2nd, 1939

F.D. Roosevelt,
President of the United States,
White House
Washington, D.C.

Sir:

Some recent work by E.Fermi and L. Szilard, which has been communicated to me in manuscript, leads me to expect that the element uranium may be turned into a new and important source of energy in the immediate future. Certain aspects of the situation which has arisen seem to call for watchfulness and, if necessary, quick action on the part of the Administration. I believe therefore that it is my duty to bring to your attention the following facts and recommendations:

In the course of the last four months it has been made probable - through the work of Joliot in France as well as Fermi and Szilard in America - that it may become possible to set up a nuclear chain reaction in a large mass of uranium,by which vast amounts of power and large quantities of new radium-like elements would be generated. Now it appears almost certain that this could be achieved in the immediate future.

This new phenomenon would also lead to the construction of bombs, and it is conceivable - though much less certain - that extremely powerful bombs of a new type may thus be constructed. A single bomb of this type, carried by boat and exploded in a port, might very well destroy the whole port together with some of the surrounding territory. However, such bombs might very well prove to be too heavy for transportation by air.

Manhattan Project

The Manhattan Project was established in June 1942. The project was given the overall responsibility of designing and building an atomic bomb. At the time it was a race to beat the Germans who, according to intelligence reports, were building their own atomic bomb.

Under the Manhattan Project, three large facilities were constructed. At Oak Ridge, Tenn., huge gas diffusion and electromagnetic process plants were built to separate uranium 235 from its more common form, uranium 238. Hanford, Wash., became the home for nuclear reactors which produced a new element called plutonium. Both uranium 235 and plutonium are fissionable and can be used to produce an atomic explosion.

Los Alamos was established in northern New Mexico to design and build the bomb. At Los Alamos many of the greatest scientific minds of the day labored over the theory and actual construction of the device. The group was led by Dr. J. Robert Oppenheimer who is credited with being the driving force behind building a workable bomb by the end of the war.

The project was the best-kept secret of the war and the greatest construction project as well. Total cost was $2 billion.

This letter dated Aug. 2, 1939, from Albert Einstein to President Roosevelt explained the significance of fusion and warned that an atomic bomb might be feasible to build. The government did take action on this matter, perhaps one of the most ominous decisions in history.

-2-

The United States has only very poor ores of uranium in moderate quantities. There is some good ore in Canada and the former Czechoslovakia, while the most important source of uranium is Belgian Congo.

In view of this situation you may think it desirable to have some permanent contact maintained between the Administration and the group of physicists working on chain reactions in America. One possible way of achieving this might be for you to entrust with this task a person who has your confidence and who could perhaps serve in an inofficial capacity. His task might comprise the following:

a) to approach Government Departments, keep them informed of the further development, and put forward recommendations for Government action, giving particular attention to the problem of securing a supply of uranium ore for the United States;

b) to speed up the experimental work,which is at present being carried on within the limits of the budgets of University laboratories, by providing funds, if such funds be required, through his contacts with private persons who are willing to make contributions for this cause, and perhaps also by obtaining the co-operation of industrial laboratories which have the necessary equipment.

I understand that Germany has actually stopped the sale of uranium from the Czechoslovakian mines which she has taken over. That she should have taken such early action might perhaps be understood on the ground that the son of the German Under-Secretary of State, von Weizsäcker, is attached to the Kaiser-Wilhelm-Institut in Berlin where some of the American work on uranium is now being repeated.

Yours very truly,
A. Einstein
(Albert Einstein)

West stands of Staggs Field at the University of Chicago where the world's first self-sustaining chain reaction was achieved on Dec. 2, 1942, in a graphite uranium pile. NATIONAL ATOMIC MUSEUM

J. Robert Oppenheimer was appointed director of the Los Alamos laboratory in March 1943. Oppenheimer was the principal scientist responsible for the development of the bomb. NATIONAL ATOMIC MUSEUM

Brig. Gen. Leslie R. Groves, U.S. Army Corps of Engineers, was in charge overall of the Manhattan Project from Sept. 17, 1942, to its completion in 1945. NATIONAL ATOMIC MUSEUM

A 70-square-mile site near Clinton, Tenn., was acquired by the government in 1942 for the establishment of a massive gaseous diffusion plant for the production of enriched uranium. The name Oak Ridge would eventually become synonymous with atomic energy. NATIONAL ATOMIC MUSEUM

Entrance to the Oak Ridge facilities. Security was very tight at all installations involved in the research and production of atomic materials.
NATIONAL ATOMIC MUSEUM

Temporary housing at the isolated Los Alamos laboratory, located 30 miles northwest of Santa Fe, N.M. Within a short time it became the best-equipped physics laboratory in the world, and the center for the greatest scientific undertaking in history.
NATIONAL ATOMIC MUSEUM

The other major production facility built from scratch for development of the atomic bomb was located in a semi-desert area of south-central Washington State. This photo shows the first plutonium production pile, called 100B under construction in late 1943 at the Hanford Works. NATIONAL ATOMIC MUSEUM

The McDonald Ranch at the Trinity Site, where the plutonium core of the first atomic bomb was assembled. NATIONAL ATOMIC MUSEUM

Assembling the bomb at the base of the 100-foot tower in preparation for the July 16, 1945, test. On July 14 the bomb was raised to the top of the tower. As the bomb was being lifted by a slow-moving hoist nervous workers stopped the operation. They drove to base camp and brought back as many mattresses as they could find. When the bomb raising continued they placed mattresses under it just in case it fell. Once on top of the tower the bomb's detonators were installed. NATIONAL ATOMIC MUSEUM

"Fat Man" was the second, and last, nuclear weapon used, detonated over Nagasaki, Japan, Aug. 9, 1945. Its 23 kiloton yield (23,000 tons of TNT) caused two square miles of devastation and approximately 45,000 immediate fatalities. This was an implosion device in which a subcritical mass of plutonium-239 was surrounded by high explosives. When detonated, inward pressure squeezed the plutonium, producing a supercritical mass. The introduction of neutrons from a suitable source initiated a chain reaction leading to an explosion. This complex detonation method was tested July 16, 1945, at Trinity Site, N.M. Plutonium was selected for the implosion because this fissionable element was in greater supply than the U-235 that was used for the Little Boy bomb. Also, plutonium was unsuitable for the gun-type method because fissioning of plutonium could not be achieved in that manner. The shape of the two weapon cases is different because of the method used to detonate them. Fat Boy's dimensions were length, 128 inches; weight, 10,800 lbs. and diameter, 60 inches. NATIONAL ATOMIC MUSEUM

The first nuclear weapon used in warfare was the "Little Boy" bomb. It was delivered by a B-29 aircraft, the "Enola Gay," and detonated about 1,800 feet in the air over the Japanese city of Hiroshima on Aug. 6, 1945. Four square miles of the city were devastated and casualties were in excess of 70,000. Little Boy was not tested prior to its use. This weapon was a gun-type weapon, using uranium-235. The scientists were sufficiently confident in its capabilities, so a test was not necessary. In a gun-type weapon, two amounts of active materials located at opposite ends of a "gun barrel" were shot together to cause a mass increase which induced the active material to reach criticality. The dimensions of Little Boy were length, 10 feet; weight, 8,900 lbs. (fully assembled) and diameter, 28 inches with a yield of 13 kilotons. NATIONAL ATOMIC MUSEUM

New Mexico Test
July 16, 1945

The earth's first atomic explosion occurred at what is now called the "Trinity" site on the White Sands Missile Range. At the time of the test, the site was part of the Alamogordo Air Base, 120 miles southeast of Albuquerque. A tense group of renowned scientists and military men gathered in the desert lands of New Mexico to witness the end results of the $2 billion Manhattan Project.

Tension before the actual detonation was tremendous. Failure was an ever-present possibility. Some present envisioned a success that might mean an uncontrollable, unusable weapon.

Assembly of the bomb began on July 12, 1945, in an old ranch house (McDonald Ranch). On Saturday, July 14, the entire unit was elevated to the top of a 100-foot steel tower.

The test was first scheduled for 4 a.m. Sunday, July 15, 1945, but was delayed because of weather. Actual detonation occurred at 5:30 a.m. MST. The nearest observation point was 10,000 yards south of the tower where the controls for the test were located. At a point 17,000 yards from the tower, many of the key figures in the project observed the detonation. These included James R. Oppenheimer, Vannevar Bush, head of the Office of Scientific Research and Development, and James B. Conant, president of Harvard. Brig. Gen. Leslie Groves observed the test from another location because of the principle that he and Oppenheimer should not be at the same location during potentially dangerous situations.

At 5:30 a.m. there was a blinding flash lighting up the whole area, brighter than the brightest daylight. A mountain range three miles distant stood out in relief. Then came a tremendous sustained roar and a heavy pressure (shock) wave. Immediately thereafter a huge multi-colored surging cloud boiled to an altitude of 40,000 feet.

Recorded by the press later was the experience of a blind girl near Albuquerque, who, when the sky lit up, exclaimed, "What was that?"

While there were many expressions of joy and a celebration by the scientists witnessing the test, there was also an air of mixed feelings. Many of the scientists had previously expressed the hope that some scientific principle would be uncovered which would make nuclear explosions impossible. Such was not the case. The nuclear genie had been let out of the bottle, a tremendous accomplishment in a short time. An air of urgency existed throughout the project because of the concern that the Germans and Hitler would obtain the bomb first. Fortunately for the Allies, Hitler had put very few of his resources into the atomic bomb project. This was not known until after the surrender of Germany in June 1945. Now the bomb originally intended for use against Germany would be used against Japan to quickly end the war in the Pacific.

Trinity Site is where the first atomic bomb was tested at 5:29:45 a.m. Mountain Time on July 16, 1945. The 19 kiloton explosion not only led to a quick end to the war in the Pacific, but also ushered the world into the Atomic Age. The 51,500-acre area was declared a national historic landmark in 1975. The landmark includes base camp, where the scientists and support group lived; ground zero, where the bomb was placed for the explosion; and the McDonald ranch house, where the plutonium core to the bomb was assembled. The site is located 85 miles north of Alamogordo, N.M., and is open to visitors only on the first Saturdays in April and October.

The name "Trinity Site" is popularly attributed to Robert Oppenheimer, director of Los Alamos. When the question of naming came up he was supposedly mulling over some John Donne poetry, specifically a devotional poem with the line, "Batter my heart, three person'd God....," and he directed Ken Bainbridge, the test director, to call it "Trinity." There are other versions. One is that the test at Trinity would be the culmination of the work of three facilities (a triad or trinity) created during World War II to build the bomb - Oak Ridge, Hanford and Los Alamos. The green, glassy substance, Trinitite, which can still be found at Ground Zero takes its name from the site.

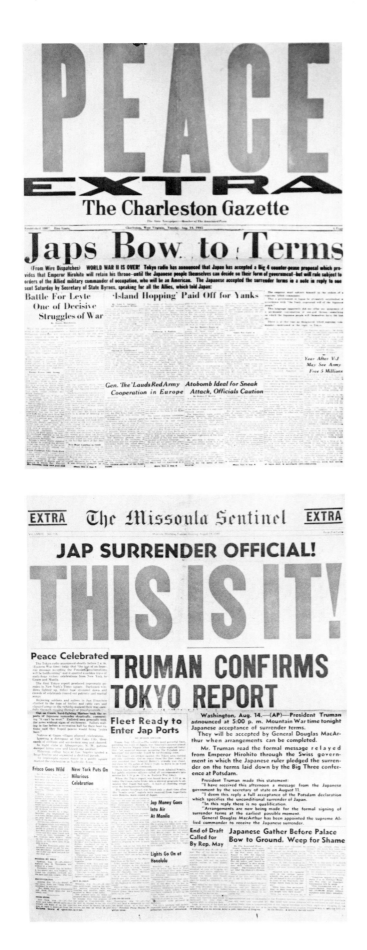

PEACE
EXTRA
The Charleston Gazette

Japs Bow to Terms

(From Wire Dispatches) WORLD WAR II IS OVER! Tokyo radio has announced that Japan has accepted a Big 4 counter-peace proposal which provides that Emperor Hirohito will retain his throne—until the Japanese people themselves can decide on their form of government—but will rule subject to orders of the Allied military commander of occupation, who will be an American. The Japanese accepted the surrender terms in a note in reply to one sent Saturday by Secretary of State Byrnes, speaking for all the Allies, which told Japan:

Battle For Leyte One of Decisive Struggles of War

'Island Hopping' Paid Off for Yanks

Year After V-J
May See Army
Free 5 Millions

Gen. 'Ike' Lauds Red Army Cooperation in Europe
Atobomb Ideal for Sneak Attack, Officials Caution

EXTRA   The Missoula Sentinel   EXTRA

JAP SURRENDER OFFICIAL!
THIS IS IT!

Peace Celebrated

TRUMAN CONFIRMS TOKYO REPORT

Fleet Ready to Enter Jap Ports

Washington, Aug. 14.—(AP)—President Truman announced at 5:00 p. m. Mountain War time tonight Japanese acceptance of surrender terms.

They will be accepted by General Douglas MacArthur when arrangements can be completed.

Mr. Truman read the formal message relayed from Emperor Hirohito through the Swiss government in which the Japanese ruler pledged the surrender on the terms laid down by the Big Three conference at Potsdam.

President Truman made this statement:
"I have received this afternoon a message from the Japanese government by the secretary of state on August 11.
"I deem this reply a full acceptance of the Potsdam declaration which specifies the unconditional surrender of Japan.
"In this reply there is no qualification.
"Arrangements are now being made for the formal signing of surrender terms at the earliest possible moment.
General Douglas MacArthur has been appointed the supreme Allied commander to receive the Japanese surrender.

Frisco Goes Wild
New York Puts On Hilarious Celebration

Jap Money Goes Into Air At Manila

Lights Go On at Honolulu

End of Draft Called for By Rep. May
Japanese Gather Before Palace Bow to Ground. Weep for Shame

-402-

Victory news comes to Portland, and this soldier and a jeep full of girls aren't holding back on celebrating as word of the Japanese surrender blares from radios in cars. Intersections were jammed with laughing, crying and awestruck soldiers and civilians when the official announcement came through. OHS

Aug. 14, 1945, V-J Day, inTimes Square, New York City. FDR

V-J Day on Bishop Street in Honolulu, Hawaii. HAWAII ARCHIVES

The "V" for Victory sign on V-J Day in Honolulu. U.S. ARMY MUSEUM HAWAII

A conga line on V-J Day. FDR

New York City on V-J Day. NA 80-G-377090

Three sailors and their girls celebrate the announcement of Japan's surrender while riding through the streets of Washington, D.C. NA 80-G-377103

A soldier and his family in Washington, D.C., read early reports of Japan's surrender prior to the official announcement on Aug. 14, 1945. NA 80-G-377102

Hundreds and hundreds of American bombers await their fate on the Arizona desert at Kingdom in 1947. This was just one example of the production capacity of American industry which overwhelmed the Axis during the war.
COURTESY WILLIAM LARKINS

This unusual photo taken in 1946 at Hill Air Force Base in Salt Lake City, Utah, shows obsolete PT-13 Stearman trainers stacked like cordwood. UTAH STATE HISTORICAL SOCIETY

Greeting a shipload of returning veterans from the European theater is American Red Cross clubmobile worker, Eileen Lipkin, of Staten Island, May 1945. ARC

A replica of the *U.S.S. Missouri* was built at the Los Angeles Coliseum in October 1945 to re-create the Japanese surrender and as a tribute to the American victory.

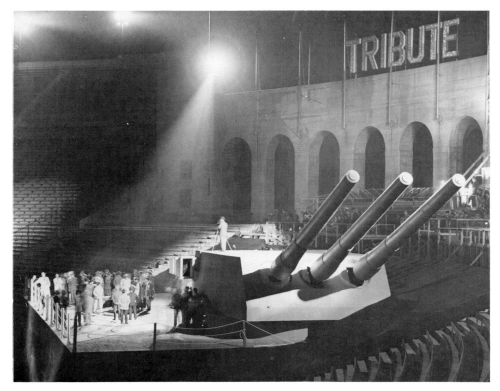

Selected Bibliography

Bishop, Eleanor C., *Prints in the Sand, The U.S. Coast Guard Beach Patrol During World War II*, Pictorial Histories Publ. Co., Inc., Missoula, Mont., 1989.

Brown, DeSoto, *Hawaii Goes to War, Life in Hawaii from Pearl Harbor to Peace*, Editions Limited, Honolulu, 1989.

The Californians, The Magazine of California, for a free sample write 5720 Ross Branch Road, Sebastopol, Calif. 95472.

Casdorph, Paul, *Let the Good Times Roll, Life at Home in America During WWII*, Paragon House, New York, 1989.

Frank, Miriam, Marilyn Ziebarth, Connie Field, *The Life and Times of Rosie the Riveter*, Clarity Educational Productions, Emeryville, Calif., 1982.

Gentile, Gary, *Track the Gray Wolf, U-Boat Warfare on the U.S. Eastern Seaboard, 1942-1945*, Avon Books, New York, 1989.

Groueff, Stephane, *Manhattan Project: The Untold Story of the Making of the Atomic Bomb*, Bantam Books, New York, 1967.

Harris, Mark Jonathan, Franklin Mitchell & Steven Schechter, *The Homefront, America During World War II*, G.P. Putnam's Sons, New York, 1984.

Hoyt, Edwin P., *U-Boats Offshore, When Hitler Struck America*, Scarborough House, Chelsea, Mich., 1978.

Keim, Albert N., *The CPS Story: An Illustrated History of Civilian Public Service*, Good Books, Intercourse, Pa., 1990.

Lingeman, Richard R., *Don't You Know There's A War On? The American Home Front, 1941-1945*, G.P. Putnam's Sons, New York, 1970.

McCombs, Don & Fred L. Worth, *World War II Super Facts*, Warner Books, New York, 1983.

Reisdorff, James J., *North Platte Canteen, An Account of Heartland Hospitality Along the Union Pacific Railroad*, South Platte Press, David City, Neb., 1986.

Reynolds, Clark, *America At War, 1941-1945 The Home Front*, Gallery Books, New York, 1990.

Rhodes, Anthony, *Propaganda, The Art of Persuasion: World War II*, The Wellfleet Press, Secuacus, N.J., 1987.

Rogers, Donald I., *Since You Went Away, From Rosie The Riveter To Bond Drives, World War II At Home*, Arlington House, New Rochelle, N.Y., 1973.

Webber, Bert, *Silent Siege, Japanese Attacks Against North America in World War II*, Ye Galleon Press, Fairfield, Wash., 1984.

About the Author

The author is pictured at his desk in 1944. His contribution to the war effort was collecting and hauling newspapers to his grade school collection station during the last year of the war.

He was born in Charleston, West Virginia, in 1938 and obtained a B.S. degree in Geology from West Virginia University. After working for many years as a consulting geologist, in the ski business and as a historical park director, he established Pictorial Histories Publishing Company in 1976. Since then the company has become a large publisher of military and other subjects with over 140 titles published including 40 written or co-written by the author. Over 40 of the titles deal with the World War II era.

He resides in Missoula, Montana, with his wife, Anne and spends his leisure time skiing, collecting paper ephemera and antique cars and traveling the world to visit World War II sites.

About the Cover Artist

Stanley C. Hughes is a professional artist and illustrator whose work has appeared in numerous books and national magazines. He has won several awards for his art, including the prestigious Jurors' Choice Award at the C.M. Russell Art Show. Hughes and his family reside in Missoula, Montana.